C000002938

The British Hotel through the Ages

Mary Cathcart Borer

The Lutterworth Press

The Lutterworth Press

P.O. Box 60
Cambridge
CB1 2NT
United Kingdom

www.lutterworth.com
publishing@lutterworth.com

Paperback ISBN: 978 0 7188 9580 8
PDF ISBN: 978 0 7188 4843 9
ePub ISBN: 978 0 7188 4842 2

British Library Cataloguing in Publication Data
A record is available from the British Library

First published by The Lutterworth Press, 1972, 2021
Copyright © Mary Cathcart Borer, 1972

Contents

Acknowledgments

I should like to thank the Archivist of the British Railways Board, British Transport Hotels, Ltd., the Youth Hostels Association (England and Wales), Trust Houses Forte, Limited, Butlin's, Ltd., and the staff of the London Library for all the help they have given me during the writing of this book.

In addition, I should like to thank the publishers listed below for their permission to quote the following passages: on pages 50–51 from *The Legacy of England*, Ivor Brown's chapter on 'The Inn' (Batsford), on pages 91–93 from *Sophie in London —1786*, translated by Clare Williams (Cape); on page 192 from *Brighton, Past and Present* by Clifford Musgrave (a Pitkin 'Pride of Britain' book); and on pages 207–211 *César Ritz* by Marie Louise Ritz (Harrap).

Thanks are also due to the following organizations for permission to reproduce the photographs and prints for which they hold the copyright: Bath Municipal Libraries and the Victoria Art Gallery (Plate 8 *top*); Buckinghamshire County Museum, Aylesbury (Plate 8 *bottom*); Charles Ritz (Plate 15 *top left*); City of Sheffield Museums Department (Plate 11 *top*); The Grand Hotel, Brighton (Plate 13 *bottom*); Grantham Public Library and Museum (Plate 9 *top*); Greater London Council Print Collection (Plates 3, 4 *bottom*, 5, 6, 7, 11 *bottom*, 12 *bottom*, 13 *top*); Guildford Museum (Plate 10); Hilton Hotels (U.K.) Ltd. (Plate 16 *top*); Leicester Museum and Art Gallery (Plate 1); Mary Evans Picture Library (Plates 4 *top left*, and 9 *top*); The Public Records Office (Plate 14); Radio Times Hulton Picture Library (Plates 2 *top*, 4 *top right*, and 15 *top right*); Royal Museum and Public Library, Canterbury (Plate 2 *bottom*); The Savoy, London (Plate 15 *bottom*); and Trust Houses Forte, Ltd. (Plates 12 *top* and 16 *bottom*).

M.C.B.

List of Plates

Foreword

FEW READERS TODAY will be familiar with the name Mary Cathcart Borer, and yet she was one of the twentieth-century's most prolific writers, across many genres. Those who do know of her work are probably most familiar with the volumes on walks and sites in London, published in the 1980s, especially her *Illustrated Guide to London in 1800*. They are, however, but a tiny part of her output.

Mary Cathcart Borer was born in 1906 in London. Her father was a hospital secretary and she graduated with a B.Sc. from University College in 1928. She first worked as a scientific researcher at what was then called the Wellcome Historical Medical Museum, and for a few years was married to an archaeologist, Oliver Myers, travelling to Luxor with him. The marriage did not last, however. In 1940 she took up screen-writing and script-editing for film and television, and continued in this field until the 1960s, working on a huge number of productions, many of them relating to children. Between 1937 and 1955 she published in book form 20 or 30 fictional stories and novelisations of some of the film scripts on which she had worked, the most famous of which was 'The Little Ballerina' published in 1949. Throughout the period from the late 1930s to the 1980s she also wrote at least 40 non-fiction books, largely with historical themes. She used at least two pseudonyms, especially for the film scripts – Molly Myers and Egan Storm. She died in 1994, aged 88.

The non-fiction titles show an amazing breadth of interest, research and knowledge. Her histories of geographical places ranged from Africa to Agincourt, from Palestine to the city of

London, and the studies of famous people from Joan of Arc to Hereward the Wake. Her books were extremely popular. The publishers were varied and included some of the most prestigious names in the business, such as Pitmans, Longmans, Michael Joseph and, of course, The Lutterworth Press.

Mary Cathcart Borer's writing shows her deep-seated interest in people, how they functioned, earned their keep and related to each other. This is very clear in *The British Hotel Through The Ages*: the layout and architectural appearance of buildings are surely subjects of explanation and discussion, but the questions that emerge most powerfully relate to why people were and still are in need of what we now describe as 'hospitality', and therefore why the various manifestations of it were designed in particular ways.

Hospitality enables travel, which for centuries was hard, wearisome and full of 'travail', as Borer points out. In this book, she takes us on a long journey, with many stops on the way. We glimpse the soldiers of Rome and the estate stewards of Roman villas travelling the long straight roads of imperial construction; the winding mud-filled tracks of the medieval countryside; the spartan conditions of pilgrims and other travellers seeking shelter and safety in monasteries; and the elaborate coaching inns, which catered not only for private travellers but also the public mail and the complexities of horse hiring, often working as meeting-places for locals – drinking clubs, theatrical plays, dances, gambling, and cockfighting.

The book also demonstrates how the need to travel relates to changes in technology. Borer identifies many of these, with particular attention to the development that made most impact over a short time: the introduction of the railway network, which ended the heyday of the coaching inns in the 1820s-40s (aided by the spread of macadamised road surfaces) that followed. To the surprise of even the railway companies, a vast new public went on the move, not only business men but also wealthy families and the participants in the newly popular railway 'excursions'. The companies built elaborate hotels at their main termini – elaborate both in their architecture and the level of services offered. Independent luxury hotels followed, whilst other more modest accommodation was provided for the less wealthy in smaller, quiet, and comfortable hotels as well as the so-called 'residential' and 'temperance' hotels and 'dormitories'.

The story of the roadside inn was not finished, however. Their fortunes were revived by the arrival of the bicycle and later the motor car, with the associated fashion for 'touring', which saw the birth of the 'motor hotel' complete with garage accommodation, forerunner of the modern motel. The idea that even the less wealthy deserved holidays led to the rise of boarding and guest houses in holiday venues, and eventually in the 1930s and 1940s the birth of the Youth Hostels Association and companies such as Butlins. At the other end of the social scale, Borer ends her story with both some of the larger companies that established highly respected chains throughout the country, and the extravagant luxuries of the great city hotels of the 1960s and 1970s.

Mary Cathcart Borer[1] did not write for an academic audience, and she surely did much to open up the genre of well-written and well-researched popular reading. She wrote with a long view in mind, providing the context to more closely focused specialised studies; and she wrote with ease and fluidity. She's earned her readers' respect, as an early woman science graduate working in a new and tough industry. The fact that much of her earlier output was designed for or about children and that in other cases she often used a male-sounding pseudonym may raise questions about the difficulties she had to overcome. There can be no better memorial to a remarkable writer than the reprint of two her books by one of her original publishers (*The British Hotel Through The Ages* and *Willing to School*, on the history of women's education)..

The appearance of this reprint is timely. It is impossible to ignore the fact that for a reader in the early 2020s a history of hotels has, in many cases, a bitter twist. Restrictions on frequent travel and holiday-making have moved us back centuries. Nonetheless, the long view presented by Mary Cathcart Borer is salutary – there have been many changes, good and bad, over

---

1.   If you would like to learn more about Mary Cathcart Borer, see: https://bearalley.blogspot.com/2011/01/mary-cathcart-borer, bookaddictionuk.wordpress.com/ 2019/12/11/mary-cathcart-borer, www2.bfi.org.uk/Egan Storm.

the centuries, and undoubtedly there will be more to come. So while we read about the hotels of our past, let us also wonder what historians of the future will have to say about the hotels of the present.

Pamela Sambrook, PhD, FSA,
historian and writer
March 2021

Chapter One

THE FIRST INNS

THE FIRST INNS in this country, where travellers could eat, drink and sleep after a day's journey, were built before the English ever arrived here, for they were introduced by the Romans.

Aulus Plautius and his legionaries landed on the Kent coast in A.D. 43 and after capturing their first objectives set about the problem of advancing through the rest of primitive Britain.

Their immediate task was to clear the wooded valleys for cultivation and build roads for their advancing armies. Government was difficult and made possible only by the maintenance of the miles of lonely roads, which were vital for the unification of the country, and the establishment of facilities for the long journeys of government officials, soldiers and road-builders. Posting houses were built, where horses could be changed. Ordinary drinking taverns inevitably followed, and in addition to these, inns or *diversoria* were established, where men and horses could refresh themselves and take a night's rest.

Along the roads, these inns were very simple affairs, but in the towns which soon came into being they were often important, well-equipped buildings. At Silchester, the Roman city built on the hill site of the original Celtic fortress of the Atrebates, roads converged from Cirencester, Exeter, Dorchester and Winchester, and amidst the wattle and daub cottages of the British there arose pagan temples, a forum and basilica, baths, stone villas and an important inn.

Though considerably larger and with more accommodation than the ordinary Roman villa, the inn seems to have been built on similar lines, arranged round two courtyards. The first, the atrium, opened from the public roadway, with sleeping quarters leading from one side, kitchens and the stoke-hole from the other, the dining-room occupying the fourth side, opposite the entrance. The far side of the dining-room opened on to the second courtyard or peristyle, which was an enclosed garden surrounded by colonnaded walks, with perhaps another reception room on the far side, opposite the dining-room.

Although there were public baths in Silchester, the inn was important enough to have its own system of baths, adjoining the stoke-hole. They were built with under-floor heating and, as in a Turkish bath, the bather went through a succession of steam-heated rooms of increasing temperatures, ending with a massage and cold plunge in the first room—the *frigidarium*.

Seneca, writing in A.D. 57, brings vividly to life something of the scene which must often have taken place at the Silchester inn when a party of weary and dusty travellers arrived for a night's lodging. 'I am living near a bath', he wrote. 'Sounds are heard on all sides. Just imagine for yourself every conceivable kind of noise that can offend the ear. The men of more sturdy muscle go through their exercises, and swing their hands heavily weighted with lead: I hear their groans when they strain themselves, or the whistling of laboured breath when they breathe out having held in. If one is rather lazy, and merely has himself rubbed with unguents, I hear the blows of the hand slapping his shoulders . . . or there is someone in the bath who loves to hear the sound of his own voice.'

The Romans liked their creature comforts, and after the bath and the massage, there was good food at the inn and also wine, but whether the wine was locally grown or imported is not certain. Wine was once produced in the southern part of Britain in considerable quantities and there were vineyards in and around London until the eighteenth century, but wine was also one of the earliest imports of the Roman city of London.

Chess was a favourite diversion of the Romans and the chequer board was an early inn sign. In the years to come, when most of the Roman buildings had been destroyed by the English invaders or had fallen into ruin through neglect and disuse, the sign of the chequer board lingered on in the memory of the inn-keepers and was often used, the chequer pattern being painted on the door post, and to this day it is a common enough sign for an inn.

While the Roman inns displayed the chequer board for a sign, the ordinary drinking places, of which there must have been hundreds, displayed a garland of ivy leaves or vine leaves, in honour of Bacchus, tied to the end of a long, projecting, horizontal pole.

In A.D. 410 Rome fell, captured and sacked by the Goths, and the great days of the Empire were over. The Romans departed from Britain and the Anglo-Saxon invaders swarmed over the country. The lovely villas of Roman Britain, the pleasant farm houses, the inns, shops and market places, the pagan temples and the newly-dedicated Christian churches were all forsaken and then pillaged, till they crumbled away into ruin and desolation. The halls of the British chieftains were left 'without fire, without light, without songs'.

The English way of life was completely different from that of Roman Britain, for the English were solitaries who disliked city life. 'None of the Germanic people dwell in cities, and they do not even tolerate houses which are built in rows', wrote Tacitus. 'They dwell apart, and at a distance from one another, according to the preference which they may have for a stream, the plain or the grove.'

They lived in scattered, heavily-defended family settlements and the waste lands outside their boundaries were places to be feared, the haunts of evil spirits, will-o'-the-wisps and dragons. In this unfriendly, pagan country, where every stranger was a potential enemy, there was no place for the friendly inn and none existed.

During the next two centuries, while the flame of British resistance flickered and died in despair, the English made England their own country. The fertile lands of the east and south gave an ease and plenty of living which, to some extent, subdued their harsh temper. They increased their trade with Europe and trading centres became small towns, many of which, including London, were rebuilt on the ruins of former Roman cities.

In A.D. 589 Pope Gregory sent St. Augustine and his band of monks to begin a Christian mission in Kent. The Christian Church made rapid progress in England and the country soon became once more part of a great cultural empire, based on Rome. European traders followed the Christian missionaries and England extended her European commerce. The quays of London were rebuilt and there was far more movement throughout the country than in the early days of the Dark Ages. Once more provision had to be made for travellers.

At first this was supplied by the monasteries, which during the seventh and eighth centuries were built in increasing numbers in England, for hospitality to strangers as well as succour and charity to the needy were regarded as one of the first principles of Christianity, the fourth of the 'seven works of mercy'.

There were several monastic orders in England but the largest and earliest was that of the Benedictines, which had been founded in the sixth century and to which St. Augustine of Canterbury had belonged. Travellers were always given food and a bed at a Benedictine monastery. The visitors' quarters were divided into three categories, based on social distinction. There was simple accommodation for the poorer guests and pilgrims, better rooms for merchants and men of similar social standing, and apartments for visiting nobles, which usually adjoined those of the abbot. No charge was made, but travellers were expected to contribute what they could afford to the Abbey funds.

As well as these havens for travellers, scores of wayside ale-houses and wine-houses were also established along the roads. The sign of the ale-house was the 'ale-stake', very similar to the Roman sign, for it was a bush or besom tied to the end of a long, horizontal pole: and here you could buy ale, mead, cider or perry. The wine was probably of local manufacture, for Bede, writing from the monastery of Jarrow, early in the ninth century, described Britain as an island 'which excels for grain and trees and is well adapted for feeding cattle and beasts of burden. It also produces vines in some places. . . .' As for game and fish, he said that the country 'has plenty of land- and water-fowls of several sorts; it is remarkable also for rivers abounding in fish and plentiful springs. It has the greatest plenty of salmon and eels; . . . besides many sorts of shell-fish, such as mussels, in which are often found excellent pearls. . . . There is also a great abundance of cockles, of which the scarlet dye is made. . . . It has both salt and hot springs, and from them flow rivers which furnish hot baths, proper for all ages and sexes arranged according.'

During the ninth and tenth centuries came the invasion of the Norwegian and Danish Vikings, and it was they who promoted the popularity of ale, so that it soon became the daily drink of nearly all Englishmen. Scores more ale houses were opened throughout the country and restrictive measures had to be passed, controlling price and quality, while fines were imposed on any men who 'quarrelled and beat another in an ale-house'. Yet accommodation for travellers on the roads was still very scarce. The monasteries would lodge them for as long as three days, if necessary, but if, in the course of their journey, they did not come upon a monastery or a friendly and hospi-table household before nightfall, they had no alternative but to sleep in the open air.

When Duke William landed in England, in 1066, the

population of the country was something between a million
and a half and two million souls, most of them living in their
small, isolated, scattered villages. William professed himself a
devout Christian and built many more churches throughout
the country as well as monasteries, thus providing more accommodation for travellers. However, he also built more towns and
cities, and trade, both inland and overseas, developed steadily.
This meant that there were more travellers on the roads, as
well as hundreds of pilgrims visiting the numerous holy shrines.

By the twelfth century the Cistercians and Carthusians were
also established in England, but the Cistercians were a more
austere order than the Benedictines and the Carthusians were a
silent order, so it was the Benedictines who did most of the
entertaining.

Most travellers were generous to the monasteries, but some
took advantage of their open-handed hospitality, so that in the
years to come they were to run into financial troubles. For
example, when King John visited Bury St. Edmunds, during
the thirteenth century, with his retinue of grooms, fowlers
and squires, and his horses and hounds for hunting and hawk-
ing, 'he availed himself of the hospitality of St. Edmund, which
was attended with enormous expense', wrote Jocelin of Brake-
land, 'and upon his departure bestowed nothing at all, either
of honour or profit, upon the Saint, save thirteen pence sterling,
which he offered at mass on the day of his departure.'

The Benedictine monasteries at this time were nearly all to
a pattern, built round a courtyard with a gatehouse. On either
side of the gatehouse were the almoner's office and the visitors'
quarters. Leading from the north and south sides of the courtyard were the stables and granaries, kitchens, bakehouses and
breweries. The church opened from the east wall of the
courtyard, its west door being usually opposite the gatehouse,
and on the sunny, south side of the church were the cloisters,
with the refectory close by. Other vital parts of the monastery
were the chapter house, the scriptorium and the infirmary,

which usually had its own chapel and kitchen. There was an outer parlour, where the monks received visitors, including merchants with whom they had business, and an inner parlour for their own diversions, with their dormitory above, which had easy access to the church for the services held throughout the night. In the monastery gardens they grew their own produce, vegetables and fruit as well as culinary and medicinal herbs, and had their fish ponds.

In addition to the abbot, the prior and sub-prior, the precentor, the sacristan and the steward, there was a hospitaller to look after the guests and an infirmarer to tend the sick.

After hours of walking or riding along the lonely, rough and dangerous roads of medieval England, the monasteries, which were the first English hotels, were blessed havens for exhausted travellers from all walks of life, and the infirmarers saved the lives of hundreds of sick and destitute peasants, nursing them back to health and giving them money to help them on their way.

Another important officer of the monastery was the cellarer, for the monasteries brewed their own ale. As early as the twelfth century, the abbey at Burton-on-Trent had acquired a high reputation for its ale, but according to the old rhyme, the abbot was canny.

> The Abbot of Burton brewed good ale
> On Fridays when they fasted
> . . . . .
> But the Abbot of Burton never tasted his own
> As long as his neighbour's lasted.

Ale at this time was made by fermenting an infusion of malt, made from barley or oats, and it was flavoured with ground-ivy or costmary. Beer was regarded as a superior kind of ale and it cost nearly twice as much, for it was much stronger, being made from the first mashing of the malt.

The monastic brewers marked their barrels X, XX and

XXX, according to the strength of the beer, the original form of the cross being like a crucifix and a sign that the monks had sworn on the Cross that their beer was of good quality and of the strength indicated.

It was during the fourteenth century that Flemish immigrants introduced hops into the brewing of beer, but at first the English heartily disliked the flavour. Hops were considered to be an adulterant and regarded with grave suspicion. The Common Council of the City of London petitioned against their use, protesting that they ruined the flavour of the beer and endangered life, whereupon Henry VI forbade brewers to use them. Henry VIII, who also liked his beer unhopped, repeated the prohibition, but the decrees of even that autocratic monarch were by no means always obeyed. Beer was brewed with hops and people gradually acquired the taste for them, so that before long they were being grown extensively, particularly in Kent. A Kentish squire of Tudor times announced: "From Bohemia cometh this goodly vine that I am minded to plant in the county of Kent. With its aid is made that good drink that we call Brunswick Mum. But the Almains call it 'Bier', for it is made from the bere or barley plant. It is like our ale but not so sweet."

For a long time the beer brewers, who used hops, kept themselves apart from the ale brewers, who were the original members of the Brewers' Company, but in time the term 'beer' came to be used for all types of malt liquor.

Chapter Two

MEDIEVAL INNS

As THE POPULATION and trade of medieval England
slowly increased, so did the number of travellers on
the roads. Royal couriers had to make long journeys
across the country. Merchants travelled from town to town
collecting orders for their merchandise or buying goods to
equip their trading vessels. Landlords' agents rode long distances collecting rents from the estates. Local government
officials had to take money to the Royal Exchequer in London.
London merchants travelled each year to the Cotswold and
Pennine sheep countries to buy wool, which was baled and
sent by pack horse trains back to the London warehouses for
export. Merchants and private travellers, many of them
foreign buyers, visited the annual trade fairs, including the
large autumn fair at Stourbridge, near Cambridge, which had
been licensed by King John, St. Bartholomew's cloth fair in
London, St. Giles's fair at Oxford and the numerous smaller
fairs which were held at most of the important towns throughout the country, at times best suited for the selling of the local
products. Here people would often buy a year's supply of such
goods as they could not obtain in their local markets or from
the itinerant pedlars.

And there were always the pilgrims, travelling to the sacred
shrines—the tomb of Edward the Confessor at Westminster,
of St. Alban at St. Albans, the holy tree at Glastonbury, St.
Cuthbert's shrine at Durham Cathedral, St. Edmund's at Bury

St. Edmunds, Walsingham with its miraculous statue of Our Lady and the relic of the Virgin's milk, and Thomas Becket's shrine at Canterbury.

Travel was difficult and dangerous, for the roads were few and ill-made. In places the old Roman roads were still in existence but it was nobody's business to maintain them and most villages and towns were connected by rough tracks which became so muddy in winter that they were almost impassable. Even the roads called highways were little better, for they often passed through mile after mile of wild and wooded country and dense forests which, more often than not, were infested with robbers and outlaws. In Hertfordshire the roads were so bad that the Abbot of St. Albans provided a special armed patrol to accompany travellers on the way from St. Albans to London, and in 1285 a law was passed decreeing that all high roads between large market towns were to be widened, so that no bushes, trees or ditches were left within two hundred feet on either side.

If it had been enforced, this would have ensured that travellers at least had a fair warning of any approaching marauders, but the work was made the duty of landowners, who were held responsible for any robbery that took place, or else by the parishes—the kind of law which was easier to frame than to operate, and it was very soon forgotten.

By the twelfth century a simple farm cart had been designed, drawn by a pair of oxen fitted with a shoulder yoke, but it was for carting purposes only. For general travel, wheeled vehicles were far too uncomfortable and impractical on the rough, rutted roads. People rode or walked. Ladies of quality sometimes rode postilion, behind a manservant, or were carried in litters, the poles being fitted to the saddles of two postilions riding fore and aft, and the luggage of wealthy travellers was carried by an accompanying train of packhorses and sometimes a luggage cart as well.

For both companionship and safety, people preferred to ride

in groups, and they were sometimes several weeks on the road together.

And all these people needed accommodation for the night. The monasteries soon found it difficult to find room for them all and before long they were building separate lodging houses for their visitors, which were called inns. 'Inn' is a Saxon word meaning a chamber, but it came to have two other meanings. It was used to describe a mansion. Thus Clifford's Inn was the mansion of the Clifford family, Lincoln's Inn of the Earls of Lincoln and Gray's Inn the home of the Grays. The town house of the Earls of Warwick, in Warwick Lane, was known as Warwick Inn, and when Warwick the King-maker came to London in 1458 he lodged a retinue of six hundred men there.

The inn also came to mean a house used as a lodging house. The inns and halls of Oxford and Cambridge were the lodging houses of the students, before the colleges were built, and the Inns of Court were the lodging places of the law students.

Glastonbury became such a popular place of pilgrimage that in the fifteenth century the Pilgrim Inn was built, outside the abbey precincts, for the ordinary run of pilgrims, though the nobility were still housed in the abbot's guest hall. The New Inn at Gloucester was another monastic inn and also the Star at Alfriston, which belonged at one time to Battle Abbey. Along the road to Walsingham there were dozens of chapels and pilgrim hostels, for the shrine was almost as popular as Canterbury and the pilgrim trade as highly organized, to the sour amusement of the porter at Croyland Abbey who used to misdirect pilgrims asking him the way to Walsingham, 'out of sheer malice' and for the pleasure of watching them trudge away in the wrong direction.

A few secular inns were also built, but they were mainly in the wool towns, as, for example, the George Inn at Norton St. Philip, near Frome, dating from 1397, where in the large upper room the cloth merchants would meet and conduct their sales. The George at Salisbury was a secular inn built from timbers taken from a pilgrim inn at Old Sarum, and an inventory of 1473 lists thirteen guest chambers, though they included both living-rooms and sleeping-rooms, for in each of the thirteen rooms were several truckle beds. People seem to have had no concern about going to bed in one of the living-rooms of an inn while other visitors were still sitting there, and the custom seems to have lasted longer in France than in England, for as late as 1630 Lieutenant Hammond of Norwich described seeing a French girl riding alone to Canterbury. When she arrived at the inn where he was staying, 'this pretty she rider at that time held it no nicety, nor point of incivility, to disrobe and bed her little tender, weary'd corps in our presence, which I understood afterwards is common and familiar amongst them of that nation.'

Another famous medieval inn was the Blue Boar at Leicester, where Richard III slept on the eve of Bosworth. The next day, his body, naked and thrown across his horse's back, 'like a hog', was brought back to Leicester and exhibited at the Town Hall in Blue Boar Lane, close to the inn where the day before 'he had lived in regal pomp'.

Yet inns were still all too few for the number of travellers, and people finding themselves still on the road at nightfall, a long distance from a town, had to hope for a monastery lodging or the hospitality of a manor house.

The manor houses of the thirteenth and fourteenth centuries, which were built when the old castle strongholds became obsolete and unnecessary, were large and very hospitable, and they willingly accepted strangers for a night's lodging. They expected no payment but the origin of tipping servants when visiting a country house may well have come from the time when strangers were given this generous hospitality. The medieval manor houses were more practical to live in and vastly more comfortable than the castles, though in the early part of the thirteenth century many were still partly fortified and also moated, for life was still hazardous outside the walled cities, and they had to be prepared still for attacks from armed robbers or enemies.

As an alternative to the monasteries or monastic hostels, they served as hotels. The house was often surrounded by a stone wall, with an outer battlemented wall, the space between housing the stable, forges and workshops. The keep of the old castle reappeared as a turreted tower to one side of the house and the main door was approached by a covered stairway which led into one end of the screened passageway at the end of the great hall. This hall, with its high, timbered ceiling, was still the main feature of the house. To the right of the entrance was the kitchen, with a cellar below and a room above, usually approached by a ladder, which often gave access to the minstrels' gallery over the hall screens. At the opposite end of the hall was the dais where the family and distinguished guests took their meals, the rest of the household and less important visitors eating in the main body of the hall, below the high table, at long trestle tables set along either side, which were easily removed when the meal was over.

Leading from the dais was the family withdrawing-room or solar, where they lived and slept. The chapel led either from the solar or the dais and also the washing apartment. The ground floor underneath the great hall was used for stores and sleeping accommodation for the household servants, while the guests usually slept on straw in the great hall.

By the fourteenth century the design of the manor house had changed. It was still surrounded by a strong stone wall, with a guarded gatehouse leading into a courtyard, and there was often a kitchen courtyard at the back, but the entrance and great hall were now on the ground floor. The hall was still the same lofty room, with a fireplace in the centre or in one of the outer walls, and it was approached from the entrance porch by way of a passage formed by the screens. A staircase led from the porch to the minstrels' gallery and beyond to the battlemented roof. The kitchen, buttery and pantry were at this end of the house and roofed separately from the hall, as were the solar and adjoining buildings at the opposite end.

The kitchen was very large and often octagonal, with tall windows and an opening in the vaulted roof for steam and smoke to escape. It had several huge open fireplaces, one for boiling great joints of salted meat, in cauldrons hanging from iron hooks, another with a revolving spit, usually turned by a small boy, for roasting beef and haunches of venison, capons and all manner of game, and a third, with ovens built into the thickness of the walls, for baking bread and pies.

With the passing years, extra accommodation was added to the manor houses. Near the entrance a small winter parlour with bedrooms above it were built and bedrooms were also added round the solar, while the kitchen, buttery and pantry were often grouped round a separate courtyard. There were many more windows and the first oriel windows appeared, while carved wooden panelling replaced the painted walls and tapestries.

In the largest households, the chief steward was responsible for the servants, seeing that 'their livery be clean, neat and comely worn, and that their shoes be good also'. A clerk, usually a monk, looked after the accounts and records of the household, and his assistants checked all the rent payments of either goods, labour or money, due from the tenants of the estate. The usher was in charge of the groom of the hall, the pages and the groom of the fires. The duty of the groom of the hall was to supervise its cleaning. The pages arranged the elm-wood trestle tables for meals and removed them afterwards, issued straw for visiting strangers to sleep on and saw to the regular changing of the rushes on the floor, thereby ensuring that there was not, as in most of the poorer households, 'an ancient collection of beer and grease, fragments of fish and everything that is nasty, hidden beneath'. The groom of the fires attended to the supplies of logs and saw that the torches and candles were in good order. The butler laid the tables and his instructions were to 'have three sharp knives, one to cut bread, one to square it and one to trim it into trenchers. . . . Look that your knives be bright polished and your spoon cleaned. . . . When you brooch a pipe of wine put in the tap upwards of four fingers above the bottom of the cask—so shall leys and dregs of wine not arise and pour out.'

The high table was covered with a linen cloth and the butler was instructed to 'let all the table cloths be fair folded and kept in a chest or hanged up on a perch'.

The grooms of the bedchambers saw to the cleaning of the bedrooms and brought in bowls of hot water, together with towels and home-made soap.

In these enormous households no stranger or traveller was ever turned away hungry, provided he could give a satisfactory account of himself. Moreover, quantities of food were distributed each day from the kitchen to the local peasants, with particular thought for the old and sick.

Many visitors arrived with vast retinues of servants and attendants. 'There came to dinner John of Brabant, with thirty horses and twenty-four valets at wages, and the two sons of the lord Edmund, with thirty horses and twenty-one valets, and they stay at our expense in all things, in hay, oats and wages', ran one household book of late medieval times, and the Book of Alicia de Brienne records the arrival of a visitor with his wife and daughter, two knights, two valets and three squires.

During the fifteenth century, three hundred and nineteen strangers are said to have dined with the Duke of Buckingham on the Feast of Epiphany, and on the same day two hundred and seventy-nine guests sat down to supper.

The manor houses kept vast supplies of food in their stores. The recorded contents of the larders in one household, during the fourteenth century, included 'the carcases of twenty oxen and fifteen pigs, of herrings eight thousand, twenty pounds of almonds, thirty of rice, barrels of lard, enough oatmeal to last till Easter, two quarters of salt.'

Fish was fairly expensive but there was plenty of variety, both fresh and salted, including herrings and hake, salmon, haddock, halibut, eels, ling, conger eel, sturgeon, cod, dog-fish, mackerel, lampreys, oysters, mussels, trout, perch and, for special occasions, whale, porpoise and swan: and there was every kind of roast and boiled meat—mutton, beef, pork, venison, veal, ham, capon, pheasant, ducks, geese and peacocks.

The cooks made elaborate tarts and pastries and all manner of sweetmeats flavoured with cinnamon, ginger and cloves—spices which had been introduced from the East by the Crusaders—while savoury dishes were spiced with peppercorns and vinegar and sometimes cooked in wine or ale to give them extra flavour. The pastry, like modern pie pastry, was made from boiling fat and flour, and the cases, called coffins, were filled with venison, pigeons or chicken, or with fruit—quinces spiced with ginger and cloves or apples with saffron and raisins.

Bacon, ham, pork and mutton were preserved in a variety of ways, soaked in brine or rubbed with honey, vinegar, salt and spices and then hung in great joints to smoke in the kitchen chimneys.

The dough of the bread was made up as rolls, loaves or trenchers, the trenchers being flat bannocks which, split in half, were usually used instead of plates. The butter was churned in a deep, narrow tub, with a long-handled wooden plunger, and patted into slabs or melted into large casks for storage and heavily salted.

Amongst the wealthy, food became an important preoccupa-tion and recipes were passed from one household to another and often recorded. For making a sausage roll, for example, the instructions were 'to take breadcrumbs and eggs and swing them together with ham; add sage, saffron and salt; wrap it up in a cloth and cast into boiling broth.' Another form of sausage was made from chicken and pork. 'Hewe it small and grounde it alle to dust. Then mix it with breadcrumbs, yolk of eggs, and pepper and then boil with ginger, sugar, salt and saffron.' Fig pancakes were made by adding figs to a 'batture of flour, ale, pepper, saffron and spices', the mixture being 'cast upon an iron pan'. Blancmange was originally meat or fish boiled in almond milk, and marchpane was a form of hard marzipan which was moulded into all manner of highly decorative table ornaments by the ingenious cooks.

Amongst the peasants, home-brewed ale was the most popular drink, with cider and perry in the apple and pear producing districts, but wine was the drink of the noble households, a favourite being piment, made from a light claret mixed with honey, borage and spices.

It was not until the thirteenth century that the English acquired a taste for vegetables, salads and fruit, and then, while the staple diet of the peasants remained rye bread and cheese with meat, fish or game when they could afford it or poach it, the rich were growing all kinds of root vegetables as well as beans, peas and lettuces, and buying dried fruits imported from the Mediterranean, raisins, figs, currants, dates, pomegranates and candied orange peel, as well as ginger from China.

In the houses of the great the cooks attained a high degree of skill. Soups and stews were darkened with toast crumbs or dried ox-blood, and sweetmeats were coloured pink with strawberry juice or pale green with spinach.

Dinner was at ten o'clock in the morning and the evening meal began about five o'clock and continued as the main source of diversion for the rest of the evening, the household and guests being entertained by a resident band of minstrels and tumblers or a group of strolling players and musicians, who assembled in the gallery to perform and also to recount the news of the day in improvised ballads or spoken poems.

Serving dishes were of wood or pewter, plates were wood, pewter or merely trenchers of bread, but small birds were served on wooden skewers. Each course was carried in ceremoniously on a wooden platter and offered to every member of the company in turn, to help himself, with his own knife. He placed it on his trencher and ate with his fingers and a spoon, tossing the bones and other fragments on to the rushes of the floor, for the dogs.

At the high table there was a display of confits and sweet-meats in gold and silver boxes and also of costly salt cellars, the most valuable, of gold or silver, inlaid with enamel and jewels, being placed before the most important person present, and smaller ones before each of the other guests. The centre-piece was the wassail bowl, which was passed round for the drinking of toasts. This was usually of maple wood, with a costly lid of wrought gold or silver.

The table was lit by wax candles and flaming torches blazed from the flambeaux on the walls.

A *Book of Curtasye* was issued in the thirteenth century, to help the unsophisticated with their table manners. 'When come to a feast', it advised, 'greet the Steward who shows you where to sit—you will find bread laid for you and perhaps a platter also—for soft food. There will be drinking cups upon the board and a salt cellar. When the food is brought around you will be served on your trencher or platter. Eat quietly, and, as you share plates and cups, do not leave your spoon in the food—or drink with your mouth full—lest you soil the cup. Don't stroke the dog or cat under the table but keep your hands clean. Don't blow on hot food—but talk awhile pleasantly to your waiting friends while it cools. Don't put your elbows on the table or turn your back upon your neigh-bour—do not inconvenience your host by calling for unserved dishes. Be sedate and courteous if you sit among gentlefolk—and tell no tale that would harm or shame any other guest that so the feast may be pleasant to all.'

By the time John Russell wrote *The Book of Nurture*, in 1460, manners had changed in some details and although it was usual to gnaw bones with one's teeth it was considered ill-bred to throw them on the rushes for the dogs and cats.

The hospitality of smaller households was as generous as that of the larger establishments and the rich merchants of the towns maintained as much of the splendour of the country mansions as they could achieve in a more limited space, while the great town houses of the nobility served as hotels for visiting noblemen to London.

In 1246 Henry III presented to his wife's uncle, Count Peter of Savoy, a piece of land between London and Westminster, along the high road 'commonly called the Strand'. The Count was created the Earl of Richmond and here, along the river bank, he built his great palace of the Savoy, where he entertained and gave hospitality to hundreds of visitors, including a number of beautiful young French noblewomen, some of whom were his wards; and for many of them he found rich English husbands.

Thus the Savoy Palace, where more than six centuries later the Savoy Hotel was to rise, can be counted London's first hotel, for it was only a mile or so outside the City boundary.

The glories of the Count's palace did not last for long, for Henry III undermined the power and wealth of the English manorial establishments by heavy taxation to pay for his expensive French court and his abortive war with France, and when Simon de Montfort led the ultimate rebellion against him, Count Peter had to flee from the Savoy, the 'fayrest Mannor in Europe'. For a time Simon de Montfort and his followers lodged there and it was from the Savoy Palace that they set forth for the battle of Evesham, during which de Montfort was killed and the royalists gained power again. Peter of Savoy was given back his lands and his palace, but he never lived again in the Savoy, which ultimately came into the possession of Edmund Cruikshank, Queen Eleanor's youngest son, and 'from that time the Savoy was reported and taken as a parcel of the Earldom and honour of Lancaster'.

Edmund's grandson, Henry of Lancaster, rebuilt the palace 'in great splendour', after the victory of Crécy, in 1346, and it passed through one of his daughters to John of Gaunt and then to his son Henry IV: and to this day the precincts of the Savoy, where the hotel and theatre now stand, are a liberty of the Duchy of Lancaster.

The great houses of the countryside maintained the tradition of their social obligations to travellers throughout the fourteenth century and if the owner of a country mansion were away from home and was still prepared to give hospitality to passing travellers, he would hang out a sign of his arms, as a token that bed and board would be provided by his servants. Some of these houses ultimately became commercial inns, as, for example, the Golden Lion at Barnstaple, once the home of the Earls of Bath, for in most families the great wealth of the Middle Ages, which made such open-handed hospitality possible, did not last. Some quarrelled with the King and were dispossessed. Many were ruined during the Wars of the Roses and lost everything. The custom, which was a relic of the Christian ideal of sharing one's possessions with those in need, foundered through sheer economic necessity.

It had almost ceased to exist in England by the time of the Restoration, but it was not entirely unknown as late as the early eighteenth century and in Scotland it lingered on even longer. In the meantime, however, more secular inns were built for travellers, and by the fifteenth century innkeepers, to guard their own interests, were actively discouraging the practice. In 1425 an act was passed forbidding, under a penalty of forty shillings fine, all travellers resorting to burgher towns to lodge with friends and acquaintances or in any place but 'hostelleries, unless indeed, they were persons of consequence, with a great retinue, in which case they could lodge personally with friends, provided the horses and servants were put up at the inn'.

The early medieval inns were built either of wood or stone and the general pattern was similar. They were built round a courtyard with a frontage on the road, the courtyard being approached by a low arch, just high enough for a horse and rider, with a door that could be securely bolted and barred at night. From the courtyard opened the sleeping quarters for the travellers and the loose boxes and stables for the horses, while the kitchen usually led from the archway.

This was the plan of the Oriental caravanserai and it has been suggested that the ground plan of the first public inns was brought back by the Crusaders.

Accommodation was primitive. People slept ten or twelve to a room. A traveller usually took his own food, expecting only a bed, beer or wine, and even then he had to be prepared to share his bed of straw, usually full of fleas, with one or more strangers. Sometimes the landlord provided bread and meat, but by the fourteenth century there were bitter complaints that they were charging extortionate prices and they had to be constrained by law.

Inns were still so scarce that travellers could stay only for a night or two and then had to make way for newcomers. The poor, who could not afford the penny charge for a night's lodging, still found accommodation in the monasteries, and they were also used by the rich, if there were no manor house nearby, for the common inns were, generally speaking, too rough for gentlefolk.

There are very few records of journeys across England during the fourteenth century but in 1331 the Warden and two Fellows of Merton College, Oxford, had to make a journey to Durham and back, on business connected with the college property, and they left an account of their expenses. Accompanied by four servants, they travelled on horseback, spending twelve nights on the road, both going and returning. The ferry across the Humber cost the party 8d. They spent 2d. a day on beer, $1\frac{1}{4}$d. on wine, $5\frac{1}{2}$d. on meat, $\frac{1}{4}$d. on candles and 4d. on bread: and fodder for the seven horses came to 10d. a night.

By this time the plan of the secular inn was more elaborate. It was built with two and sometimes three storeys and round the upper floors of the courtyard ran galleries approached by outside staircases, from which the bedrooms opened. Sometimes there was a colonnaded walk beneath the lower gallery and in the more important inns the stabling was housed in a separate courtyard at the back, with its own door on to a lane behind the inn.

The Tabard at Southwark was a galleried inn, one of many which came to be built in the Southwark High Street for the accommodation of pilgrims to Canterbury; as late as the sixteenth century, Stow listed the Spurre, the Christopher, the Bull, the Queen's Head, the George, the Hart and the King's Head, all within a relatively short distance of the Tabard. It was at the White Hart that Jack Cade arrived in 1450 and lodged for the night, after being refused entry to the city, and one of his followers was beheaded there. 'At the Whyt Harte, in Southwarke, one Hawaydyne, of Sent Martyns, was beheddyd', but Chaucer has made the Tabard the most famous of all the Southwark inns.

It was an ecclesiastical foundation, for it was built in 1307 by an Abbot of Hyde, near Winchester, part of the building being a town residence for himself and a guest house for brother clergy visiting London to attend the Bishop of Winchester, at his palace close by on Bankside. Adjoining the Abbot's house was the inn for pilgrims, which was given the sign of the medieval herald's coat—the Tabard.

It stood where the roads from Sussex, Surrey and Hampshire all met the Dover Road—the Pilgrim's Way—and here, in the rush-strewn reception room, assembled one day in April, 1383, on the eve of their journey to Canterbury, the twenty-nine pilgrims of the *Canterbury Tales*—the brave, courteous knight, his son, the squire, and their yeomen, the lawyer and the doctor, the franklin, the merchant, the miller, the wife of Bath, the drunken cook, the reeve, the London burghers, the kindly ploughman, the prioress and her chaplain, the monk, the friar and the pardoner, with his wallet 'bret-full of pardons—come from Rome all hot'.

In Elizabethan times the inn was largely rebuilt and some beautiful fireplaces and carved oak panelling added, but it was destroyed in 1676, when a disastrous fire broke out in an oil-man's shop between the Tabard and the George. The Tabard was rebuilt on the same plan, with its galleried courtyard, pilgrims' room and sleeping quarters, but by this time its name had been changed to the Talbot, and in 1874 it was pulled down.

In Chaucer's day, the landlord of the Tabard was his friend Harry Bailly, a man of substance and education who had twice stood as Member of Parliament for Southwark and had the manner and authority to order his inn competently and preside over the motley collection of guests who came there, representing so many different ranks of society.

Pilgrims either walked or rode, and for the riders there was a regular service of horses for hire, both at Southwark and Rochester, all of them branded with the owner's name. The first day's journey from Southwark brought the pilgrims to Dartford, a distance of fifteen miles. Here there were several hostels where they could spend the night, one, similar to the Tabard, standing on the site of the later Bull Inn. Their second night was spent at Rochester, perhaps at an inn in the High Street where the George was later to be built, for beneath the mundane, modern George is a magnificently vaulted thirteenth-century crypt, which suggests that it was once part of an ecclesiastical building.

After Rochester, the pilgrims had twenty-seven miles to travel, and their next stopping place was Ospringe, a mile from Faversham, where there was a Maison Dieu for their lodging, maintained by the Knights Templars and Brethren of the Holy Ghost. It had been there for many years, for during King John's lifetime a room had been set apart especially for his use when he was passing through to Canterbury. At one time there were eight brethren in residence at Ospringe, to entertain the pilgrims, but gradually their numbers dwindled, through lack of funds, and by 1480, long before the Reformation, the Maison Dieu, one of many throughout the country, had become derelict.

From Ospringe it was only nine miles to the end of the pilgrimage, so pilgrims who had spent the night there could safely count on reaching the walled city of Canterbury before the gates were locked at sunset. For any who were delayed on the road, however, and arrived at the great west gate after nightfall, there was no hope of admission. Even before the gate was rebuilt, in 1380, with its massive and formidable drum towers, it had been almost impregnable, and no one was allowed through after curfew. In the early days, the late-comers amongst the pilgrims had been forced to spend the night as best they could, sheltering against the outside of the city walls or finding refuge in the fields, but before long an inn was built outside the west gate, in the suburb of St. Dunstan's, and on the site of this inn now stands the Falstaff.

Inside the city walls there were a great many pilgrim inns, though traces of only a few of them can be found today. At the Fountain Inn, Earl Godwin's wife once stayed, and nearly a hundred and fifty years later it was the secret meeting place of the four knights who planned to challenge Thomas Becket: and later that day they set forth from the inn to murder him on the chancel steps of the Cathedral.

The Fountain must have been a good deal more comfortable than most medieval inns, for in 1299 it received a warm compliment from the German ambassador who was lodged there on the occasion of the marriage of Edward I to his second wife Margaret, sister of Philip IV of France. 'The inns in England are the best in Europe, those of Canterbury are the best in England, and The Fountain, wherein I am now lodged as handsomely as I were in the King's Palace, the best in Canterbury', he wrote. Even allowing for the fact that he was a diplomat, this was high praise indeed.

Another famous Canterbury inn was the Chequers of the

. The Blue Boar at Leicester, where Richard III slept on the eve of his death at
he Battle of Bosworth in 1485.

2. Two inns used by the Canterbury Pilgrims. The Tabard Inn (*above*) in Southwark High Street, at the start of the Dover Road. (*Below*) The Chequers of the Hope at Canterbury.

Hope, 'that every man doth know', on the east side of Mercery Lane. It was a very big house and the pillars which supported the open gallery round its wide courtyard formed a colonnade which ran the entire length of Mercery Lane. The Fleur de Lys in the High Street is one of the oldest inns in Canterbury still standing, for it was built in the early fifteenth century, and although the courtyard has now been roofed, there is still one fifteenth-century window looking on to it—long and narrow and supported by carved wooden brackets.

The pilgrim business became debased, in many ways, by the end of the fourteenth century, for a large number of pilgrims regarded their journeys to the shrines and the over-night stops on the way, at the free or extremely inexpensive pilgrim hostels, as a holiday jaunt.

William Thorpe, the Lollard, complained that pilgrims 'will ordain beforehand to have with them both men and women that can well sing wanton songs; and some other pilgrims will have with them bagpipes, so that every town they come through, what with the noise of their singing, and with the sound of their piping, and with the jangling of their Canterbury bells, and with the barking of dogs after them, they make more noise than if the King came'.

If a man vowed to take a pilgrimage, it was solemnly binding, and if he were unable to fulfil his promise he would seek absolution from his bishop. Sometimes he sent a deputy or left provision in his will for a professional pilgrim to undertake the visit on his behalf, to the shrine of his choice, for a suitable payment.

Gild members were given every encouragement when they set off on pilgrimages, their fellow members often giving them money for the journey and accompanying them to the town gates in a joyful procession, to the accompaniment of pipes and tabors. In some cities, the gilds provided hostels for pilgrims. At Coventry, for example, during the fourteenth century, there was a hostel with thirteen beds, maintained by a gild merchant, who also provided a master and a woman to attend to the pilgrims' needs and wash their feet, and this was only one of many, where pilgrims could pass the night, either for nothing or at a very small cost.

About three weeks was the usual leave of absence from work allowed for an English pilgrimage, but for a pilgrimage to Rome sixteen weeks were given and for Jerusalem a year. The more distant a shrine and the more inaccessible, the higher it rated in the final assessment of a man's virtue, and a scale of values was established. The journey to the shrine of St. David in Pembrokeshire was particularly long and difficult and two pilgrimages to St. David equalled a visit to Rome, while three rated as high as a visit to the Holy Land.

Chapter Three

TUDOR INNS

By TUDOR TIMES most of the large feudal manor houses, which in medieval times had offered hospitality to passing travellers, were in decline. During the sixteenth century, the dissolution of the monasteries meant that the second alternative a traveller might use for a night's lodging also disappeared, although by the time of the Reformation, despite the fact that many monasteries were still immensely wealthy, some had already become impoverished by over-generous hospitality, which had sometimes been flagrantly imposed on them. In 1475 the Duchess of York, for example, arrived at the Abbey of St. Benet's at Holm in Norfolk, with her entire household staff, with the intention, according to the Paston letters, of making a long stay 'if she liked the air'. St. Albans Abbey had long been famed for its lavish hospitality and at one time had stabling for three hundred horses, but by the end of the fifteenth century even visiting nobles were sent to lodge at the George Inn. At Abingdon all but the most important visitors were sent to the 'new hostelry', a secular inn which had replaced the old Abbey hospice.

There remained the few secular inns and the monastic hostels, some of which came into the possession of secular landlords, although those on the roads to remote shrines, where there was nothing else of any particular interest, disappeared altogether. During Cromwell's time, a baron of the Exchequer wrote to him on behalf of the City of Canterbury, to ask for the grant of a windmill which had once belonged to St. Augustine's Abbey, 'since the inn holders and victuallers had suffered so great a loss by the cessation of pilgrim traffic to the Shrine of St. Thomas'.

Travel became increasingly difficult and hazardous. The very word is derived from 'travail'. The roads were still appallingly bad. It is true that with the end of the pilgrim traffic there were fewer people using them, but this in itself proved a disadvantage, for the crowds who had used the pilgrim routes kept them in a tolerable state of repair, and they now fell into neglect and actually deteriorated.

The transport of heavy goods was made by sea or river wherever possible and otherwise by pack horse or pack mule trains. The only wheeled traffic was the medieval farm cart and, very occasionally, a horse litter used by women and children, and the usual method of travel was still by horse, while itinerant pedlars, minstrels and companies of actors covered long distances on foot.

With the accession of Queen Elizabeth I in 1558, the upper classes and rising middle classes of England's four million people began a half-century of splendid achievement and prosperity, during which they enjoyed the liberating thought and culture of the Renaissance. With the sea voyages of exploration and the capture of the Netherlands trade, when Northern Europe was overrun by Spain, London became the financial centre of Europe, in place of Antwerp. Inevitably many foreign visitors came to England and there was a need for more inns.

When Thomas Gresham built the Royal Exchange in London, a bourse similar to those which had been so busy and prosperous in Venice and Antwerp, before the decline of those cities as Europe's commercial centres, Stow wrote that the arcades were 'crowded with merchants, grave and sober men, walking within in pairs, or gathered in little groups. Amongst them were foreigners from Germany, France, Venice, Genoa, Antwerp and even Russia, conspicuous by their dress.'

Towards the end of the sixteenth century a *Manual of Foreign Conversation For the Use of Travellers* was published in Flanders, for the guidance of commercial travellers in foreign countries. It gave, in seven languages, specimens of conversation suitable for the traveller when he arrived at his inn, which were intended to cover all contingencies.

When the Netherlander arrived at an English inn he was advised to make polite opening gambits on the topics of trade and wars, and when he wished to go to bed he was told to broach the subject to his landlord by saying: "Sir, by your leave, I am sum what ill at ease", whereupon the following routine would follow naturally. The landlord, in this purely hypothetical conversation, would reply: "Sir, if you be ill at ease, go and take your rest, your chambre is readie. Joan, make a good fier in his chambre, and let him lacke nothing."

The traveller was then given instructions in his handbook for a long and demanding conversation with Joan, the chamber-maid.

Traveller: My shee frinde, is my bed made? Is it good?

Joan: Yes, Sir, it is a good fedder bed, the scheetes be very clean.

Traveller: I shake as a leafe upon the tree. Warme my kerchif and bynde my head well. Soft, you binde it to harde, bring my pillow and cover me well: pull off my hosen and warme my bed: drawe the curtines and pin them with a pin. Where is the chamber pot? Where is the priuie?

Joan: Follow me and I will show you the way: go up straight, you shall finde them at the right hand. If you see them not you shall smell them well enough. Sir, doth it please you to haue no other thing? Are you Wel?

Traveller: Yes, my shee frinde, put out the candel and come nearer to me.

Joan: I will put it out when I am out of the chamber. What is your pleasure, are you not well enough yet?

Traveller: My head lyeth to lowe, lift up a little the bolster, I can not lye so lowe—My shee frinde, kisse me once, and I shall sleape the better.

Joan: Sleape, sleape, you are not sicke, seeing that you speake of kissyng. I had rather die than to kisse a man in his bed, or in any other place. Take your rest, in God's name, God geeue you good night and goode rest.

Taking his rebuff in good part, the traveller meekly murmurs: "I thank you, fayre mayden" and goes to sleep, but in the morning he has recovered his spirit and is giving his orders again. "Drie my shirt, that I may rise", he shouts to the boy. "Where is the horse-keeper? Go tell him that hee my horse leads to the river."

But he does not forget Joan. "Where is ye maiden?" he asks, and when she appears he gives her a tip. "Hold my shee frinde, ther is for your paines." Then "Knave, bring hither my horse," he calls. "Have you dressed him well?" And as the boy brings him his horse, assuring the traveller that "he did wante nothing", the adventure is over and the Netherlander rides contentedly away, satisfied that he has fulfilled his social obligations and comported himself in seemly fashion.

At the beginning of the century, the furnishings of an inn were as sparse as those of a private house, but during the Elizabethan years the standard of comfort increased with the steady rise in prosperity which was enjoyed by a large proportion of the people, notwithstanding the numbers of unemployed and destitute.

The medieval chest became a settle with a back and arm rests. Stools became chairs, often beautifully carved, though they were not yet upholstered. In fact they were very hard indeed and when the Elizabethan fashion for padded trunk hose went out of favour, one sufferer had cause to complain bitterly that 'since great breeches were laid aside, men can scant endure to sit.' As separate dining-rooms became usual, the medieval trestle table developed into a draw-table with separate leaves, which could be added when the company was unusually large, and side-tables and court cupboards were made.

In the bedrooms, the old truckle beds were still in use, but now the magnificent, curtained four-posters appeared, usually approached by a short flight of steps, for they were often high enough for a truckle bed, used by a servant or child sleeping in the same room, to be pushed underneath when it was not in use.

With the four-posters came feather mattresses and pillows, linen sheets, blankets and embroidered coverlets.

Although in the poorer houses the practice of covering the beaten earth floor with straw and rushes persisted into the next century, in more prosperous households and in the better types of inn, the floors were made of planked wood, on which it was now fashionable to lay the Oriental carpets which had hitherto been used for wall coverings, as well as English carpets, which were just coming into manufacture.

It was in London that these luxuries were mainly to be found and here the first cushions and upholstered furniture were seen, but even the country people were beginning to discard the logs of wood they had previously used for head-rests and were taking to pillows of down and feathers.

Wall hangings of tapestry were still to be found, and they were becoming increasingly costly and elaborate, especially those imported from France and the Netherlands, but more carved oak panelling was used to cover plain, plastered walls.

William Harrison, writing in 1598, said that the houses in England were still mainly built of wood, though stone and brick were being increasingly used, and that not only in the houses of noblemen, but in the houses of 'knights, gentlemen, merchantmen and some other wealthy citizens it is not geson to behold generally their great provision of tapestry, Turkey work, pewter, brass, fine linen, and thereto costly cupboards of plate, worth five or six hundred or a thousand pounds . . .' while even 'inferior artificers and many farmers . . . have learned also to garnish their cupboards with plate, their joined beds with tapestry and silk hangings, and their table with carpets and fine napery, whereby the wealth of our country (God be praised therefore, and give us grace to employ it well) doth infinitely appear.'

In his own village, he said 'there were old men still living who recalled the remarkable changes which had come to the country' during their lifetimes. The first change was the 'multitude of chimneys in the towns . . .' The second was 'the great (although not general) amendment of lodging', for, they said, 'our fathers, yea and we ourselves also, have lain full oft upon straw pallets, rough mats covered only with a sheet, under coverlets made of dogswain or hop harlot (I use their own terms), and a good round log under their heads instead of a bolster or pillow. . . . Pillows (said they) were thought meet only for women in childbed. As for servants, if they had any sheet above them, it was well, for seldom had they any under their bodies to keep them from the pricking straws that ran oft through the canvas of the pallet and rased their hardened hides.'

The third great change they recalled was in table ware, the wooden trenchers and spoons of medieval days giving place to pewter platters and spoons of silver or tin.

These changing standards of comfort were to be found in the inns as well as private houses and by the end of the century the furnishings of the inns were said to compare favourably with those in any small manor house, while the food and service made them famous throughout all Europe.

Fynes Moryson, the Lincolnshire traveller of the early seventeenth century, who had visited scores of inns throughout Europe, declared that: 'The world affords not such inns as England hath, either for food and cheap entertainment after the guests' own pleasure, or for humble attendance on passengers, yea even in very poor villages. For as soon as a passenger comes to an inn, the servants run to him, and one takes his horse, and walks him till he be cold, then rubs him and gives him meat. . . . Another servant gives the passenger his private chamber, and kindles his fire; the third pulls off his boots and makes them clean. Then the host or hostess visit him; and if he will eat with the host, or at a common table with others, his meal will cost him sixpence, or in some places but four pence; yet this course is less honourable and not used by gentlemen. But if he will eat in his chamber, he commands what meat he will, yea the kitchen is open to him to command the meat to be dressed as he best likes. And when he sits down at table, the host or hostess will accompany him, or if they have many guests will at least visit him, taking it for courtesy to be bid sit down. While he eats, if he have company especially, he shall be offered music, which he may freely take or refuse. And if he be solitary, the musicians will give him good day with music in the morning. . . . A man cannot more freely command in his own house than he may do in his inn. And at parting, if he give some few pence to the chamberlain and ostler, they wish him a happy journey.'

This all sounds idyllic but it was, in fact, too good to be entirely true in many instances. There was another side to the picture. The accommodation for humbler travellers and servants was as primitive as it had been a century earlier. "I think this be the most villainous house in all London road for fleas," grumbled the carrier in the inn yard at Rochester, in Shakespeare's *Henry IV*. "I am stung like a tench."

Moreover there was a good deal of conniving and conspiracy between inn servants and highway robbers. Harrison complained of the practice 'by serving men whose wages cannot suffice so much as to find their breeches' giving information to highwaymen of the route that travellers were taking, and even the innkeepers were sometimes involved, 'to the utter undoing of many an honest yeoman as he journeyeth on his way.'

All travellers were armed, said Harrison: 'Seldom shall you see any of my countrymen above eighteen or twenty years old go without dagger at the least at his back or by his side. . . . The honest traveller is now forced to ride with a case of dags at his saddle-bow. . . . Seldom also are they or any other way-faring men robbed, without the consent of the chamberlain, tapster, or ostler where they bait and lie, who feeling at their alighting, whether their capcases or budgets be of any weight or not, by taking them down from their saddles, or otherwise see their store in drawing of their purses, do by-and-by give intimation to some one or other attendant daily in the yard or house, or dwelling hard by, upon such matches, whether the prey be worth the following or no. If it be for their turn, then the gentleman peradventure is asked which way he travelleth, and whether it please him to have another guest to bear him company at supper, who rideth the same way in the morning that he doth, or not. And thus if he admit him, or be glad of his acquaintance, the cheat is half wrought. And often it is seen that the new guest shall be robbed with the old, only to colour out the matter and keep him from suspicion. Sometimes, when they know which way the passenger travelleth, they will either go before and lie in wait for him, or else come galloping apace after, whereby they will be sure, if he ride not the stronger, to be fingering with his purse. And these are some of the policies of such shrewd or close-booted gentlemen as lie in wait for fat booties by the highways, and which are most commonly practised in the winter season, about the feast of Christmas, when serving-men and unthrifty gentlemen want money to play at the dice and cards, lewdly spending in such wise whatever they have wickedly gotten, till some of them sharply set upon their chevisances, be trussed up in a Tyburn tippet, which happeneth unto them commonly before they come to middle age. Whereby it appeareth that some sort of youth will oft have his swing, although it be in a halter.'

Harman, a contemporary of Harrison, thought that nearly all ostlers were dishonest. 'Not one amongst twenty of them but have well left their honesty,' he declared.

In *Henry IV*, Shakespeare describes just such an incident as Harrison, when the chamberlain of the inn at Rochester appears and whispers the news to Falstaff's men that "there's a franklin in the wild of Kent hath brought three hundred marks with him in gold; I heard him tell it to one of his company last night at supper: a kind of auditor; one that hath abundance of change too, God knows what. They are up already, and call for eggs and butter; they will be away presently."

The penalty for those who were caught was the gallows, but Harrison complained that 'selfish men, and even constables, in the country, won't leave their work to follow up thieves and take them to prison.'

Despite the prosperity of much of Elizabeth's reign, rogues and vagabonds, beggars and vagrants became an increasing menace. There were a number of economic reasons for this, including the change from arable farming to sheep-rearing during the mid-century wool boom, the restrictive practice of the gilds against men who came to the towns to seek alternative work, and the system of enclosures. All these causes produced hundreds of destitute people. At one time the number was estimated at ten thousand, and many of them turned to robbery in order to keep alive, thereby increasing the hazards of honest travellers. The creation of the Elizabethan poor laws, the founding of hospitals, schools and almshouses, helped the situation but did not solve the problem.

Stow described an inn in London where training for the business of picking pockets was given professionally, by a man called Wotton, who must have been the model for Dickens' Fagin.

'One Wotton, a Gentleman born, and sometime a Merchant of Good Credit, but falling by Time into Decay . . . kept an Alehouse at Smart's—very near Billingsgate. . . . And in the same house he procured all the Cutpurses about the City to repair to his House. There was a School-house set up, to learn young boys to cut Purses: two Devices were hung up, the one was a Pocket, the other was a Purse. The Pocket had in it certain Counters, and was hung about with Hawk's bells, and over the top did hang a little Scaring Bell. The Purse had silver in it. And he that could take out a Counter without any Noise was allowed to be a public Foyster. And he that could take a piece of silver out of the Purse without Noise of any of the Bells was adjudged a judicial Nypper, according to their Terms of Art. A Foyster was a Pickpocket, a Nypper was a Pickpurse or Cutpurse.'

Travelling was still a very slow business. In Henry VII's day a royal messenger took six days to ride from Greenwich to Stirling. A King's Messenger, riding on urgent state business, had the power to impress fresh horses on his route, but in Queen Elizabeth's reign the first posting houses were established at inns along the main highways, where the innkeepers, for a small salary paid by the Crown, were prepared to have fresh horses ready for the royal couriers. In times of emergency, a special messenger would ride ahead, to warn the post-master of the inn at the next stopping place of the approach of the courier, but if the journey were off the beaten track, the riders had to present a warrant to the mayor, authorizing the requisition of post-horses immediately, and sometimes the horses had to be hurriedly unharnessed from a plough or farm cart. It was an expensive business, for the charge of impounding horses was about 1s. 8d. a post of between ten and fifteen miles and in 1589 the cost of the Queen's messengers amounted to £5,000 a year, but the horse-owners benefited and there was competition amongst the inn-keepers to become post-masters, not so much because of the profits from hiring horses or the small income they received, as for the extra custom it brought to their inns. The service was soon being used by private travellers, although this was not officially allowed until 1583, when a fixed charge of twopence a mile was made, but people using this 'Through Post' were obliged to use a guide, at a charge of fourpence a post, whose duty was to see the traveller to the next posting house, which often had a horn, or the painted sign of a horn, hanging outside. The guide had to carry the passenger's luggage, provided it did not exceed 14 lbs., and to blow his horn 'so oft as he meeteth company' through towns and villages, or at least three times in a mile in open country.

No horse was allowed to be ridden for more than one stage, without the consent of the owner, and the postmaster had to have at least four horses and two horns in readiness and keep a record of all users of the post.

In 1603 the charge was raised to 3d. a mile and a few years later innkeepers were allowed to make their own terms with travellers, for there were many complaints that horses were ridden too hard. Englishmen were not considered to be good riders. 'The English generally are observed by all Nations, to ride commonly with that speed, as if they rid for a midwife or a Physician, or to get a pardon to save one's life as he goeth to execution . . . which made them call England the Hell of Horses', wrote Howell, and advised all those who could to learn to ride in Italy. English saddles were also disliked by many visitors and a German traveller took one home with him to show 'how very wretched and hard to ride upon' it was.

One of the first carriers in England was Tobias Hobson, an innkeeper of Cambridge, who in 1568 inherited a cart and eight horses from his father. Besides hiring horses he began a carrier service for the transport of both people and goods which became famous throughout East Anglia. Then he began a carrier service between Cambridge and London which was licensed by the University, his place of call in London being the Bell Inn, Bishopsgate Street Within.

He was a man of character and something of an eccentric. 'He kept a stable of forty good cattle, always fit and ready for travelling,' said *The Spectator*, 'but when a man came for a horse he was led into the stable, where there was a great choice, but was obliged to take the horse which stood nearest to the stable-door; so that every customer was alike well served, according to his chance, and every horse ridden with the same justice.' Thus the traveller had no opportunity to choose for himself but had to accept 'Hobson's choice'.

Within a few years a number of these stage-waggons were in service. They were nothing more than the old four-wheeled waggons of earlier days, which had been used for the transport of goods, but they were now provided with a cloth hood and used as conveyances for fare-paying passengers as well. They were drawn by 'seven or eight horses in file, one behind the other, with plumes and bells, and embroidered cloth coverings' and sometimes twenty or thirty passengers were crammed in, to make themselves as comfortable as they could amongst the bales and boxes and bundles which made up the carrier's normal load. By 1637 the names and routes of more than two hundred carriers travelling the main roads of England were listed in the *Carrier's Cosmography*.

The first coach was not built in England until 1555 and the following year Queen Mary bought one. Queen Elizabeth also had a coach but disliked it intensely and it was many years before she could be persuaded to ride in it again after the first trial. She preferred to make her long progresses on horseback, her baggage train, amounting at times to three hundred heavily laden carts, plodding behind. These were usually two-wheeled carts, drawn by five or six horses, for the four-wheeled carrier waggons, with their iron-shod wheels, were too heavy for steep roads in the hilly districts or the sticky clay soils of the south. It was not until late in her reign that she could be persuaded to trust herself again to a coach, and then a new one was specially made for her journey through London to St. Paul's, to give thanks for the victory of the Armada. It was a very magnificent-looking affair, but in construction it was nothing more than a box on wheels. It was open at the sides but the back and front were curved into magnificent scrolls, elaborately carved and painted, and they were surmounted by a regal-looking dome, all a-flutter with plumes.

More coaches were built towards the end of the century but for several years there was little development in design. They remained like boxes and had no springs. They were provided with a canopy, but the sides were open, though fitted with curtains for privacy and to keep out the rain. They were carved and brightly painted, and their gay appearance belied the extreme discomfort the passengers must have endured. At first they were drawn by two and sometimes four horses, harnessed abreast, the coachman riding postilion. Later they were drawn by six horses, a postilion riding one of the leaders and the coachman, by this time provided with a seat, driving the others.

Although in and around London and other large towns, these unsprung coaches gradually came into use, they were no good for long journeys on the rough, narrow country roads, and until the end of Tudor times the innkeepers were catering only for horse-riding travellers.

The medieval inns prospered and many more were built during the sixteenth century, in the towns and villages along the main roads, for the increasing numbers of travellers, whose journeys would have been impossible without a plentiful supply of inns.

In London the Southwark inns, including the Tabard, received travellers and goods from Kent, Surrey and Sussex. To the Bull and Mouth,[1] near St. Martin's-le-Grand, and the inns of Aldersgate came the travellers and carriers from the Midlands and the North, and in Bishopsgate and Aldgate were inns to receive the travellers and goods from East Anglia.

Apart from London, York and Bristol, the towns and cities of Elizabethan England were very small and few if any had any public buildings, so that goods were brought to the inns by the carriers, to await collection. The function of the inn developed until many became important business centres for the town and surrounding countryside, and the innkeepers provided not

[1] The name is a corruption of Boulogne Mouth—the mouth of Boulogne harbour.

only special rooms for distinguished visitors, but rooms and offices where business could be transacted.

J. K. Fowler has left a valuable description of the White Hart Inn at Aylesbury which, long before the coaching days, had become more important to the social and business life of Aylesbury than the beautiful medieval King's Head close by. The White Hart, which was pulled down in 1863 to make way for the Corn Exchange, was a galleried inn which had been built in the fifteenth century and became an important Yorkist meeting place during the Wars of the Roses. It stood in the market square, the front composed of three gables, surrounded by carved timbers, the first floor overhanging the ground floor and the second floor the first floor. 'In the centre was a large gateway, the floor above supported by great fluted posts, with heavy hanging oak gates, which could be closed when required. This confronted a spacious yard, one half of which was bounded by an open, covered gallery, into which the bedrooms opened. This gallery was supported on strong oak pillars: a broad covered staircase rose from near the entrance into the gallery, and formed the main approach to the principal sitting and bedrooms. There were large rooms on either side of the entrance, and adjoining was the business portion of the inn. . . .

'On one side of the gateway was the room called the "Change", where the principal business transactions of the town were discussed, on the other side the "Crown", where the customs, excise, and other duties were periodically collected. Another room was the "Mitre", where the Bishop of the Diocese had for three hundred years collected his ecclesiastical fees and dues by his chancellor, as also the archdeacon did the same by his apparitor. There was also the "Fountain", a name often appertaining to old inns; this sometimes gave the name to the inn itself. There has always been much speculation and doubt as to the origin of this term, but we know it often existed with inns of this importance.'

3. The Bull and Mouth Inn at St. Martin's-le-Grand, London. (*Left*) Courtyard of the old inn and (*below*) the façade of the new Bull and Mouth after reconstruction, when the name was changed to the Queen's Hotel.

4. (*Above left*) Tobias Hobson, a sixteenth-century innkeeper of Cambridge w one of the first carriers in England. (*Above right*) Examples of seventeenth-centu hackney coaches (the 'Hackney Hell-Carts') and (*below*) the early nineteenth-centu London to Birmingham Tally-Ho coach.

The Fountain was, in fact, very probably the equivalent of the modern bar.

The kitchen of the White Hart filled one end of the yard and the cellars were under the front part. The garden at the back included a full-sized bowling green, flanked by giant elms and a row of walnut trees. Beyond was an orchard of apple and pear trees and three very ancient mulberries 'at least three centuries old', wrote J. K. Fowler, in 1892. 'The orchard contained the cow-house, piggeries, and a hospital for horses when lame or ill. This orchard was bounded by a mill stream and in the midst was a large shallow pond, called a "stew", for fresh-water fish, in which was kept an eel trunk, consisting of a strong, iron-bound box about four feet long and two feet wide and deep, perforated with holes, and a lid fastened with a lock and key, the latter kept by the man cook, who was the head of the servants. In this trunk were kept live eels, the trunk having a strong iron chain attached to it, which was fastened to the base of a large tree adjoining; this enabled the trunk to be hauled up a sloping bank . . . when company required fish. Two or three big perch, with the same number of tench, were also kept there. A rookery was established in the elms. . . . The stables were stalled. . . . The lofts for hay, straw and corn, being over the stables, generally a considerable quantity of corn and fodder was kept for some weeks' consumption.' There was accommodation for about fifty horses, with harness rooms and rooms for the ostlers and post-boys, and the whole establishment covered nearly six acres.

On public holidays and other festive occasions a stage was built in the courtyard for sparring matches and cock-fighting.

There are no records of plays having been performed at the White Hart, but it was in Tudor times that they were first given in inn-yards. After the production of the first English comedy, *Gammer Gurton's Needle*, at Cambridge, in 1566, the fashion for the play spread quickly. Schools and universities and also the Inns of Court all put on their own plays and a few professional companies appeared for the first time, each sponsored by a rich nobleman. They gave their performances in the courtyards of inns, with privileged spectators ranged in the surrounding galleries and the rest crowded below, round the stage.

With the Vagrancy Act of 1572, the position of the actors was difficult, and the Puritans in particular disapproved of them, but two years later the Queen gave a licence for a few of the companies to act throughout the country, and within the next few years there were six companies of actors based in London, who acted in the inn courtyards and from time to time toured the country. Although the companies had wealthy patrons, they had a struggle to make ends meet, for the inns took the money from the gallery audiences and the actors had to collect what they could from the courtyard.

The Puritans were not able to prevent the performance of plays, but managed to exercise a strict censorship on the choice of the play and the place of its performance by limiting the issue of licences. They complained of dangerous overcrowding in the inns and the risk of spreading infection and plague: and as the performances were held during daylight hours, they bemoaned the fact that people were tempted to take time off from work to watch them.

After 1576, when James Burbage built the first London theatre, the practice of performing plays in the inn courtyards gradually disappeared, but the first theatres were very much like the courtyards, being open to the sky and surrounded by covered galleries, while the stage was a platform projecting into the auditorium, so that the audience surrounded it on three sides.

'When the theatre architect began to build regular play-houses, he accepted the tradition of the inn-yard play-boys', wrote Ivor Brown. 'The first English professional theatres were direct descendants of the hostelry into whose court the players had drawn their platform and properties. A platform, with a pent-house, arose as it were amid the galleries of a tavern, which surrounded this platform-stage almost entirely. The lords, ladies, and wealthy patrons went to occupy seats aloft. The groundlings stood in the relics of the coach-yard. Dramatists must compose their play to suit their premises, and the free-and-easy motion and the rhetorical splendour of the Elizabethan drama were conditioned by the large platform-stage, absence of frontal curtain, and lack of roof in the theatres which had sprung from the inn-yard. Consequently, it is no exaggeration to say that, among the many gifts brought to English life by the English inn, was the cut and shape of Shakespeare's plays.'

Chapter Four

INNS OF STUART ENGLAND

ONE OF THE first acts of the reign of James I pronounced that 'the ancient and principall True use of Innes and Victualling Houses is for the Receipte, Relief and Lodginge of wayfaring people travelling from place to place.' Both innkeepers and alehouse-keepers were required to 'keep one or more spare Beds for lodging of strangers' and if they refused, without good cause, a constable could force admittance for the traveller, although the constable's manual at the time very rightly remarked that 'how the officer shall compell him is not yet set down'. Tavern-keepers, on the other hand, were forbidden to 'harbour travellers' and in 1599 a tavern-keeper of Hitchin had been charged with using 'lodging for pack men, whereas in truth the same house was never hitherto used as an inn'.

He was probably just unlucky, for in practice people did very much what they felt inclined about receiving travellers and there were very few constables about to enforce the letter of the law, which had been framed in the first place in an attempt to keep track of people's movements. One chronicler, Nicholas Brooks, a fishmonger of Southwark, recorded that he left his home in December and lodged the first night of his journey at the Fleur-de-Lys in St. Albans. The two following nights he stayed at the Redd Lyon at Luton, but when, on the following afternoon, he reached Wheathampstead, the host of the Bull could not, or would not, accommodate him and he had to bribe a John Skale with a quarter of a pound of tobacco and two flagons of beer before he would lead him to the Tinn Pott, where he found 'good entertainment for himself and his two horses'. Otherwise he would have had to spend the night 'under a hedgerow'.

Despite the political troubles of the seventeenth century, England's economy steadily expanded, which meant that more people needed to travel about the country, thereby creating the need for more inns. Many more were built but travellers were still often hard put to find accommodation, especially in the more remote parts of the country. Nor, when a landlord was making a fair enough living by the sale of liquor to the locals, and did not want to bestir himself by preparing a bed and a meal, were they always welcomed, for although this was the century of the Puritans, there was undoubtedly 'inordinate hauntinge and tiplinge in Innes, Alehouses and other Victual-linge Houses' which kept the innkeepers prosperous and busy.

A broadsheet was published giving rules for innkeepers and their guests, 'meet to be fixed upon the wall of every Chamber'. Innkeepers were told that it 'must not be accounted a small matter to afford house roome, lodging, rest and food to the comfort of God's children' and they must 'account honest men your best guests: ever hold their company better than their roomes. Content yourselves with an honest gaine, so using your guests as they may have an appetite to return to you when they are gone from you, and make choice of good servants', while the advice to guests included a reminder that 'ye are in the worlde as in an Inn to tarry for a short space, and then to be gone hence. Eat and drink for necessity and strength, and not for lust. At table let your talk be powdered with the salt of heavenly wisdom, as your meat is seasoned with material and earthly salt. At night when you come to your Inne thank God for your Preservation: next morning pray for a good journey.'

There was plenty of justification for this last piece of advice, for travelling was still an arduous and very chancy business, mainly because the English roads remained in a deplorably neglected state throughout the whole of the Stuart period, and the slow development of wheeled traffic and coaches did little to ease the hardships of the travellers.

The medieval law decreeing that the highways should be cleared on either side had lapsed through being consistently ignored. If land running by the roadside were good and fertile, it was surreptitiously enclosed, which made the road even narrower. 'There is good land where there is foul way,' remarked Cotton shrewdly. It was still the business of each parish to maintain the high roads within its boundaries, and landowners were responsible for the by-ways through their properties, but boundaries were ill-defined and the easiest way to avoid the responsibility of maintaining a road was to enter into lengthy litigation about ownership, which could drag on for months and even years.

Farmers were expected to give their services free for road maintenance or pay a tax in proportion to the size of their holding. The local Justice of the Peace appointed a surveyor who usually collected the money from the unwilling parishioners and then hired, or more often impressed, labourers, who could ill-afford to lose a day's wages, to patch up the roads as best they could. They filled in the ruts with whatever came to hand—usually loose stones and scrub—and made an attempt to cut back the undergrowth, but it was all very haphazard, and the workmen, who were dignified by the title of the King's Highwaymen while they were on the job, were usually so idle that they were known as the King's Loiterers and spent most of their time begging from passing travellers. Pepys, during his journey to Bath, mentions on one or two occasions giving money to the road-menders. One day it was sixpence and three days later as much as two shillings.

The roadmen's task was a thankless one, for no one had yet thought of building hard roads comparable with the old Roman roads, which were still the most reliable in the country; and where stone was not easily available, the winter ruts were sometimes ploughed level in the spring, only to become just as bad again with the next autumn rains.

Sometimes the road consisted of a narrow, fairly solid causeway with wide ditches of mud on either side, so that when a rider met a waggon train or a coach coming in the opposite direction he was forced into the mud, sometimes up to his saddle-bags. In summer ruts were deep enough to overturn a coach or throw a rider, and the floods and ice of winter sometimes made the roads impassable for weeks at a time.

There were constant protests and many proposals for improving the roads, one suggestion being to 'remove the obstructions, clean the ditches, let in the sun and air, and the roads will grow better of themselves', which was an odd philosophy at a time when the Age of Reason was considered to be supplanting the Age of Belief.

Nothing really useful was done about them until the latter part of the eighteenth century, when Blind Jack of Knaresborough built miles of roads across the hills of northern England and McAdam built roads with a hard core of broken stone: and it was not until the early years of the nineteenth century and the heyday of the fast stage-coaches that Thomas Telford built roads with a firm base on carefully chosen, practical routes which avoided the steeper hills.

But in Stuart times people floundered through the mud or were pitched and tossed over the deep, dried ruts, and it is remarkable that they survived as well as they did.

A great deal of travelling was still on horseback but coaches gradually became more practicable, and both private and 'hackney' or hired coaches came increasingly into use. A rank for the first hackney coaches—the Hackney Hell carts— appeared in London in 1634, forming at the Maypole in the Strand. In the narrow, crowded streets they caused frightful traffic jams and when two met head-on, there was no room to give way, even if either coachman had wanted to, which he seldom did. Amidst shouts and oaths, wheels came off and coaches overturned, to the delight of the onlookers and the mortification of the passengers. Drivers haggled over fares and drove too fast. The situation had not changed when Pepys was writing thirty years later. 'Thence by coach, with a mad coachman, that drove like mad. Everybody through the street cursing him, being ready to run over them.'

By 1635 there was an attempt to suppress coaches, but the coachmen had no intention of going out of business and within a few weeks, after much argument and protest, fifty hackney coachmen were fully licensed again, being allowed twelve horses each. It was about this time that sedan chairs appeared in London, and while some people welcomed them as a possible solution to London's traffic problem, it was a long time before they became fashionable, for there was at first a 'loathing that men should be brought to as servile a condition as horses' and it was not until Queen Anne's reign that there were some three hundred licensed carriers in London, as well as many privately-owned sedan chairs, whereas by 1669 there were eight hundred hackney coachmen in London and Westminster, plying for hire.

During the first part of the seventeenth century the number of privately-owned coaches steadily increased, but at first they were still heavy and cumbersome, with a square body and domed roof, covered with black leather and studded with brass nails. They were suspended by leather straps from upright posts attached to the axle trees and there was accommodation for two passengers in the back and front boots, which were the spaces between the coach and the wheels.

The coachman sat precariously on a cross-bar, his feet resting on the carriage pole, and he was as uncomfortable as the unfortunate boot passengers.

The exact date of the beginning of a public coach service is not certain but by 1637 two coaches were running each week between St. Albans and the Bell Inn, Aldersgate, and there were also services to Hertford and Cambridge, which were probably made by coach during the summer and waggon in the winter.

There was little development of the coaching services during the Civil War, but by 1647 there was a regular service between Rochester and Gravesend, the place of embarkation for the 'Long Ferry' to London. The following year Taylor, the water poet, with a party of friends, hired the coach 'which comes weekly to the Rose at Holborn Bridge' to make the three-day journey to Southampton, in order to visit the King at Carisbrooke Castle: and by 1655 stage coaches seem to have been established on many of the main highways from London. This was the year that Marmaduke Rawdon, a Yorkshireman, hired an entire coach to take himself and a party of friends from Exeter to London: and when the young and attractive Mrs. Fax arrived from Plymouth at the Exeter inn where Rawdon was staying, also hoping to take the coach to London, she was dismayed to learn that it was fully engaged, as she had urgent business in London 'which could not wait a week'.

Choosing her moment when they were just about to leave and were in a mellow mood, taking their early morning claret in the inn kitchen, Mrs. Fax presented herself to Rawdon and his friends and asked whether they could find room for her as well. And as she was 'a proper hansome young woman' there was no difficulty. Rawdon not only agreed, but gave her the best place at the 'brood end' of the coach. He would take no money for her fare and entertained her handsomely to dinner and supper at all the stopping places on the way.

By 1656 there was a coach service from London to York and in 1657 a public coach to Chester, the port for Ireland, was running three days a week. It left the George Inn, Aldersgate, every Monday, Wednesday and Friday and arrived four or five days later at the Bear and Billet in Chester. This was an excellent inn which had once been a mansion belonging to the Earl of Shrewsbury and it offered travellers good entertainment whilst awaiting a fair wind for the passage across the Irish Sea. For this journey the advertisement announced the innovation that fresh horses would be used once a day, for up till this time, though riders had ridden post for many years, the coach horses were not changed. This was a first step towards speeding up the journey, but it was to be many more years before coach horses were changed at every post.

By the year of the Restoration, there were coaches running to Durham and Newcastle, to Preston, Lancaster and Kendal, and to Exeter and Plymouth. These services were established by the innkeepers, who were quick to see the possibilities of increasing their business. At first the proprietors of the coach services were mainly based on the London inns and as their business increased so did the comfort and service of their inns, but those at the stopping places on the roads were not always so good and the coaches were still extremely uncomfortable. Many of them were discarded private coaches, of obsolete design and still without springs, which the innkeepers had bought up cheaply. There were usually six inside passengers, sitting three abreast, facing each other, on hard wooden benches, with their feet buried in straw for warmth. There were no windows and in winter they were protected by leather curtains: but three or four passengers, travelling at half fare, were accommodated in 'the conveniency behind', which was a straw basket suspended over the boot, with no protection from the wind and weather, and in some coaches a boot to carry four people, sitting in pairs, back to back, was built on to the back part of the coach.

After the Restoration, there was a great improvement in the design of private coaches. They were provided with glass windows and proper doors in place of the leather flaps, and coach-builders, helped by the experiments of some of the members of the Royal Society, began to investigate the problem of springs. Many more coaches were built for private owners and by the 1670s there were an estimated six thousand in and around London alone, and many more throughout the rest of the country, though where the roads were exceptionally bad, a footman had to walk ahead with an axe, to clear the way.

The Company of the Coach and Harness Makers was founded in 1677 and coaches became very elegant, often heavily gilded and beautifully painted. In fact they became so ornate that a law was passed forbidding the use of gilding, as it was considered a waste of gold, but it had little effect and a handsome coach became a matter of social prestige.

The public coach services were extended and by 1680 every town of any importance within a radius of twenty to twenty-five miles of London had a service of one or more coaches running once or twice a week, at a cost of twopence or threepence a mile. The journey from London to Stanmore took from between four and six hours, the 'Flying Coach' from London to Oxford a day.

Yet the roads were still bad and travelling in the boot was purgatory: and there are far more stories about the trials of coach travelling during these years than of the comfort or discomfort of the inns. In 1663 the Reverend Edward Parker made the journey from Preston to London. 'I got to London on Saturday last', he wrote home. 'My journey was noe way pleasant, being forced to ride in the boote all the waye. . . . My journey's expense was 30s. This travell hath soe indisposed me, yt I am resolved never to ride up again in ye coatche. I am extremely hott and feverish. What this may tend to I know not. I have not yet advised my doctor.'

Four years later the Bell Savage Inn on Ludgate Hill announced the opening of their service by 'Flying Machine' to Bath.

All those desirous to pass from London to Bath, or any other Place on their Road, let them repair to the Bell Savage on Ludgate Hill in London, and the White Lion at Bath, at both which places they may be received in a Stage Coach every Monday, Wednesday and Friday, which perform the Whole Journey in Three

Days (if God permit), and sets forth at five o'clock in the morning. Passengers to pay One Pound five shillings each, who are allowed to carry fourteen Pounds weight—for all above to pay three-halfpence per Pound.

Bath was not yet at the height of its fashion but the therapeutic properties of its mineral waters were becoming increasingly valued, and it was a shrewd move on the part of the proprietor of the Bell Savage to open the coach service.

The Bell Savage, later to be known as the Belle Sauvage, was one of the most important inns in the City of London. In the time of Henry VI it had been owned by a John French and was known as the Bell on the Hoop, but during the reign of Queen Elizabeth it came into the possession of Isabel Savage and acquired its new name. Its courtyard was a popular place for the performance of plays and Queen Elizabeth's favourite comic actor, Tarleton, was often on the bill. He was a little man, with a flat nose and a squint, the kind of comedian who gets a laugh the minute he appears on the stage. He was famous for his miming, dancing and singing and was the original of Shakespeare's 'poor Yorick', whom Hamlet lamented.

There was also a school of dancing held at the Bell Savage and a variety of entertainments including wrestling matches, cock-fighting and bear-baiting, while at one time it had a small menagerie, which included Marocco, the famous performing horse.

The inn was built round two courtyards, the outer one opening on to Ludgate Hill and containing several private houses, while the inn itself, advertising forty rooms, good cellarage and stabling for a hundred horses, was built round the three galleries of the inner courtyard.

At one of the houses in the outer courtyard lived the young Grinling Gibbons, and as a sign of his craft he carved a little pot of flowers in wood, which stood on his windowsill. The work was so delicate that the petals of the flowers used to quiver as the coaches passed by. John Evelyn was one of the first to notice the young woodcarver's masterly work and it was he who recommended him to Charles II and Queen Catherine and set him on the road to fame.

The George Inn at Aldersgate soon followed the lead of the Bell Savage by offering coach services to Salisbury in two days, Blandford and Dorchester in two and a half, Axminster and Exeter in four days. Soon it extended its routes to Newark, Doncaster and York, Birmingham, Wolverhampton and Shrewsbury, and was offering the run to Edinburgh once a fortnight for £4.

The George became as important and busy as the Bell Savage and there were a dozen or more flourishing coaching inns to the west of the City, several of which had been built after the Restoration, such as the George in Holborn and the Blue Boar close by, where prisoners on their way to Tyburn were allowed to stop for a final dram.

It was in 1673 that John Cresset published his famous diatribe against coaches. It was inspired perhaps by the disgruntled horse-dealers who feared they would be selling fewer riding horses and the equally worried innkeepers who were missing the coaching business.

Cresset estimated that at this time fifty-four people were travelling each week by coach between London, York, Chester and Exeter. The yearly figure he put at 1,872, which implies that some coaches were not yet running during the winter months.

'What advantage is it to a Man's health to be called out of their Beds into these Coaches an hour before day in the morning, to be hurried in them from place to place, till one hour, two, or three within night?' he wrote. 'Insomuch that, after sitting all day in the summer-time stifled with heat, and choacked with dust; or in the Wintertime, starving and freezing with cold, or by Torchlight, when it is too late to sit up to get a Supper: and next morning they are forced into the coach so early, that they can get no breakfast: What addition is this to

men's Health or Business, to ride all day with strangers, often-
times Sick, ancient deseased Persons, or young Children
crying; to whose humours they are obliged to be subject. . . ,
and many times crippled by the crowd of Boxes and Bundles?
Is it for a Man's Health to travel with tired Jades, to be laid fast
in the foul Wayes, and forced to wade up to the knees in mire;
afterwards to sit in the cold, till Teams of Horses can be sent
to pull the Coach out? Is it for their health to travel in rotten
Coaches, and to have their Tackle, or Pearch, or axletree
broken, and then to wait three or four hours (sometimes half
a day) to have them mended again, and then to travel all night
to make good their stage? Is it for a Man's pleasure, or advan-
tagions to their health and Business, to travel with a mixt
Company that he knows not how to converse with; to be
affronted by the rudeness of a surly, dogged, cursing, ill-
natured Coachman, necessitated to Lodge or Bait at the worst
Inns on the Road, where there is no accommodation fit for
Gentlemen; and this merely because the Owners of the Inns,
and the Coachmen, are agreed to cheat the Guests?'

John Cresset's eloquence fell on deaf ears, for the innkeepers
prospered. He had suggested that many roadside inns which had
catered for the post-horse riders would lose custom because
of the speed of the coaches which would pass them by, but in
practice, throughout the whole of the seventeenth century, the
riders were faster than the coaches. In that same year, 1673,
the journey to Exeter, which in 1658 had been advertised as
taking only four days, was now taking eight days in summer
and ten in winter, perhaps to placate the innkeepers on the route.

As coaches became increasingly comfortable, the public
coach services were expanded by the innkeepers. De Laune, in
The Present State of London, dated 1681, lists a hundred and
nineteen public coaches, between sixty and seventy for long
distances and the rest for journeys of twenty to twenty-five
miles from London. There were five coaches a week to Bath
and Bristol, four to Exeter, three to Guildford and two each to

Cambridge, Braintree, Canterbury, Chelmsford, Gloucester, Lincoln and Stamford, Norwich, Oxford, Portsmouth, Reading, Saffron Walden and Ware.

Chamberlayne, in the 1684 edition of *The Present State of Great Britain*, wrote that 'There is of late such an admirable commodiousness for both men and women to travel from London to the principal towns of the country, that the like hath not been known in the world; and that is by stage-coaches, wherein any one may be transported to any place, sheltered from foul weather and foul ways, free from endamaging of one's health and one's body by hard joggling or over-violent motion, and this not only at the low price of about a shilling for every five miles, but with such velocity and speed in one hour as that the post in some foreign countries cannot make but in one day.'

'Those townes that we call thorowfaires have great and sumptuous innes builded in them,' Harrison had written late in the previous century, 'for the receiving of such travellers and strangers as pass to and fro. . . . Our inns are also verie well furnished with naperie . . . for beside the linnen used at the tables, which is commonly washed dailie . . . each commoner is sure to lie in cleane sheets, wherein no man hath beene lodged since they came from the laundresse. . . . If the traveller have an horse, his bed doth cost him nothing, but if he go on foot he is sure to paie a penie for the same: but whether he be horseman or footman if his chamber be once appointed he may carie the kaie with him, as of his own house so long as he lodgeth there.'

During the seventeenth century and the beginning of coaching days, many of the coaching inns maintained this tradition of a high standard of comfort and service and amongst those which became famous for the elegance of their appointments was the White Hart at Aylesbury.

During the Civil War the Earl of Rochester had taken shelter there with Sir Nicholas Armorer. They had been seen entering the inn and the Justice of the Peace was warned. He called at the White Hart, saw the two horses in the stable and was satisfied of the identity of the owners. He warned Gilvy, the innkeeper, 'that he should not suffer those horses nor the persons to whom they belonged, to go out of the house, till he, the said Justice, came thither in the morning, when he would examine the gentlemen, who they were, and from whence they came.'

He made a mistake to postpone the examination, or perhaps he did not relish it, for as soon as he had departed, Gilvy warned the Earl and his companion. Leaving their own horses in the stable, he produced two more and the Cavaliers were able to make their escape from the back of the inn.

At the Restoration, the Earl of Rochester returned to Aylesbury and as a token of gratitude to Gilvy he arranged for the building of the beautiful Rochester room at the White Hart. It was on the first floor, a magnificent chamber forty-two feet long by twenty-three wide and twelve feet high, panelled with recessed classical murals by Verrio, a painted ceiling and large, elaborately carved fireplace.

However, inns in remote parts of the country fell very far short of these high standards. John Taylor made many journeys of exploration through England and when he arrived at the Rose and Crown at Nether Stowey, one hot summer's day in 1649, he found that the host was drunk and the hostess nowhere to be seen. The rooms were full of smoke and the walls and ceilings hung with 'rare spiders' tapestry'. The host offered him 'powdered beef' and carrots for supper, which Taylor gladly accepted. Then he went and sat in the street to wait for it. After three hours he returned to the inn, his 'hungry selfe half starv'd with expectation', but found that the fire had gone out, there was no boiled beef, the host was asleep and the maid feeding the pigs. He woke the host, demanding his beef, and was asked to content himself with eggs fried with parsley. He went up to his room, which was a poor sort of place, 'suitable to the rest of the house', and there waited for another two hours, but at nine o'clock the host came up to tell him there were no eggs to be had, so poor Taylor bought himself a piece of bread and butter and went to bed, to be tormented by 'an Ethiopian Army of Fleas'. He dispatched them as best he could, but just as he was dropping off to sleep three children began to cry. They kept him awake for another hour and by the time they had been quietened the dogs began to bark and continued till daybreak, when the hogs woke up and cried for their breakfast, whereupon Taylor arose and 'almost sleeping' continued his journey.

It was a different picture from that drawn by kindly old Isaak Walton, whose long life spanned nearly the whole of the seventeenth century. His love and knowledge of the country and country pursuits, particularly fishing, were nurtured in the fields and rivers to the north-east of London, mainly around Tottenham and Waltham, and in his *Compleat Angler* the fishermen, after a day's sport, repair to an inn[1] where they find 'a cleanly room, lavender in the windows and twenty ballads stuck about the wall'. The hostess is clean, handsome and civil and knows how to dress the fish after Piscator's own fashion. Having made an excellent supper of their gallant trout, they pass a happy evening drinking ale, singing ballads and exchanging fishing stories with a fellow angler who drops in to join them, and at last go to their beds, 'the linen of which looks white and smells of lavender.'

In June, 1668, Pepys set out for Bath, travelling by coach. At Newport Pagnell they were comfortable and rose the next day at four o'clock. 'A few people in the town; and so away. Reckoning for supper, 19/6d; poor 6d. Mischance to coach, but no time lost.' At Salisbury they stayed at the George Inn, where he lay 'in a silk bed; and very good diet.' The following morning they went to visit Stonehenge. 'Not being able to hire coach-horses, and not willing to use our own, we got saddle-horses, very dear.'

[1] *The Thatched House*, Hoddesdon.

He paid 6d. to the boy who went to fetch the saddle-horses and 4d. to the shepherd woman who guided them to the temple, but they could make little of the ancient stones. 'God knows what their use was,' observed Pepys.

They returned to the George for dinner 'and that being done, paid the reckoning, which was so exorbitant, and particularly the rate of my horses, and 7s. 6d. for bread and beer, that I was mad, and resolved to trouble the master about it, and get something for the poor; and come away in that humour. . . .

'Thence about six o'clock, and with a guide went over the smooth plain indeed till night; and then by a happy mistake, and that looks like an adventure, we were carried out of our way to a town where we could lye, since we could not go so far as we would. And there with great difficulty come about ten at night to a little inn, where we were fain to go into a room where a pedlar was in bed, and made him rise; and there my wife and I lay, and in a truckle bed Betty Turner and Willett.[1] But good beds and the master of the house a sober, understanding man, and I had good discourse with him about the country's matters, as wool, and corne, and other things. And he also merry and made us mighty merry at supper. . . . By and by to bed, glad of this mistake, because it seems, had we gone on as we intended, we could not have passed with our coach, and must have lain on the Plain all night.

'The following morning—Up, finding our beds good, but lousy; which made us merry. We set out, the reckoning and servants coming to 9s. 6d.; my guide thither, 2s.; coachman, advanced, 10s. So rode a very good way, led to my great content by our landlord, to Philips-Norton, with great pleasure. . . .'

But what the pedlar said, who was so rudely awakened and summarily turned out of his bed, was never recorded.

At some of the inns on that journey, Pepys mentioned that they were awakened with morning serenades outside their

[1] Their servants.

bedroom door, the custom which Fynes Moryson had described earlier in the century, and charming enough it must have been when the musicians were moderately competent, but at one inn Pepys complained that the music was 'the worst we have had, coming to our chamber-door, but calling us by wrong names, so we lay'.

The price of lodgings varied a great deal throughout the country and was far less in the north of England than in the south. In 1665, when Sir Ralph Verney's sister, Lady Elmes, fled, with a party of friends, from the plague in London to Knaresborough, they paid only ten shillings a week each 'en pension' and seven shillings a week for each servant, 'with lodgens in', but they had a miserable time there. In a letter to her brother at Claydon she wrote about 'the horrid sulfer water . . . as bad as is possible to be imajined' and everything about the house was 'horidly nasty and crowded up with all sorte of company, which we Eate with in a roome as the spiders are ready to drope into my mouthe, and sure hathe nethor been well cleaned nor ared this doseven yerese, it makes me much moare sicke than the nasty water. . . . Did you but see me, you woulde laughe heartily att me but I say little of it to whot I thinke. Then to mend all this, the(y) goe to supper att halfe an ower after six, soe I save a bitt and supp bye myselfe 2 owers after them, which is the pleasantest things I doe heare.'

Later she moved to Astrop Wells in Northamptonshire, a small watering place where the waters were considered to have valuable therapeutic properties, but 'instead of the sweet woodbine and jessamine att Claydon, I have the stincke of sower whay and cheese, which is so strong in my chamber I know not what to doe . . . not a coale of fyer can I get to burne one small bitt of perfume, fast I must at night, heare not being athor [either] master or maide att home, candle there is not a bit, soe I have sent to borrow one.'

It was in the 1690s, during the reign of William and Mary, that the redoubtable Celia Fiennes set out on her travels through England, one of the first women explorers. She covered well over a thousand miles, during which she visited every county in the country. She also crossed into Scotland and Wales, but she was so dismayed at the poverty she found in both countries that she did not venture far over the borders. She travelled alone except for two servants and covered most of the way on horse-back, riding side-saddle, and only very occasionally did she take a coach. The account of her adventures shows that the roads of England were little improved. Several times her horse stumbled or fell and when she was making her way through Hampshire 'the Little raines I had in the morning before I left Newtownbury made the wayes very slippery, and it being mostly on Chaulk way a Little before I came to Alsford forceing my way out of the hollow way his feete failed and he Could noe wayes recover himself, and soe I was shott off his neck upon the Bank, but noe harm I bless God. . . .'

Whenever possible, she stayed with friends or relations, but very often she had to make use of whatever inns or lodgings she could find: and in many parts of the country she had to employ a guide, for roads were only just being sign-posted. She first noticed them in Lancashire and made a note in her journal that 'at all crossways there are posts with hands pointing to each road with the names of the great town or market town that it leads to', but in remoter parts of the country things were not so easy. In Cornwall, for example, she found that 'people were ill guides and knew little away from home'. And again, 'you are forced to have Guides . . . in all parts of Darbyshire, and unless it be a few that use to be guides the common people know not above 2 to 3 miles.' To ford the sands of the Dee at low tide she had to have two guides, for the fording place changed with the loose, shifting sands.

She complained often of the high charges at the inns. At Mansfield she remarked that 'there is nothing remarkable here but the dearness of the Inns'. At Doncaster she was well entertained at the Angel. At York, she ate 'very good Cod fish and Salmon and that at a pretty Cheape rate tho' we were not in the best inn, for the Angel is the best'. In Scarborough she found that 'most of their best Lodgings are in Quakers hands, they entertain all people soe in Private houses in the town, by way of ordinary, so much a Meale, and their Ale every one finds themselves, there are a few Inns for horses only'.

At Hemsworth she could find no lodgings at all but two miles farther on 'made use of the hospitality of a Clergyman one Mr. Ferrar which was a very genteele man and gave us a civil entertainment and good beds, he has a very good house and genteelly fitted, good Hall and Parlour, and the Garden very neate'.

Of Buxton she had nothing good to say. 'The house thats call'd Buxton Hall which belongs to the Duke of Devonshire its where the warme Bath is and Well, its the largest house in the place tho' not very good, they are all Entertaining houses and its by way of an Ordinary, so much a piece for your dinners and suppers and so much for our Servants besides; all your ale and wine is to be paid besides, the beer they allow at the meales is so bad that very little can be drunk, you pay not for your bed room and truely the other is so unreasonable a price and the Lodgings so bad, 2 beds in a room some 3 beds and some 4 in one roome, so that if you have not Company enough of your own to fill a room they will be ready to put others into the same chamber, and sometymes they are so crowded that three must lye in a bed; few people stay above two or three nightes its so inconvenient. . . .'

Sir Thomas Browne's son, Edward, had no better opinion of this house at Buxton. 'We had nothing but oatcakes and mutton,' he said, 'which we fancied to taste like dog.'

At Derby, Celia was charged 5s. 8d. for her lodgings, though her dinner was 'but a shoulder of mutton and bread and beer'. Lancashire offered her only 'sad entertainment' and in Carlisle her landlady 'ran her up the largest reckoning for allmost nothing. . . . It was the dearest lodging I met with and she pretended she could get me nothing else, so for 2 joynts of mutton and a pinte of wine and bread and beer I had a 12 shilling reckoning but since, I find, tho' I was in the biggest house in town I was in the worst accommodation, and so found it, and a young giddy landlady that could only dress fine and entertain the soldiers.'

So Celia rode valiantly on, till she reached the Scottish border at Addison Bank. Here, at the only lodging she could find, every room, including the parlour and buttery, contained two or three beds, 'and notwithstanding the cleaning of their parlour for me I was not able to beare the roome' and 'I could not bring myself to sit down: my Landlady offered me a good dish of fish and brought me butter in a Lairdly Dish with the Clap bread, but I could have no stomach to eat any of the food they should order.'

So she paid for the fish and went to bed without any supper, though she took some of their wine 'which was exceeding good Claret which they stand conveniently for to have from France. . . .'

A day or two later she ran into more trouble, for the only inn at Haltwhistle had no hay for the horses and refused to fetch any, and when Celia's servants procured some on their own initiative, the people at the inn 'were angry and would not entertain me, so I was forced to take up in a poor cottage, which was open to the thatch and no partition but hurdles plaister'd: indeed the loft as they called it which was over the other roome was sheltered but with a hurdle, here I was forced to take up my abode and the Landlady 'brought me out her best sheetes which serv'd to secure my own sheetes from her dirty blanckets . . . but noe sleepe could I get, they burning turff and their chimneys are a sort of flews or open tunnels that the smoake does annoy the rooms.'

She was well pleased with her inn at Durham and enjoyed her stay at Whitchurch, at the Crown Inn, but she had a bad time at Ely where, though her chamber was 'nearly 20 Steppes up I had froggs and slow worms and snailes in my Rooms, but suppose it was brought up with ye faggots.'

On her way to the west country she found the roads very bad, but she enjoyed her west country tart at St. Austell. 'I was much pleased with my supper,' she wrote, 'tho not with the custome of the country, which is a universall smoking both men, women and children have all their pipes of tobacco in their mouths and soe sit round the fire smoking, which was not delightful to me when I went down to talke with my Land-lady. . . .'

In all her long journeys she seems only once to have encountered any highwaymen and that was on the way to Whitchurch. '2 fellows all on a sudden from the wood fell into the road, they look'd truss'd up with great coates and as it were bundles about them which I believe was pistolls, but they dogg'd me one before the other behind and would often look back to each other and frequently jostle my horse out of the way to get between one of my servants horses and mine, and when they first came up to us did disown their knowledge of the way and would often stay a little behind and talke together then come up againe, but the Providence of God so order'd it as there was men at work in the fields hay makeing, and it being market day at Whitchurch as I drew near to that in 3 or 4 miles was continually met with some of the market people, so they at last called each other off and soe left us and turned back.'

Along the four great post-roads of England, the London to Dover road, the road to the west from London to Plymouth, and the roads to Scotland and to Holyhead, by way of Chester, the inns were generally good, but Celia's adventures show that away from these relatively frequented routes the standard of comfort in the inns of late seventeenth century England was variable: and even in the large towns the inns were very over-crowded during the Assizes, at election times or during important race meetings, so that the chance traveller often had great difficulty in finding accommodation.

With communication still so difficult, inns had, of course, to rely on supplies of food available in their immediate vicinity, and the meals often fell below the standard which the sophisticated traveller expected. In 1695 Thomas Brockbank described his dinner at the Angel's Wings, at Sleaford in Lincolnshire. 'I . . . had a curious piece of roasted beef set before me . . . and it look'd as like a piece of rotten horse as anything I know. Vinegar I call'd for, 'twas brought in a Cruet delicately besmear'd with grease, not very deep for I co'd discern Ye Cruet was glass'. When he dined at the Cock at Salisbury, however, he had two beautifully cooked trout and found that this was the 'ordinary', and in London he was more than satisfied with the fare at the Eagle and Child in St. Martin's Lane, for he had ale and toast for breakfast, an excellent dinner of beef and cabbage, a pudding, pigeons, Westphalia ham, chicken and wine, and was still able to face a supper of mutton steaks and pigeons, washed down with sack.

During Queen Anne's time there was little change in the hazards of travel. In 1708 Ralph Thoresby, the antiquarian, prepared for a journey to York, setting out from the Black Swan in London. 'Lord Grant thy favourable presence and protection from sin and all dangers!' he wrote in his diary. And after his arrival he recorded: 'We found the way very deep, and in some places dangerous for the coach (that we walked on foot) but the Lord preserved us from all evil accidents, that we got to our journey's end in safety, blessed be God!'

He visited the Archbishop, with whom he had business, and then made his way to the inn, which he found 'crowded with vast multitudes', for it happened to be the day of the election of the Knights of the Shire. There were so many people about that he 'could have no opportunity for private prayer, but happily found in my walks one church open, where I retired.'

He returned to the inn but it was more crowded than ever and 'most lay three in a bed'. He managed to find private lodgings in the town, but even so he didn't get much sleep for he had to be up again between three and four in the morning, as the departure time of the coach had been brought forward on the demand of 'Captain Crome (whose company we had) upon the Queen's business, that we got to Leeds by noon; blessed be God for mercies to me and my poor family!'

Chapter Five

GEORGIAN ENGLAND

THE EIGHTEENTH CENTURY saw a great extension of coach traffic and with it the development of the posting inns, which were a vital part of the service. During the great fire of London the danger of the medieval timber and plaster buildings had been all too apparent. Wren's new London of brick and stone had already arisen and throughout the country many of the old inns were now faced with brick and stone and given rows of neat sash windows, although much of the old timbering was left at the back and in the buildings round the courtyard. A large number of new inns were also built at this time, all very much to a pattern, with plain fronts and trim sash windows, and still the archway leading to the courtyard.

In the early part of the century, before outside passengers were usual on the coaches, the arch was low, but as the 'outsiders' became customary the arches were raised so that they could pass in and out of the courtyard in safety, thus avoiding any danger of the sad story recounted by Jingle in *Pickwick Papers* about the old Golden Cross. 'Terrible place—dangerous work—other day—five children—mother—tall lady, eating sandwiches—forgot the arch—crash—knock—children look round—mother's head off—sandwich in her hand—no mouth to put it in—head of a family off—shocking, shocking!'

In Queen Anne's time roads were little better than they had been during the seventeenth century and coaches drawn by six horses were still very cumbersome, so that although travelling in a coach, particularly in bad weather, saved exposure to the wind and rain and the ruination of one's clothes, it remained a mixed blessing, and for those who travelled at a reduced fare in the basket, which soon became known as the rumble-tumble, it was often a torture.

The public coach was not an aristocratic method of travel. The rich used their private coaches or lighter post-chaises or else hired a coach to themselves, while the poor, if they could not afford a cheap seat in the basket, still used the old post waggons, or their later developments the 'Flying Stage Waggons' and the 'Caravans'. The innkeepers inevitably made a distinction between their wealthy clients arriving in their private coaches, who were given the best rooms, and the mixed bag of public coach travellers, particularly if they were stopping only for a meal. The humbler ones were often shown into the kitchen and when the coachman was in a hurry to be off again on his journey there was usually a scramble to be served in time. In some places the inns became so grand that they catered only for private travellers, but in most important towns there were at least two inns, sponsoring rival coach services, and a little healthy competition kept the standard of food, accommodation and service reasonably high. The stage-waggon people usually used the 'penny-hedge inns' where the fastidious ones could pay sixpence extra for clean sheets and a bed to themselves, and the others bedded down as best they could.

The first Turnpike Trusts of the eighteenth century gradually brought about an improvement in the roads. These were trusts formed by groups of people who took control of certain stretches of road and kept them in good order, obtaining money for the work by charging a toll collected by the keeper at the toll gates. Each trust was legalized by an act of Parliament and throughout the century hundreds were passed, sixteen hundred between 1730 and 1780 alone.

Harder and better roads came into existence but only very

slowly. Henry Purefroy, writing to Bath in 1742 from his home near Buckingham, doubts whether he will ever reach there that year, for 'I am afraid the Roads will be bad,' and writing to a shopkeeper in Brackley in 1744 he thanks him for mending the road but says 'there is since that a quick sand in the lane that my coachman with his coach horse was like to be mired in it as hee will tell you, and that prevents me from coming to Brackley.'

His mother, in a letter to her nephew, who was coming to stay with them at Shalstone Manor, tells him that: 'The Ailesbury stage coach goes out from the Bell Inne in Holborn every Tuesday at 6 in ye morning and comes to Ailesbury that night, next day it comes to the Lord Cobham's Arms in Buckingham and there our Coach may meet you. But how you get from Shalstone to Northampton I know not . . . neither do I know whether that is the road to Lincoln or no.'

During the 1760s, the Reverend Mr. Cole of Bletchley often rode because the roads round Bletchley were too bad to travel in his chaise, and when he moved into Cambridgeshire most of his furniture went by river, by way of Bedford: and even so the roads were so bad that he had to wait two or three days before it could be moved even from the rectory as far as the river.

Yet sometimes the coaches fared better on the open roads than in the cobbled streets of the towns. Ned Ward, who wrote *The London Spy*, said of his arrival in London: 'Our Stratford tub outran the smoothness of the road and entered upon London stones with as much rightful rumbling as an empty hay-cart, our leather conveniency having no more sway than a funeral hearse or a country waggon, so that we were jumbled about like so many peas in a child's rattle, running in a great hazard of dislocation at every jolt.'

As the design of coaches gradually improved, someone thought of providing seats for passengers on top of the coach, as well as in the basket. Places were made for three on the roof of the front part, their feet resting on the coachman's box, with a fourth passenger sitting on the box beside him. Another three were perched on the back part of the coach roof, with nothing more to support them than their own will for survival, until a small hand-rail was provided for them.

Carl Philippe Moritz, the young German pastor who visited England in 1782, described the horrors of this form of travel in no uncertain terms, after travelling on an outside seat from Leicester to Northampton. 'This ride I shall remember as long as I live,' he said. 'The coach drove from the yard through a part of the house. The inside passengers got into the coach from the yard, but we on the outside were obliged to clamber up in the street, because we should have had no room for our heads to pass under the gateway. My companions on the top of the coach were a farmer, a young man very decently dressed, and a blackamoor. The getting up alone was at the risk of one's life, and when I was up I was obliged to sit just at the corner of the coach, with nothing to hold on by but a sort of little handle fastened on the side. I sat nearest the wheel, and the moment that we set off I fancied I saw certain death before me. All I could do was to take still faster hold of the handle, and to be strictly careful to preserve my balance. The machine rolled along with prodigious rapidity over the stones through the town of Leicester, and every moment we seemed to fly into the air, so much as that it appeared to me a miracle that we stuck to the coach at all. . . . This continual fear of death at last became insupportable to me, and therefore, no sooner were we crawling up a rather steep hill, and consequently proceeding slower than usual, than I carefully crept from the top of the coach, and was lucky enough to get myself snugly ensconced in the basket behind . . . as long as we went on slowly up the hill, it was easy and pleasant enough, and I was just on the point of falling asleep, when on a sudden the coach proceeded at a rapid rate downhill. Then all the boxes, iron-nailed and copper-fastened, began . . . to dance round me; everything in the basket appeared to be alive, and every moment I received such violent blows that I thought my last hour had come. . . . I was obliged to suffer horrible torture for nearly an hour, which seemed to me an eternity. . . . At last we came to another hill, when, quite shaken to pieces, bleeding and sore, I ruefully crept back to the top of the coach to my former seat.'

Shortly afterwards it began to pour with rain and poor Moritz ended the journey soaking wet as well as shaken in spirit and body.

Early in the century coaches did not change horses in the course of their day's journey. This was for a number of reasons, one being that they sometimes diverged from their published routes to oblige passengers and this made it difficult to establish regular posting houses. However, in May, 1734, the Newcastle 'Flying Coach' announced that 'A coach will set out towards the end of next week for London or any place on the road. To be performed in nine days, being three days sooner than any other coach that travels the road: for which purpose eight strong horses are stationed at proper distances.'

It was the beginning of the stage coach and the proprietors of other routes soon adopted the idea, so that journeys took far less time. The Edinburgh coach reached an average speed of forty-four miles a day compared with its previous record of twenty-eight, and spent only eight nights on the road instead of thirteen. Innkeepers became worried and some lost business, but this sudden burst of speed was not maintained, perhaps, as in the previous century, because of an agreement between the proprietors of the service and the innkeepers along the route.

By 1754 there was a vast improvement in the design of stage-coaches and they became more like private carriages, the driver handling four horses and a postilion riding one of the two leaders, yet where the roads were not properly made coach services were still inevitably restricted.

Until the 1750s stage-coaches were forbidden to travel on Sundays and passengers in the middle of their journeys had to spend the day at the inn where they had arrived on the Saturday night, but in 1750 the first licences were granted for a few of the coaches to travel on Sundays.

When Count Frederick Kielmansegge visited England in 1761, to attend the coronation of George III, he and his brother landed at Harwich at nine o'clock at night. They had to leave all their luggage on board to be examined by customs in daylight and went to the Three Cups for the night, 'the host being one of those who had met us on shore and had taken pains to persuade each passenger to come with him. He tried to make sure of success by actually taking possession of an overcoat, which one of the company allowed him to carry, thus securing those of us who did not wish to separate. At his house we found everything we could wish for; a good cup of tea, bread and butter, and well-aired and clean beds, which my brother and I were glad to occupy, this being the first of ten nights on which we are able to undress and lie between two sheets.' The following day they hired a landau and drove the seventy-two miles to London by post, and the Count commented that 'no country is so well arranged for comfort and rapid travelling as this.'

In the course of the next few days they went sightseeing through England. Between Buckingham and Oxford they encountered bad roads and their coachman said he needed two extra horses, so they sent him back with one of the servants and the riding horse, and took 'two post-chaises, with two horses each, and made our two servants ride. . . . This mode of travelling is a little more expensive, but it has the advantage, not only of enabling you to travel as you like, but of saving the payment to the coachman of his 27s. a day, when you stop for that time anywhere; on the other hand, you can do double the distance in one day with a post-chaise, and are not forced to stop at inns on the road for feeding purposes and meals. . . .

'We took two days to make the 108 miles from Bath to London, but the journey can be accomplished in one day by starting a little sooner than we did, especially if you change horses every ten miles; or better still, if you take four horses, by which means you can accomplish the whole journey without trouble in eleven hours. We changed horses, however, only eighteen or nineteen miles, besides riding for an hour and a half, and making use of the post-chaises also for two hours; nine to ten miles an hour can easily be accomplished without over-working the horses, so in this way 200 miles can be covered in twenty hours without much trouble. We spent the night at Maidenhead Bridge, in a good inn, near the bridge over the Thames, 26 miles from London.'

When they went to Portsmouth to see the departure of the fleet, under the command of Lord Albemarle, they arrived at Godalming at half past eight in the morning, barely half an hour after Prince Charles of Mecklenburg and his party had left the same inn, taking with them twenty fresh horses. The rest were being kept for the Duke of York, who was expected later in the morning, which meant that there were none available for the Kielmansegges.

The hostess of the inn suggested that they took seats in the 'flying machine', which the Count described as a 'kind of post-coach, which travels with remarkable speed from one place to another, as, for instance, between London and Ports-mouth. Eight of these are on the road daily, four passing each way. Each of the four starts in the morning from its appointed house in London, has its own change of horses and stopping places for breakfast, dinner, and tea, and arrives between 6 and 7 p.m. in Portsmouth, a distance of seventy-two miles from London. In such a carriage there is room for six persons; one can sit on the box, three or four behind, on the great back seat, and, in cases of necessity, two more can sit on the top.'

The Count and his brother were at first appalled at the idea of travelling in a public conveyance, but there being no alterna-tive, they at last agreed. When the coaches arrived they were almost fully occupied and they had to travel separately. Kiel-mansegge's brother was not so fortunate as the Count in his travelling companions 'as all the way he had the company of a fat English innkeeper's wife, who kept her brandy bottle handy, two sailor's wives and one other man who was the only one of the party with whom he could converse, and who left the coach after the first four miles. As each coach has its own special stopping places, my brother and I did not see each other again until we arrived at our destination.'

The Count fared better and obviously took a great fancy to one of his travelling companions, the 'young and handsome wife of a captain in the service of the East India Company' with whom he was soon in conversation, and 'thus I passed the day without being bored.' Another diversion was a quarrel with a cart-driver who refused to make way for the coach. 'This occasioned a fight, which was settled by three of the men passengers in the coach and my servant, who was sitting behind, coming to the aid of the coachman and making the carter get out of the way by using force and administering a good licking, thus gaining the victory. Meanwhile I, as a careful strategist, guarded the baggage and coach with the lady inside, and formed the *corps de reserve*, so as to cover the retreat in case of necessity.'

In order to avoid similar trouble with the post horses on the return journey to London they stayed in Portsmouth that night, while Prince Charles of Mecklenburg departed for Godalming: and in the evening they went to the Assembly Rooms at Portsmouth with the Duke of York, where the Count danced 'with the young lady whom I had met on the journey, and as she had the honour of both starting the minuets and the English dances, she opened the ball with me'.

Of the town of Portsmouth, said the Count, 'it is one of the worst in England; the houses are bad, the streets narrow, and the inns especially, which are not by any means equal to those usually to be found in England, are dirty and bad. The only good things we found in ours were clean and good beds in a bad bedroom.'

It was twenty years later, in 1782, that Carl Moritz arrived in England, but he had some very different experiences from the aristocratic Kielmansegges, for he had very little money, and apart from his alarming drive on the roof of the coach from Leicester to Northampton, he made most of his tour on foot, which provoked many a cool reception from the more snobbish English innkeepers.

He landed at Dartford and took a post-chaise to London. Passing through the villages on the way, he was first struck by 'the amazing large signs which, at the entrance of villages, hang in the middle of the street, being fastened to large beams, which are extended across the street from one house to another opposite to it . . .; these sign posts have the appearance of gates, or of gateways, for which I at first took them, but the whole apparatus, unnecessarily large as it seems to be, is intended for nothing more than to tell the inquisitive traveller that there is an inn. At length, stunned as it were by this constant rapid succession of interesting objects to engage our attention, we arrived at Greenwich, nearly in a state of stupefaction.'

After a stay in London, Moritz decided to explore the country, making first for Derbyshire. Leaving his trunk with a German friend, to avoid the expense of keeping it at his lodging, he set out with four guineas in his pocket, some linen, his English book of the roads, a map and pocket-book and a copy of Milton's *Paradise Lost*. He took a stage-coach from the White Hart to Richmond. 'These coaches are, at least in the eyes of a foreigner, quite elegant,' he wrote, 'lined in the inside; and with two seats large enough to accommodate six persons: but it must be owned, when the carriage is full, the company are rather crowded.' At first his only companion was an elderly lady, 'but as we drove along, it was soon filled, and mostly by ladies, there being only one gentleman, and myself. The conversation of the ladies among themselves, who appeared to be a little acquainted with each other, seemed to me to be but very insipid and tiresome. All I could do, was, I drew out my book of the roads, and marked the way we were going.'

He was enchanted with the rural tranquillity of Richmond

and after booking in at his inn went for a long walk. When it was time to return for supper he had forgotten the name of his inn and had great difficulty in finding it again, and when he did he was none too comfortable, for 'the landlady of this house was a notable one; and talked so much and so loud to her servants, that I could not get to sleep, till it was pretty late. However, I was up next morning at three o'clock: and was now particularly sensible of the great inconveniences they sustain in England by their bad custom of rising so late: for, as I was the only one in this family who was up, I could not get out of the house. This obliged me to spend three most irksome and heavy hours till six o'clock; and I rushed out, to climb Richmond Hill.'

He returned for breakfast and then set out on his 'romantic journey on foot'.

That morning he reached Eton and began to feel hungry. 'As I entered the inn and desired to have something to eat, the countenance of the waiter soon gave me to understand that I should there find no very friendly reception. Whatever I got, they seemed to give me, with such an air, as shewed too plainly how little they thought of me; and as if they considered me but as a beggar. I must do them justice to own, however, that they suffered me to pay like a gentleman. No doubt this was the first time this pert bepowdered puppy had ever been called on to wait on a poor devil, who entered their place on foot. I was tired and asked for a bedroom where I might sleep. They showed me into one, that much resembled a prison for male-factors. I required that I might have a better room at night. On which, without any apology, they told me, that they had no intention of lodging me, as they had no room for such guests; but that I might go back to Slough, where very probably I might get a night's lodging.

'With money in my pocket, and a consciousness moreover that I was doing nothing that was either imprudent, unworthy, or really mean, I own it mortified and vexed me, to find myself obliged to put up with this impudent ill usage from people, who ought to reflect, that they are but the servants of the public; and little likely to recommend themselves to the high, by being insolent to the low. They made me, however, pay them two shillings for my dinner and coffee. . . .'

Moritz did not return to Slough. He went on to Windsor and caught a glimpse of the King driving into the castle. He found himself opposite a very attractive-looking inn, where 'many officers and several persons of consequence' were going in and out, and decided to see what his reception would be. Contrary to all expectations, the landlord received him with great civility and kindness. He asked to be shown a room where he might 'adjust his dress a little' and the innkeeper ordered a maid to direct him, but on the way Moritz could hear her 'mutter and grumble'. Undismayed he tidied himself and returned to the coffee room by the entrance of the inn, and later in the day had an evening bathe in the Thames, which he thoroughly enjoyed. Happily he returned to the inn, looking forward to a comfortable night's rest, but found that the waiters '(who from my appearance, too probably expected but a trifling reward for their attention to me) received me gruffly, and as if they were sorry to see me again. This was not all: I had the additional mortification to be again roughly accosted by the cross maid, who had before shewn me to the bed-chamber; and who, dropping a kind of half-courtesy, with a suppressed laugh, sneeringly told me, I might look out for another lodging, as I could not sleep there, since the room she had by mistake shown me, was already engaged. It can hardly be necessary to tell you, that I loudly protested against this sudden change. At length the landlord came and I appealed to him: and he with great courtesy, immediately desired another room to be shown me: in which, however, there were two beds; so that I was obliged to admit a companion. Thus was I very near being a second time turned out of an inn.'

His room mate arrived very late and very drunk, but 'at length though not without some difficulty, he found his own bed; into which he threw himself just as he was, without staying to pull off either clothes or boots.'

The following morning he went for another walk in Windsor and on returning to the inn 'I received from the ill-tempered maid, who seemed to have been stationed there, on purpose to plague and vex me, the polite welcome, that on no account should I sleep another night there.'

Luckily that was not my intention, observed Moritz, with admirable forbearance. They charged him 6s. for the old fowl that had been his supper and 3s. for the shared bedroom. To the waiter who hovered expectantly near the doorway of the inn he gave 1½d., on which 'he saluted me with the heartiest God damn you, sir, I have ever heard.' Even the cross maid had the effrontery to murmur 'Pray remember the chamber-maid', but that was too much, even for the mild-tempered Moritz. ' "Yes, yes", said I. "I shall long remember your most ill-mannered behaviour, and shameful incivility"; and so I gave her nothing. She strove to stifle her anger by a contemptuous horse laugh.'

Despite his rebuffs, the weather was so fine that Moritz decided to continue his journey on foot. At Henley no inn would take him in so he walked a further five miles to Nettle-bed. By this time it was getting dark and he was very tired. At the far end of the village he saw an inn with a large beam across the road to the opposite house, 'from which hung an astonishingly large sign and the name of the proprietor.'

They took him in but showed him into the kitchen and sat him down to take supper with the servants and some soldiers, but he found it very comfortable. The kitchen range where they were roasting and boiling was cut off by a wooden partition and the rest of the room was used as a sitting-room and dining-room. All round it 'were shelves with pewter dishes and plates, and the ceiling was well stored with provisions of various kinds, such as sugar-loaves, black-puddings, hams, sausages and flitches of bacon.'

While they were at supper a post-chaise drove up and caused

a great stir. Even though the new arrivals wanted only a couple of pots of beer, they were given 'every possible attention because they came in a post-chaise', observed Moritz, but he had no cause for complaint for 'though this was only an ordinary village, and they certainly did not take me for a person of consequence, they yet gave me a carpeted bedroom, and a very good bed.'

The next morning he put on clean linen and made himself look so presentable that he was shown into the parlour and addressed as Sir instead of Master, which was the form of address to farmers and 'quite common people'. It was Sunday and all the family were dressed in their Sunday clothes. Moritz took such a liking to them all, and also to Nettlebed, that he went to church with them and stayed to dinner, departing about three o'clock for Dorchester.

Here his courage failed him. He saw several ladies 'with their heads dressed' and decided that the place was altogether too elegant to welcome a travel-worn walker. So he walked on to Nuneham. It was quite dark when he arrived there but he saw an inn with its sign across the street and boldly walked in and announced that he intended to sleep there that night.

'By no means! It was utterly impossible', they told him. 'The whole house was full, and all their beds engaged; and as he had come so far, he might as well walk on the remaining five miles to Oxford.'

He asked for something to eat and was told that as he could not stay there the night it would be better for him to sup where he lodged. For ready money only, they unwillingly supplied him with a pot of beer but refused even a piece of bread.

'Such unparalleled inhospitality I really could not have expected in an English inn,' wrote Moritz, 'but, resolving, with a kind of spiteful indignation, to see how far their inhumanity would carry them, I begged that they would only let me sleep on a bench, and merely give me house-room; adding, that if they would grant me that boon only, I would pay them the same as for a bed; for, that I was so tired, I could not possibly go any farther. Even in the moment that I was thus humbly soliciting this humble boon, they banged the door to full in my face.'

Luckily it was a fairly warm night. Poor Moritz took himself to a nearby field and was just choosing a spot where he could lie down and sleep when, out of the darkness, a stranger spoke to him. Though the man could not justify the folk at the inn refusing Moritz the elementary hospitality of a piece of bread, he explained that the inn really was full and suggested that they walk together to Oxford. He introduced himself as Mr. Maud of Corpus Christi, a clergyman like Moritz, who had been preaching at Dorchester.

During that happy five-mile walk in the dark, Moritz forgot all his troubles and when they reached Oxford Mr. Maud took him to the Mitre. It was nearly midnight and he was shown into a large room on the left of the entrance which, to his astonishment, was 'full of clergymen, all with their gowns and bands on, sitting round a large table, each with his pot of beer before him'.

Moritz was now with people of his own kind and they sat drinking and talking, toasting each other and debating, until the small hours, and when the party at last broke up 'the people of the house made no difficulty of giving me lodging, but, with great civility, showed me a very decent bed-chamber.'

The following morning he woke with a sore head and stayed late in bed, but once he was on his feet again he began to enjoy himself and remained in Oxford for the next two days. Compared with his treatment at Windsor, he found 'Prince-like' attendance at the Mitre. They washed his linen for him—for 'no people are so cleanly as the English; nor so particular about neat and clean linen.' He dined with the family and a few other visitors, but they admitted that they would not have received him had it not been for Mr. Maud's introduction, for anyone travelling on foot was considered 'either a beggar, or a vagabond, or some necessitous wretch, which is a character not much more popular than that of a rogue.' 'A poor peripatetic is heardly allowed even the humble merit of being honest', observed Moritz in his diary.

Mr. Maud showed him round Oxford and when Moritz returned to the Mitre he said that 'there was hardly a minute, in which some students, or others, did not call, either to drink, or to amuse themselves in conversation with the daughter of the landlord,' who 'was not only handsome, but sensible, and well-behaved.'

As he was preparing to leave, he was strongly advised to take a post-coach for the rest of his journey to Derbyshire and was assured that the farther he travelled from London the cheaper he would find the inns. His bill at the Mitre he considered not unreasonable, bearing in mind the good service he had received. Supper, bed and breakfast was 3s., and he gave 1s. to the waiter. Then he took an inside seat on the post-coach to Birmingham, where he soon fell into conversation with a friendly young fellow traveller. Moritz asked him why Englishmen 'who were so remarkable for acting up to their own notions and ideas, did not, now and then, merely to see life in every point of view, travel on foot. "O," said he, "we are too rich, too lazy, and too proud." And most true it is, that the poorest Englishman one sees, is prouder and better pleased to expose himself to the danger of having his neck broken, on the outside of a stage, than to walk any considerable distance, though he might walk ever so much at his ease. I own, I was frightened and distressed, when I saw the women, when we occasionally stopped, get down from the top of the coach. One of them was actually once in much danger of a terrible fall from the roof, because, just as she was going to alight, the horses all at once unexpectedly went on.'

'From Oxford to Birmingham is sixty two miles' he noted, 'but all that was to be seen between the two places was entirely lost to me, for I was again mewed up in a post-coach.'

After a brief stay in Birmingham he determined to continue

his journey on foot, but he became over-sensitive about the possible reception he might meet when bed-time approached. Two miles from Lichfield he saw an inn which he felt was humble enough to accept him. It was the Swan at Sutton, kept by Aulton, a brick-maker. Moritz was disheartened when he was addressed as 'master' and shown into the kitchen, but there he found the landlady suffering from toothache and he was so sympathetic that she actually invited him to stay the night and made him very comfortable. Furthermore, he was charged only 1s. for his supper, bed and breakfast, and the daughter of the house who was also the chambermaid, was pleased with her 4d. tip.

By the time he reached Burton he was very tired and longed for a bed but Burton proved inhospitable. He became a victim of English xenophobia and had some very unpleasant experiences. People stared and pointed at him and he hated it all. He trudged on towards Derby and then his luck changed. A friendly farmer overtook him and gave him a lift on his horse as far as his own village, setting him down at the Bear Inn, where he was given a welcome and courteous attention. The landlord called him 'Sir' and ordered a separate table to be laid for himself and Moritz, for, he said, he could see plainly that Moritz was a gentleman.

He spent a pleasant evening at the Bear and in the morning set off for Derby, Matlock and the Peak district. Here he spent several days, but his reception at the inns was variable and he did not greatly enjoy the food. In the Peak district he found a solitary inn 'and dined on cold meat and sallad. This, or else eggs and sallad, was my usual supper, and my dinner too, at the inns at which I stopped. It was but seldom that I had the good fortune to get anything hot. The sallad, for which they brought me all the ingredients, I was always obliged to dress myself. This, I believe, is always done in England.'

After Derbyshire, Moritz made his way to Nottingham and Leicester, and it was from here that he made his disastrous trip to Northampton. From Northampton to London he took the precaution of securing an inside seat, though he was sorry not to see more of the places on the route—Newport Pagnell, Dunstable, St. Albans, Barnet and Islington. For the rest of his stay in England he lodged first at the Freemason's tavern, where 'the bill for eight days lodging, breakfast and dinner, came to one guinea and nine shillings, and ninepence. Breakfast, dinner, and coffee, were always without distinction, reckoned a shilling each. For my lodging I paid only twelve shillings a week; which was certainly cheap enough.' For the last few days he moved to St. Catherine's, 'one of the most execrable holes in all this great city, where I am obliged to stay, because the great ships arrive in the Thames here, and go from hence, and we shall sail as soon as the wind changes.'

The lodging at St. Catherine's was a 'Publick-house . . . of which the master is a German; and where all the Hambro' Captains lodge' and it was even cheaper than the Freemason's Tavern—only half-a-guinea a week for food, drink and lodging, but it was in a miserable, narrow, dirty street, amidst a 'mass of ill-built, old, ruinous houses', forming, for anyone landing there 'no very favourable idea of this beautiful and renowned city.'

In the cheap lodgings and inns where Moritz stayed during his visit to England he did not form a very good impression of English catering. 'The fine wheaten bread which I find here, besides excellent butter and cheshire-cheese, makes up for my scanty dinners,' he said. 'For an English dinner, to such lodgers as I am, generally consists of a piece of half-boiled, or half-roasted meat; and a few cabbage leaves boiled in plain water; on which they pour a sauce made of flour and butter. This, I assure you, is the usual method of dressing vegetables in England. . . . The slices of bread and butter, which they give you with your tea, are as thin as poppy leaves. But there is another kind of bread and butter usually eaten with tea, which is toasted by the fire, and is incomparably good. You take one slice after the other and hold it to the fire on a fork till the butter is melted, so that it penetrates a number of slices all at once; this is called *Toast.*'

Only four years after Carl Moritz had visited England, Sophie V. La Roche, another German visitor, arrived. She was middle-aged and comparatively wealthy, so she saw a different aspect of England, but like so many Germans, she found lodgings cheaper than inns or hotels, and while she was in London she stayed at the German Hotel in Suffolk Street. In her diary, she says little about her lodgings, but Angelica Kauffmann had also stayed in lodgings in Suffolk Street, when she had arrived in London twenty years earlier, in 1766. 'I have four rooms, one where I paint and a second where I hang my finished pictures,' she wrote to her father. . . . 'The other two rooms are very small. One of these is my bedroom . . . and in the other I keep my clothes and other such things. For the rooms I pay two guineas a week, and one guinea for the food and the servant, whose clothes I also have to provide. This is without washing and other small daily expenses. . . .'

Sophie began the diary of her English visit on August 31, 1786, while waiting with twenty-one other passengers, including Charles Wesley, at Helvoetsluys for a fair wind to Harwich. They were lodging at Mistress Norman's—an English hostess with a house alongside the harbour. 'Neither English nor Dutch cleanliness is evident in this establishment', she remarked, but the lunch was good, consisting of soup, some good-sized fish, large English roasts, vegetables boiled in salt water with melted butter, pastries, fruit, and a large and excellent cheese, served in a beautifully carved mahogany cart, and rolled on four brass castors from one guest to another.

They enjoyed their breakfast the next morning but at dinnertime there were two diversions. 'Firstly, the waiter entered bringing the gentlemen their nightcaps and hats to wear until their wigs were dressed; secondly, they put on their slippers while their boots and shoes were being cleaned so as to be presentable outdoors after lunch.' Soon after this murmurings arose about the food, 'which was not well prepared, nor was there sufficient to satisfy our appetites. . . . Mistress Norman, who came up to us quite anxiously when some of the men left to eat elsewhere, had many complaints forced upon her ears— and in the hurry could only prepare some boiled fish and potatoes in butter sauce. It was a long time before order was restored, and our only consolation was that we had heard a veritable English squabble. Wesley and his disciples did not take part, as they appeared to have no truck with the needs of the vile body.'

The party had a frightful crossing which took forty-eight hours, but once they had landed at Harwich Sophie, who was determined to enjoy herself, forgot all the troubles and dis-comforts of the boat.

On September 4 she was writing: 'The transport arrange-ments for London are excellent. From the capital to Harwich is a distance of seventy-four English miles; these are divided into five stages: from here to Mistley, twelve miles; Colchester, ten miles; Witham, fourteen miles; Ingatestone, fourteen miles; Romford, twelve miles; London, twelve miles. The host of the "Three Bumpers", our present abode, keeps horses, grooms and coaches, of which he has all kinds, letting them out for London, and he is connected with landlords at the above-mentioned localities who, if one arrives with his coach, immediately harness the best horses and put one *en route* again fast as lightning, accompanied by very well-dressed attendants. Our coach held five comfortably, was lined with fine cloth, and so well built and lacquered as befitted a stage-coach. Four horses and two postillions brought us early into Ingatestone along the best roads and through the finest of landscapes.'

Arriving in so splendid a style, it was not surprising that she was well received at Ingatestone, where she spent the night. 'We were at once given the choice of a number of well-papered rooms fitted with every possible comfort, and carpeted, as were stairs and corridors, by which means even with the house full of guests there is a kind of hushed effect, which is just as pleasant in its way as the cleanliness of everything one sees and wants. I have not better bed or table-linen than was provided here. All the bed-covers are of white cotton material with fringe decorations woven in. Everything we had was spotlessly white, and until our meal was ready we had the fun of watching the Colchester mail-coach arrive. Its name is quite rightly the Colchester Machine—seating six people inside, in front outside behind the coachman four more, and at the back, where the trunks usually go, as many again within a neat enclosure with benches, while eight people were sitting above on deck, their feet dangling overboard, holding fast with their hands to screwed-in brass rings.'

The mail coach passengers had only half an hour for supper and then were off again, but Sophie and her friends were able to take a leisurely meal. 'We enjoyed the first English supper immensely', she wrote. 'We were given slices of beef and veal, cut very thin and beaten tender, about the size of a hand, sprinkled with bread crumbs and grilled, and nicely served on a silver dish; fine big potatoes with salt butter to follow; delicious beer and a good Bordeaux wine.'

Chapter Six

THE MAIL COACHES

As LATE AS as the 1780s the mail was still carried by the post-boys, riding at about six miles an hour and costing the post office 3d. an hour, while the stage-coaches were reaching a speed of seven miles an hour and costing their proprietors only 2d. a mile.

The letter- and travelling-post was a royal monopoly, giving postmasters the advantage of being the only people legally entitled to supply horses, but after 1780 this monopoly was removed. Anyone could let horses and any innkeeper could call his inn a posting-house.

In 1782 John Palmer planned a service of mail coaches which, by means of changing horses every seven or ten miles, would increase the speed of the post to eight or nine miles an hour. By allowing passengers to ride in the mail coaches, he argued that the extra cost of the shortened posts would be offset and the postage of mails need cost no more.

After months of deliberation, John Palmer won his concession for the mails. At first no outside passengers were allowed but the mail coaches carried a guard armed with two short guns and a blunderbuss and the coachman was provided with two pistols.

The first mail coach ran from Bristol by way of Bath to London on August 2, 1784, five innkeepers having been engaged on the route to horse the coach at 3d. a mile, two at Bath, one at Marlborough, a fourth at Thatcham and the fifth the proprietor of the Swan with Two Necks, Lad Lane, London.

It was advertised as a Mail Diligence and the first advertisement announced that

> The Proprietors of the above Carriage having agreed to convey the Mail to and from London and Bristol in Sixteen Hours, with a Guard for its Protection, respectfully inform the Public, that it is constructed so as to accommodate Four Inside Passengers in the most Convenient Manner; that it well [*sic*] set off every Night at Eight O'Clock from the Swan With Two Necks,[1] Lad Lane, London, and arrive at the Three Tuns Inn, Bath, before Ten the next Morning, and at the Rummer-Tavern, near the Exchange, Bristol, at Twelve. . . . Will set off from the said Tavern at Bristol at Four o'Clock every Afternoon, and arrive at London at Eight o'Clock the next Morning.
>
> The Price to and from Bristol, Bath, and London, 28s. for each Passenger. . . . No Outside allowed.
>
> Both the Guards and Coachmen (who will be likewise armed) have given ample Security for their Conduct to the Proprietors, so that those Ladies and Gentlemen who may please to honour them with their Encouragement, may depend on every Respect and Attention. . . .

There was a postscript to this notice that the London, Bath and Bristol Coaches would run from the above Inns as usual. At the same time, other coach and inn proprietors, quick to sense dangerous competition, immediately announced that 'Pickwick, Weeks, and other Proprietors of the Coaches from Bristol, Bath and London respectfully beg leave to inform the Public that they continue to run their Coaches from the Bush Tavern in Corn Street, Bristol' and from other inns in Bristol and Bath 'with equal Expedition to any Coaches that travel the Road.'

[1] A corruption of the 'Swan With Two Nicks', the two nicks being the mark used for royal birds.

By 1785 the Norwich Mail was on the road and the first cross-posts established from Bristol to Portsmouth. Within a few months more services to London were established, the Leeds, Manchester and Liverpool mail, the London, Gloucester and Swansea, the Hereford, Carmarthen and Milford Haven, the Worcester and Ludlow, the Birmingham and Shrewsbury, the Chester and Holyhead, the Exeter, the Portsmouth, and, by the autumn of 1786, the Edinburgh mail, which ran along the Great North Road by way of York.

By this time John Palmer had been appointed Comptroller General of the Post Office. The ordinary stage coaches were as numerous as ever and the long-distance travellers who preferred travelling by day and enjoying a good bed at an inn for each night of their journey preferred them, but the mail coaches gained a prestige. Their turn-out was extremely smart and their time-keeping astonishingly accurate, while nervous travellers felt that the security of the armed guard outweighed the dangers of the ever-increasing speed at which they travelled.

The coachman was under the order of the guard but was employed by the innkeeper-contractor who horsed the coach, the coach itself being hired by the coachmaker who had the government monopoly for the building of all the mail coaches, and to whom it was regularly returned for cleaning and maintenance. The guard was a Post Office employee who, despite his magnificent appearance in the royal livery of scarlet coat and black hat, his timepiece to log the journey and his pistols and blunderbuss, was paid 10s. 6d. a week, having to rely on the usual 2s. 6d. tip from each passenger.

Palmer, determined that the mail coach should be the most efficient available, ordered that Besant's new 'patent coach' should be used exclusively for the mail. It was a coach hung very high, with a new type of patent spring, but was extremely uncomfortable. Matthew Boulton, taking a mail-coach journey from London to Exeter in 1798, thought very little of it. 'I had the most disagreeable journey I ever experienced the night after

5. The George Inn (*left*) and the White Hart (*below*) were two fine examples of galleried inns in the London borough of Southwark.

6. The Swan with Two Nicks (later corrupted to Necks), Lad Lane (*above*), w the first London inn to receive a mail coach (1784) and The Spread Eagle in Grace church Street (*below*) was another famous City coaching inn, at one time owne by the same proprietor, William Chaplin.

I left you,' he wrote to a friend, 'owing to the new improved patent coach, a vehicle loaded with iron trappings and the greatest complication of unmechanical contrivances jumbled together, that I have ever witnessed. The coach swings sideways with a sickly sway, without any vertical spring; the point of suspense bearing upon an arch called a spring, though it is nothing of the sort. The severity of the jolting occasioned me such disorder that I was obliged to stop at Axminster and go to bed very ill. However, I was able to proceed next day in a post-chaise. The Landlady in the London Inn at Exeter assured me that the passengers who arrived every night were in general so ill that they were obliged to go supperless to bed; and unless they go back to the old-fashioned coach, hung a little lower, the mail-coaches will lose all their custom.'

Besant's design had been intended 'to give an easy motion fore and aft, as well as sideways and also to be self-righting in case of a spill', Besant claiming that 'the overturning of the carriage will only set the body down on its bottom between the fore and hind wheels when they lay flat on the ground.'

Very soon after this the design was modified by Vidler, the coach-builder of Millbank, who held the monopoly for the supply of mail coaches until 1836. A seat was provided for one outside passenger but it was not till the end of the mail-coach days that more than one outside passenger was allowed, and those days were very short for Matthew Boulton, who had suffered so badly from Besant's coach, represented an un-dreamed of threat to their existence. He was the proprietor of the large Soho engineering works at Birmingham and he took as a partner James Watt, who had made a valuable contribution to the development of Newcomen's steam engine, which had been used as early as the beginning of the eighteenth century for pumping water out of coal mines. However it was not until 1830 that the threat became tangible and when the mail coaches first appeared few people thought their speed would ever be exceeded.

Innkeepers were anxious to become mail coach contractors, for although passengers were given little time to stop for a meal it was a sign of prestige to be known as a house where the Royal Mail stopped. Moreover, people sometimes used the Mail for part of a journey and would put up at the inn where it stopped to change horses before continuing in a post-chaise, so the innkeeper had a chance of additional custom.

The organization of the mail-service was very complicated, and made possible only by the efficiency of the posting inns. In 1796 Thomas Hasker, who had succeeded Palmer at the Post Office, was writing to the Hon. Charles Greville: 'I do not think it would be proper to establish a Mail Coach between Gloucester and Carmarthen . . . it would establish more coaches on the road than can live. . . .

'If the Innkeepers think the contrary, and will back that opinion, and not let it be only a word, let them Start a Coach themselves and run it three days a week from Gloster to Carmarthen for six months, and at the end of that time they shall have the mail to carry.'

During the same year he was writing to Mr. Woolmer of Carlisle about the establishment of a Mail to Dundee and Aberdeen. 'You know it must be a maxim of the Office to bring all the Mail to one Inn at a Central Town that they may assist each other. This being the case, Drysdale's must be the Inn at Edinburgh—and by way of nursing the undertaking I will intreat the Postmaster General to give the first year 2d. per mile each way—if the hills are still so bad between Bervie and Stonehaven there is another road via Lawrence Kirk—it may be right if you find it bad to report the Lawrence Kirk road.'

Thomas Hasker was extremely efficient and insisted on the mail coaches maintaining their speed and keeping to time, so that travellers had to snatch their meals in the shortest possible time. J. G. Campe, the German professor who visited England in 1801, described his journey from Yarmouth to London, after a thoroughly uncomfortable North Sea crossing, during which they had been tossed and buffeted for four days and had finally been forced to make for Yarmouth instead of Harwich.

'. . . with the English posting system,' he wrote, '. . . the pursuit of efficiency is driven to such lengths, that any traveller with a considerable journey before him, who is not rich enough to provide his own equipage and stop when he pleases, is subjected to a veritable torture. Picture to yourself that we were obliged to cover 124 English miles from Yarmouth to London in fifteen hours without a single stop, except about half-way, at Ipswich, where we were suffered to refresh ourselves for half an hour. Even the most urgent demands of nature had to be suppressed or postponed in order that there might not be a minute's delay in changing horses, which happened about every ten miles. If a traveller wished to get down and disappear for a moment, he was faced with the danger that his luggage might be carried on to London without him. The postilion seemed to recognize no other duty than to arrive punctually. Whether his travellers, whose money had very wisely been collected beforehand, arrived with him was their concern, not his. The fresh horses were harnessed in a flash, and away we dashed without any inquiry as to who was on board. It was useless to call after the postilion. Either the noise of the carriage drowned the voice, or if he heard he paid no attention, nor would he stop even for a moment. The guard who sat behind, armed with two pistols as a protection against highwaymen, has no responsibility for the passengers. They are left entirely to their own devices, and must see to it themselves that they are not left behind.

'This indifference extends also to the passengers' luggage. In order that not a second should be lost, everything—trunks, boxes, packages—were thrown into the well like balls. Whether they fell on their sides or corners, or damaged each other, or were smashed, was not even a matter for thought. A request that a little care might be taken to avoid injury was simply ignored. No one pays the least attention or even deigns to reply.

Every one is concerned with his own affairs, and has no thought except to see that the coach departs at the exact moment and arrives according to schedule. The result, so far as I was concerned, was that on arrival in London my trunk was in holes, while a sturdy box, made of oak and strengthened with iron, was stove in completely on one side down to its contents.'

Yet the guards who controlled the coachmen were themselves under strict orders from Hasker to keep up their speeds. 'Stick to your bill and never mind what the passengers say', he wrote, when passengers had complained that they were given no time to finish their meals. 'Is it not the fault of the Landlord to keep them so long? Some day when you have waited a considerable time, suppose 5 or 8 minutes longer than is allowed by the Bill, drive away and leave them behind, only take care that you have a witness that you called them out two or three times—then let them go forward how they can.'

The craze for speed, particularly towards the end of the coaching era, caused some terrible accidents, many of them fatal. In one month alone of 1835 the Post Office recorded: February 5, Edinburgh and Aberdeen Mail overturned; February 9, Devonport Mail overturned; February 10, Scarborough and York Mail overturned; February 16, Belfast and Enniskellen Mail overturned; February 16, Dublin and Derry Mail overturned; February 17, Scarborough and Hull Mail overturned; February 17, York and Doncaster Mail overturned; February 24, Louth Mail overturned; February 25, Gloucester Mail overturned.

It was small wonder that by this time the stage coaches had become as popular again as the mail coaches, for although many had increased their speed and were as fast as the mails, there were plenty available which proceeded at a more leisurely pace, still allowing their passengers overnight stops at the inns on the roads.

By the end of the eighteenth and the beginning of the nineteenth century, the principal London coaching inns were the

Bull and Mouth, St. Martin's-le-Grand, the Bell Savage on Ludgate Hill, by this time known as the Belle Sauvage, the Swan with Two Nicks, Lad Lane, the Spread Eagle in Gracechurch Street, the White Horse in Fetter Lane, the Blossom Inn, Lawrence Lane, Cheapside, the Bolt-in-Tun, Fleet Street, the Cross Keys, Wood Street, Cheapside, the Golden Cross, Charing Cross, the George and Blue Boar in Holborn, the Bell and Crown, Holborn, the Bull Inn, Aldgate, the Three Nuns, Aldgate, the Saracen's Head, Snow Hill and the King's Arms, Snow Hill.

All these inns had stabling for bringing horses in late at night and taking them out early in the morning, as well as stables for the night coach and mail horses which stayed all day in London. And the London end of the coaching business was mainly in the hands of six competitors, William Chaplin, Edward Sherman, Benjamin Horne, Robert Nelson, Mrs. Ann Nelson of the Bull Inn, Aldgate, and Mrs. Ann Mountain of the Saracen's Head, Snow Hill.

William Chaplin succeeded William Waterhouse at the Swan With Two Necks about 1825 and then acquired the White Horse, Fetter Lane and the Spread Eagle and Cross Keys in Gracechurch Street. His coaches went north, east, south and west and he also owned large stables at Purley on the Brighton Road, at Hounslow on the road to the west and at Whetstone at the beginning of the Great North Road.

Lad Lane no longer exists for it has been merged into Gresham Street, but in Chaplin's day the inn yard was in a narrow lane approached by a low arch and extremely difficult of access. The courtyard was surrounded on three sides by three tiers of galleries with outside staircases, made gay with creepers and window boxes, and so it remained until it was demolished in 1856, but as his business expanded Chaplin had underground stables built for two hundred horses. At the height of his prosperity, in the 1830s, he employed two thousand people and owned or partly-owned sixty-eight coaches and 1,800 horses.

Of the twenty-seven mails which left London every night, he horsed fourteen on the first stage out of London and the last stage in, and his annual returns were estimated at half a million pounds.

From the General Post Office in Lombard Street or the new building to which it moved in 1829 in St. Martin's-le-Grand, all the mail coaches except those bound for the west, departed every evening at 8 o'clock, having first loaded up their passengers and luggage, from the inns.

As late as the 1830s the population of England and Wales was only fourteen million, a large proportion of whom were illiterate and never received or sent a letter in all their lives, so all the letters and newspapers from London to every part of England, Wales, Scotland and Ireland were carried in the boots or on the top of twenty-seven mail coaches. To avoid congestion, passengers for the West assembled at the booking offices and inns in Oxford Street and Piccadilly or were taken there in coaches or omnibuses from their City inns, while the guards collected their mail boxes from the Post Office and drove down to the West End departure points to join the mail coaches. There was a line of inns from the City to the West End catering for these west-bound coaches and their passengers, including the Green Man and Still and the Gloucester Coffee House in Oxford Street for those using the Uxbridge Road, the White Bear in Piccadilly and the Spread Eagle, the Bull and Mouth and the Golden Cross where Piccadilly Circus now stands, and where Chaplin, Sherman and Horne had their West End offices, which were used for the Hounslow route. Hatchett's was another very popular coaching inn for travellers to the west country and the White Horse Cellar, on the corner of Arlington Street, near where the Ritz now stands, though it later moved across the road next door to Hatchett's, was at one time considered the finest inn in London.

On summer evenings crowds would gather outside the White Horse Cellar to watch the West Country mails depart.

'The finest sight in the metropolis is the setting-off of the mail coaches from Piccadilly,' wrote Hazlitt. 'The horses paw the ground and are impatient to be gone, as if conscious of the precious burden they convey. The mail carts drive up and the transfer of packages is made, and at a given signal off they start. . . . How we hate the Putney and Brentford stages that draw up when they are gone! Some persons think that the noblest object in Nature is the ship launched on the bosom of the ocean; but give me, for my private satisfaction, the mail coaches that pour down Piccadilly of an evening, tear up the pavement, and devour the way before them to *The Land's End*.'

But Hazlitt was already living in the past, for the days of coach travel were numbered by the time he was writing, although the little band of Jewish street traders still hung around the passengers selling oranges, pencils, sponges, brushes and similar sundries. Dickens took a less romantic view of the White Horse Cellar. 'The travellers' room at the "White Horse Cellar" is, of course, uncomfortable,' he wrote in *Pickwick Papers*. 'It would be no travellers'-room if it were not. It is the right-hand parlour, into which an aspiring kitchen fireplace appears to have walked, accompanied by a rebellious poker, tongs and shovel. It is divided into boxes, for the solitary confinement of travellers, and is furnished with a clock, a looking-glass, and a live waiter: which latter article is kept in a small kennel for washing glasses, in a corner of the apartment.'

Edward Sherman, who established himself at the Bull-and-Mouth, St. Martin's-le-Grand in 1823 was second only to Chaplin in the coaching business. He was the pioneer of the long-distance day coaches to Carlisle, Glasgow, Liverpool, Manchester, Holyhead and other places in North Wales, and as a result of marrying no less than three elderly and rich women in quick succession he was able to rebuild his seventeenth-century inn, with its three tiers of open galleries round the spacious courtyard, which was large enough to accommodate thirty coaches. Every Monday twenty-one coaches left his yard and twenty-one arrived, and his pride was his Manchester 'Telegraph', which first ran in 1833, and by starting from London at 5 o'clock in the morning reached Manchester the same day, at 11 p.m., covering 186 miles in eighteen hours, though it was closely rivalled by Chaplin's Manchester 'Defiance'.

The Bull-and-Mouth, which became the Queen's Hotel after the rebuilding in 1830, was the stopping place for Manchester men, and long after the coaches were off the roads it remained their favourite London inn until it was pulled down in 1887.

William Horne became proprietor of the Golden Cross early in the nineteenth century and soon acquired the Cross Keys in Wood Street and the George and Blue Boar in Holborn, as well as West End offices. By the time he died, in 1828, he was working seven hundred horses, and his son Benjamin, who succeeded to the business, made it even larger, but in 1830 the first Golden Cross, which stood in the south-eastern part of what was to become Trafalgar Square, had to be rebuilt, and no sooner was it finished than it had to come down again because of the slum clearance and rebuilding scheme which was afoot, during which the tumbledown buildings huddled round St. Martin-in-the-Field were all swept away and Trafalgar Square laid out. The third Golden Cross, designed by Smirke, went up a little to the east, opposite Charing Cross, a dignified Georgian building of five storeys with a long, narrow courtyard. Benjamin Horne also had large stables at Barnet and Finchley so that he could compete with Sherman on the north and north-western routes, and at one time he had seven mails, the old Chester and Holyhead, the Cambridge Auxiliary, the Gloucester and Cheltenham, the Dover Foreign Mail, the Norwich, the Milford Haven and the Worcester and Oxford.

There were several coaching inns in East London, serving the eastern counties, but the most important and considered one of London's best, was the Bull Inn in Aldgate, owned by Mrs.

Ann Nelson. She ran nearly all the coaches on the eastern routes and also the Exeter 'Defiance' which was driven by her son George. Charles Harper, writing in 1903, said that the Bull 'presented the picture of a typical old English hostelry, and its coffee-room, resplendent with old polished mahogany fittings, its tables laid with silver, and the walls adorned with numerous specimens of those old coaching prints that are now so rare and prized so greatly by collectors, it wore no uncertain air of that solid and restful comfort the new and bustling hotels of today . . . are incapable of giving. Everything at the Bull was solid and substantial, from the great heavy mahogany chairs that required the strength of a strong man to move, to the rich old English fare, and the full-bodied port its guests were sure of obtaining.'

At the Bull, Mrs. Nelson kept a room especially for her coachmen and guards where they 'dined with as much circumstance as the coffee-room guests, drank wine with the appreciation of connoisseurs, and tipped the waiter as freely as any travellers down the road. A round dozen daily gathered round the table of this sanctum. . . .

'The etiquette of this room was strict. The oldest coachman presided—never a guard, for they always ranked as juniors—and at the proper moment gave the loyal toast of the King or Queen. An exception to this rule of seniority was when Mrs. Nelson's second son, Robert, who drove her Exeter "Defiance", was present, as occasionally he was. Following the practice of the House of Commons, whose members are never, within the House, referred to by their own names, but always as the representatives of their several constituencies, Mrs. Nelson's coachmen and guards here assembled were addressed as "Manchester", "Oxford", "Ipswich", "Devonport", and so forth.'

When Mrs. Nelson retired her son John carried on the business and saw the dawn of the railway age and the end of the coaches, but the old Bull survived until 1868, still known as an inn and not the Bull 'Hotel', for, says Harper, Mrs. Nelson 'most resolutely set her face against that new-fangled word; and as an "inn" the house was known to the very last.'

In 1807 Robert Nelson, Mrs. Nelson's third son, took over the Belle Sauvage from Robert Gray, who moved to the Bolt-in-Tun in Fleet Street.

The Belle Sauvage was a magnificent place in Nelson's day, its galleried courtyard busy with his fast day and night coaches running to Bath, Cheltenham, Brighton, Cambridge and Manchester and the Newmarket–Norwich Mail. He kept four hundred horses in his stables and the inn was famous for its comfort and good food.

To rival Sherman, who had run Nelson's 'Red Rover' to Manchester off the road with an even faster coach, Nelson established a new service with his 'Beehive', announcing that:

Merchants, buyers, and the public in general, visiting London and Manchester, are respectfully informed that a new coach, called the 'Beehive' built expressly, and fitted up with superior accommodation for comfort and safety to any coach in Europe, will leave 'La Belle Sauvage', Ludgate Hill, London, at eight every morning and arrive in Manchester the following morning, in time for the coaches leaving for Carlisle, Edinburgh, and Glasgow. . . . In order to insure safety and punctuality, with respectability, no large packages will be taken, or fish of any description carried by this conveyance. The inside of the coach is fitted with spring cushions and a reading-lamp, lighted with wax, for the accommodation of those who wish to amuse themselves on the road. The inside backs and seats are also fitted up with hair cushions, rendering them more comfortable to passengers than anything hitherto brought out in the annals of coaching, and, to prevent frequent disputes respecting seats, every seat is numbered. Persons booking themselves at either of the above places will receive a card, with a number upon it, thereby doing away with the disagreeables that occur daily in the old style. The route is through Stockport, Macclesfield, Congleton, Newcastle, Wolverhampton, Birmingham, Coventry, Dunchurch, Towcester, Stony Stratford, Brickhill, Dunstable, and St. Albans, being the most level line of country, avoiding the danger of the steep hills through Derbyshire.

It was twenty-five years earlier than Robert Nelson's arrival at the Belle Sauvage that Parson Woodforde described his visit there. In 1782 he had travelled up from Norwich with his niece Nancy and arrived at the Swan with Two Necks, but not liking it there had taken a hackney coach to the Bell Savage where they dined, supped and slept. Here they seem to have been very comfortable, with certain important reservations, for Parson Woodforde recorded: 'They were very civil people at the Bell Savage inn by name Barton and a very good House it is. About 10 o'clock at Night we set of [sic] in the Salisbury Coach from the same Inn for Salisbury, and the Coach guarded. I was bit terribly by the Buggs last Night, but did not wake me.'

Four years later he and Nancy were again staying in London at the Bell Savage, but on June 25 he wrote: 'I was very much pestered and bit by the Buggs in the Night'. The next day they breakfasted, supped and slept at the inn, but, said Parson Woodforde: 'I was bit so terribly with Buggs again this Night that I got up at 4 o'clock this morning and took a long Walk by myself about the City till breakfast time.' They remained at the Bell Savage but that night the poor Parson, determined to get a better sleep, made his own arrangements. 'I did not pull off my Cloathes last Night but sat up in a Great Chair all night with my Feet on the bed and slept very well considering and not pestered with Buggs', he wrote. Again the following night, June 28: 'I did not pull off my Cloathes last Night again but did as the Night before, and slept tolerably well.'

And the next morning they departed for Bath, leaving at 6.45. There were four in the coach and a guard on top and it was called the 'Balloon coach on Account of its travelling so fast making it a point to be before the Mail Coach.'

Robert Nelson maintained the standards of the Belle Sauvage

until the end of the coaching days and then kept the Portland Hotel in Great Portland Street, the historic old Belle Sauvage being demolished in 1850.

The sixth important coaching proprietor of the early nineteenth century was Mrs. Ann Mountain of the Saracen's Head, Snow Hill. She had been widowed in 1818 but with the help of her son, Peter, carried on the business. In 1823 she put the Tally-Ho coach on the London to Birmingham road, which, to the fury of William Horne, travelled 109 miles in eleven hours. He quickly established his Independent Tally-Ho on the same road, arranging for it to set out an hour and a quarter before Mrs. Mountain's coach, in order to attract her customers. Her Tally-Ho was only one of thirty coaches which left the Saracen's Head each day and at the back of the inn she had a coach-factory where her own coaches were built: and other coaches built here were leased to her partners at the rate of 3½d. a mile.

It was at the Saracen's Head that Nicholas Nickleby joined Mr. Squeers and the five small schoolboys for his journey to Dotheboys Hall and found the schoolmaster breakfasting in the coffee room on a plate of hot toast and a round of beef, while the boys were provided with milk and water and thick bread and butter, and expected to be grateful.

Chapter Seven

ON THE ROADS

TRAVELLERS TO NEWCASTLE and Edinburgh by post chaise, stage-coach or mail coach used the Great North Road, and the inns on the way were considered to be amongst the best in the country. In 1734 the journey took nine days to Newcastle and three more to Edinburgh, but by 1773 the time had been halved.

The way from London lay through Islington, Holloway, Highgate and Finchley to the Red Lion at Barnet. A few miles farther on, beyond the branch road to St. Albans and Holyhead, was the Green Man coaching and posting inn and in Hatfield another Red Lion, a dignified establishment which had acquired a brick frontage by the eighteenth century but still had a great deal of ancient timbering round the stable courtyard. From Hatfield the road went through Welwyn and Stevenage and on to Baldock and Biggleswade, where the Crown and White Swan stood on opposite sides of the street, in ancient rivalry, though the passengers of the up 'Regent' coach always dined at the White Swan. At Eton Socon the Cock and the White Horse were the two important inns and it was at the White Horse that Squeers and Nicholas Nickleby stopped for 'a good coach dinner' on their way to Dotheboys Hall, though the five small new boys had to make do with sandwiches, despite the fact that it was bitterly cold, with a keen wind, and a great deal of snow had fallen.

Seven miles on stood the George at Buckden, a large Stuart

Inn which had been given a brick face and eleven sash windows on its first and second storeys: and opposite was the Lion Inn, nearly as vast. The next important inn on the road was the George at Huntingdon, fifty-nine miles from London, with its fine courtyard and gallery, where the landlord provided a good supper and bed for 2s. 6d.

On the coach went, up Alconbury Hill, to the next stage at Stilton, where the broad main street was lined with coaching inns. At one time the most famous of them all was the Bell, which was considered one of the best on the road, although it was later surpassed by the Talbot, the Angel and the Woolpack.

The Bell was a late Gothic sandstone building with an eighteenth-century frontage added, and a great sign, over six feet high, projecting far into the road. When Cooper Thornhill was the landlord, in the 1740s, he introduced Stilton cheese to the world. In the first place he bought it from Mrs. Paulet of Wymondham for the dining-room but it became so popular that he took to selling it to passing travellers at 2s. 6d. a pound as a speciality of his own dairy. Then Miss Worthington of the Angel Inn, on the other side of the road, got wind of what was happening and also began to offer 'real Stilton cheese' to her passengers: and although everyone soon knew that all the cheese was made in Wymondham, Leicestershire, the popularity of Stilton cheese was established for all time.

It is recorded in the *Torrington Diaries* that in 1745 Cooper Thornhill, for a wager of 500 guineas, rode from the Bell to the Queen's Arms, Shoreditch, in 3 hours 52 minutes and made the return journey in 4 hours 13 minutes. He had been allowed fifteen hours but did the return journey of 213 miles in 12 hours 17 minutes. 'This is deservedly reckon'd the greatest performance of its kind ever known. Several thousand Pounds were laid on the affair; and the roads for many miles lined with people to see him pass and repass.'

After Thornhill's death the Bell declined. In 1756 Mrs.

Calderwood had cause to find fault with the linen, which was all in 'perfit rags with fifty holes in each towel' and early in the next century Major Hanslip complained, after ordering some fruit at the Bell for dessert, that 'the bill was enormous and must have included the cost of repainting the sign, or at least the engraving of the sign on the billhead.'

On from Stilton, the journey took the travellers past Norman Cross, with its exclusive establishment which catered only for travellers in their own coaches or hired post-chaises. Seven miles farther on was the Wansford Bridge, spanning the Nene, and on the far side of the bridge the village of Stibbington, with its beautiful Haycock Inn which horsed the next stage. The Haycock Inn was believed to have been the largest stone-built inn of the seventeenth century. It took its name from the story of the man who, somewhere near Peterborough, fell asleep on top of a haycock. The Nene rose and carried him, still asleep on the haycock, as far as Wansford Bridge, where he was suddenly wakened by being bumped against one of the buttresses. 'Where am I?' he asked a passing farmer. 'At Wansford', said the farmer. 'In England?' asked the startled man anxiously.

The Haycock, which later became a private house, was built like a country mansion. There were two windows on each side of the central portico, on the ground and first floors, with a pedimented window over the entrance and five dormer windows in the roof. The two wings had similar sash windows and dormers in the attic floor, and there was a magnificent range of stabling.

After the Haycock, the next stop was Stamford, where the George, with its gallows sign stretching right across the road, was even more impressive.

Writing early in the eighteenth century, Defoe had very little of interest to say about inns. He seemed to accept them as part of the scenery. Dunstable, he remarked, 'is furnished with very good Inns for the Accommodation of Travellers'. Bishop's Stortford was 'Full of convenient Inns'. Puckridge was a 'little hamlet town but a great thoroughfare standing in Ermin Street where there are several good inns for travellers' and when he was travelling through Lincolnshire and approaching Stamford, all he said about the George was 'from hence we came to St. Martins, and stopped at the George, out of curiosity, because it is reckoned one of the Greatest Inns in England, and thence proceeded to Stamford.' And that is his only comment about the large and dignified George which, as Charles Harper wrote, 'is to all other inns what the Athenaeum is to other clubs'.

It stands at the approach to Stamford, a medieval inn which was given a characteristic Georgian façade in the eighteenth century, with long sash windows on the ground and first floors and smaller sashes on the second floor, and it is full of history. During the fifteenth century the daughter of the proprietor married a Stamford youth called David Cecil, and they became the ancestors of William Cecil, Lord Burghley. It was here that Charles I slept, during the Royalist march from Newark to Huntingdon. In 1714 Bolton, the landlord, was suspected of Jacobite sympathies. Queen Anne had just died and the Hanoverian George I was already on his way to England. The town was full of the King's troops and Bolton was forced to kneel down and drink to Queen Anne's memory. He knelt, but as he raised his glass a dragoon ran him through with his sabre and killed him. The people of Stamford, furiously angry, stormed round the George trying to catch the murderer, but after breaking every window in the place the 'villain escaped backway, and the tumult gradually subsided'.

The Duke of Cumberland stayed at the George, on his way back from the victory of Culloden, after the '45 rebellion, and in 1768 the King of Denmark was a guest.

It has yet another claim to fame, for in 1765 Margaret Hodgson, the daughter of the landlord, married Beilby Porteous, a clergyman who became Bishop of Chester and, in 1787, the Bishop of London.

The Blue Boar, Holborn (*above*), and the Belle Sauvage, Ludgate Hill (*below*), were both important coaching inns. In Elizabethan times the courtyard of the Belle Sauvage was used to stage plays, wrestling and other entertainments. The board outside shows the numerous coach destinations.

8. Two White Harts. The one at Bath (*above*) was opposite the Pump Room. T
one at Aylesbury (*below*) shows its eighteenth-century façade.

The George, which today is so quiet and dignified—one of only two inns out of London where E. V. Lucas liked to dine, the other being The Royal George at Knutsford—was once as busy and noisy as any inn in the country, with its two panelled rooms on either side of the central archway, the York, where the passengers for the north waited for their coach, and the London, where the 'up' passengers waited: and in 1776 the Reverend Thomas Twining wrote of the 'distracting bustle of the "George", which exceeded anything I ever saw or heard'.

During the run from Stamford to Grantham there were stops at the Greetham Inn and the Black Bull at Witham Common, where at one time forty-four coaches changed horses every day, but both these inns became private houses in the last century.

The most famous of the Grantham Inns was the Angel—now the Angel and Royal. On this site there was once an Anglo-Saxon manor house belonging to Queen Edith. By the twelfth century it had become a hostel of the Knights Templars and a *maison du roi*, where in 1213 King John held a Court. Some time in the fourteenth century the Angel was rebuilt and in the course of the next century there were many additions and alterations, but its beautiful stone façade is still intact, with its central Gothic archway, surmounted by an oriel window on a carved angel bracket, which was once bravely gilded.

The room over the archway, which is now divided into three, ran the full width of the inn, and in this magnificent, tapestry-hung hall King Richard III, on October 19, 1483, signed the death warrant of the Duke of Buckingham.

The George at Grantham was another important inn for coach travellers, a typical example of eighteenth-century inn-building, with three storeys of sash windows and a central archway into the yard.

As Nicholas Nickleby continued his journey to York, 'the night and the snow came on together, and dismal enough they were. There was no sound to be heard but the howling of the wind; for the noise of the wheels, and the tread of the horses' feet, were rendered inaudible by the thick coating of snow which covered the ground, and was fast increasing every moment. The streets of Stamford were deserted as they passed through the town; and its old churches rose, frowning and dark, from the whitened ground. Twenty miles farther on, two of the front passengers, wisely availing themselves of their arrival at one of the best inns in England, turned in for the night at the George, at Grantham. The remainder wrapped themselves more closely in their coats and cloaks, and leaving the light and warmth of the town behind them, pillowed themselves against the luggage, and prepared, with many half-suppressed moans, again to encounter the piercing blast which swept across the open country.'

The George was built in 1789, replacing a medieval building which had been destroyed by fire a few years earlier. In a private letter, Dickens described it as 'the very best inn I have ever put up at' and another enthusiast said that at the George 'you had a cleaner cloth, a brighter plate, higher-polished glass and a brisker fire with more prompt attention and civility, than at most other places'.

After Grantham the next important town was Newark, with its galleried White Horse Inn, the Clinton Arms, which later became the Kingston Arms, and the Saracen's Head. When Sir Walter Scott stayed at the Saracen's Head on one occasion he found that there was a new landlord, William Thompson, whom he considered to be a vast improvement on his predecessor, for he wrote: 'The travellers who have visited Newark more lately will not fail to remember the remarkable civil and gentlemanly manners of the person who now keeps the principal inn there, and may find some amusement in contrasting them with those of his more rough predecessor.'

From Newark the road went on to Retford and Barnby Moor, where the Blue Bell was, according to the Rev. Thomas Twining, in 1776, 'a gentlemanlike, comfortable house'. Later it became known as the Bell, and when George Clark was proprictor, from 1800 to 1842, it was famous, for he was a well-known sportsman and breeder of racehorses as well as a good innkeeper. With the coming of the railways the Bell was forced to close, for it was remote from any town or village and depended entirely on coach traffic. For many years it was a private house but in 1906 it reopened as an inn and was soon flourishing as a half-way house for motorists between London and Scotland.

The Great North Road stretches on through Bawtry and Doncaster, where the landlord of the Angel, who was also the mayor and the post-master, 'kept a pack of hounds' and 'lived as great as any gentleman ordinarily did'. North of Doncaster the road divides. Nicholas Nickleby's coach took the road to Catterick Bridge, Greta Bridge and Carlisle and it was at Greta Bridge that 'he and Mr. Squeers, and the little boys, and their united luggage, were all put down together at the George and New Inn.' The York road from Doncaster ran through Selby, and at York coach travellers stayed mainly at the Black Swann, while the county families and the wealthy, in their private coaches, went to the exclusive Harker's.

All the way to the border there were coaching inns—the Rose and Crown at Easingfold, the Fleece and the Three Tuns at Thirsk, the Three Tuns at Durham, the Plough at Alnwick.

The Holyhead road branched off from the Great North Road at Barnet and went on to St. Albans, where there was an abundance of ancient inns as well as newer ones. On Holywell Hill were the Old Crown, the White Hart, the Saracen's Head, the Angel, the Horsehead, the Dolphin, the Seven Stars, the Woolpack, the Key and the Peahen, which had been founded in the sixteenth century and, after many alterations, was rebuilt early in the present century. All along the road was a long range of stabling and behind the old Peahen was a builder's yard for coach repairs. In Chequer Street stood the Chequers, the Half Moon and The Bell, in French Row the Old Christopher and the Fleur-de-Lys. The Great Red Lion was in Red Lion Street and the George, once a monastic inn, known as the George Upon The Hupe, still survived.

The road lay through Redbourne, with the Mad Tom on one side of the way and the Bull, a substantial coaching-house, on the other. Eight miles farther on was Dunstable, with its early Georgian Sugar Loaf and the Saracen's Head: and then Hockliffe, with its White Horse Inn. Little Brickhill was six miles on, a small village which was full of inns—the George, the White Lion, the Swan, the Shoulder of Mutton and the Wagon. Fenny Stratford offered the early eighteenth-century Cock, the Bull, the George and the White Swan. The Cock and the Bull were on opposite sides of the street and passing coaches were said to call the news to each other, giving rise to 'cock-and-bull' stories, but the origin of the expression is far older than the Fenny Stratford inns. The next town was Towcester, with its Talbot, once known as the Tabard, and the stone-built Pomfret Arms, which was once the Saracen's Head. It was here that Mr. Pickwick and his friends arrived in their post-chaise after the long wet journey from Coventry, during which 'at the end of each stage it rained harder than it had done at the beginning'.

"There's beds here," said Sam Weller, "everything's clean and comfortable. Werry good little dinner, sir, they can get ready in half an hour—pair of fowls, sir, and a weal cutlet; French beans, 'taturs, tarts and tidiness. You'd better stop vere you are, sir, if I might recommend." Encouraged by the landlord, who appeared at that moment, 'to confirm Mr. Weller's statement relative to the accommodations of the establishment, and to back his entreaties with a variety of dismal conjectures regarding the state of the roads, the doubt of fresh horses being to be had at the next stage, the dead certainty of its raining all night, the equally mortal certainty of its clearing up in the morning, and other topics of inducement familiar to innkeepers', they decided to stay, and when they entered the dining-room, bright with wax candles and a cheerful fire 'everything looked (as everything always does in all decent English inns) as if the travellers had been expected, and their comforts prepared for days beforehand.'

From Towcester the Holyhead road passes through Daventry, with its old Wheatsheaf, and then Willoughby, where once stood the Four Crosses. Dean Swift, on his way to Ireland, stayed here one night in 1730 and found the landlord's wife so unpleasant, that before he left he scratched on a window-pane:

> There are three
> Crosses at your door,
> Hang up your Wife
> And you'l [sic] count Four.

At Dunchurch, farther along the road, once stood the Lion Inn, where some of the conspirators of the Gunpowder Plot awaited the signal for the Catholic rebellion, and hastily scattered when they heard that it had failed and Guy Fawkes was under arrest.

In Coventry, Birmingham and Wolverhampton there were many famous coaching inns though few signs of them are to be found today. At Shrewsbury was the magnificent Lion, an eighteenth-century, red-brick inn, four storeys high, with the arch into the courtyard on one side and an annexe on the other, an obviously much older building, where Dickens stayed as a young man. In a letter to his eldest daughter he wrote: 'We have the strangest little rooms (sitting-room and two bedrooms together) the ceilings of which I can touch with my hand. The windows bulge out over the street, as if they were little stern windows in a ship. And a door opens out of the sitting-room on to a little open gallery with plants in it, where one leans over a queer old rail.'

It was here that, a generation earlier, De Quincey had stayed and where he wrote his essay on the Mail Coach. Although he had walked from Oswestry, he was booked on the mail coach from Shrewsbury to London and was therefore received with the respect due to a coach passenger, compared with the scant courtesy usually accorded to an impecunious pedestrian. It happened that the house was being repaired, and to De Quincey's amazement he was shown into the ballroom. '. . . I was received with special courtesy,' he wrote. '. . . Four wax-lights carried before me by obedient mutes. . . . I stepped into a sumptuous room allotted to me. It was a ball-room of noble proportions—lighted, if I chose to issue orders, by three gorgeous chandeliers, not basely wrapped up in paper, but sparkling through all their thickets of crystal branches, and flashing back the soft rays of my tall waxen lights.'

This beautiful room, in the style of Adams, had been added at the back of the house by the enterprising landlord, Robert Lawrence, who was the proprietor from 1776 to 1806. It had two music galleries and a number of smaller rooms, for cards and refreshments, leading from it. The inn became so popular, not only as a meeting place for local society, but as a coaching-inn for travellers, that the route to Holyhead was diverted from Chester in order to pass through Shrewsbury and make a stop at the Lion.

He also owned the Raven, the other inns in Shrewsbury being the George, the Pheasant and the Unicorn, but Lawrence was undoubtedly the most important innkeeper in Shrewsbury of his time and when he died his friends wrote the following epitaph for his tombstone.

'Sacred to the memory of Mr. Robert Lawrence, for many years proprietor of the "Raven" and "Lion" inns in this town, to whose public spirit and unremitting exertion for upwards of thirty years, in opening the great road through Wales between the United Kingdom, as also for establishing the first mail coach to this town, the public in general have been greatly indebted, and will long have to regret his loss.'

On into Wales from Shrewsbury, the coach went through Oswestry and Llangollen, both full of inns, and then to Betws-y-Coed, where David Cox, in 1847, painted his picture of the little Royal Oak as an inn sign to please the landlady, Mrs. Roberts.

The road to Manchester and Glasgow branched off from the Great North Road at Hockliffe and ran to Newport Pagnell and Northampton, and thence to Market Harborough, Leicester, Loughborough and Derby. At all these places there were important coaching inns, the Bell at Derby having been founded in the seventeenth century and rebuilt late in the eighteenth century. Seventeen miles on, approaching Dovedale, the way passed through Ashbourne, where, at the Green Man, Boswell and Johnson hired a post-chaise in 1777 and Boswell found the landlady a 'mighty civil gentlewoman'.

The road went on through Leek, Macclesfield, Manchester and Bolton, Preston, Lancaster and Shap Fell, past inns great and small, some of which have survived and others have long since disappeared. It was at the lonely little Greyhound in Shap village that Prince Charles Edward called, during the '45 rebellion, and found the landlady to be but a 'sad imposing wife'.

At Penrith, amongst the newer inns, was the Gloucester Arms, which had once been a mansion belonging to Richard III, and opposite stood the Two Lions, which had been converted from the Tudor mansion of the Lowther family.

Carlisle was one of the biggest coaching centres in the country, with its Crown and Mitre, the Bush and the Royal, and it was only another ten miles to Gretna Green.

When the Rev. William MacRichie arrived at Gretna Green, at the beginning of his English tour, in 1795, he noted in his diary: 'Arrive at the famous Gretna-green and dine sumptuously in one of the pleasantest inns in the kingdom, where so many fond lovers have had their hearts and their fortunes united.'

After Gretna, it was another long haul of eighty-five miles to Glasgow, by way of Lockerbie, Crawford and Hamilton.

The first important stop on the Milford Haven road from

London was at Hillingdon, with its Red Lion, where Charles I stayed for the night during his flight from Oxford, the King's Head, first established in the fifteenth century, and the Chequers. At Uxbridge was the famous Crown and Treaty Inn. In Tudor times the Bennet family had built it as a private mansion and it was here, being approximately midway between the Royalist armies at Oxford and the Parliamentary armies in London that, in the early part of 1645, sixteen commissioners from each side consulted for three weeks in a vain attempt to bring an end to the Civil War.

At Beaconsfield, the Royal White Hart and the Saracen's Head were the two important coaching inns and at High Wycombe stood the stately porticoed Red Lion, which Disraeli was to make famous in 1832 and 1834, when he delivered his election speeches under the rampant Red Lion sign.

Through West Wycombe, Stokenchurch and Tetsworth, all with their flourishing inns, the traveller arrived in Oxford, where the Clarendon, the Mitre and the Golden Cross were all kept busy. On to Witney, Burford and North Leach in the Cotswolds, and then to Cheltenham, where the Plough, with its large yard and extensive stabling, had been famous for its good food and comfort since the sixteenth century. At Gloucester, the New Inn, once the pilgrims' hostel, kept its galleried courtyard and outside staircases till the end of the coaching days. At the Bell, in Southgate Street, the landlord during the early part of the eighteenth century, was Whitfield, whose son George became the great missionary of the Society for the Propagation of Christian Knowledge to the American colonies, and later an independent evangelist, building his tabernacle in the Tottenham Court Road in London.

Ross, Monmouth and Abergavenny all had their prosperous inns and the road went on through Brecon to Carmarthen, with its Boar's Head and the Ivy Bush, where Nelson often stayed and where, in 1797, the French commander was brought after the attempted French landing at Fishguard.

After Carmarthen the road forks, one arm leading to Pembroke and the other to Milford Haven.

The Exeter and Bath travellers from Piccadilly followed the same road as far as Hounslow and from there the Bath road continued straight on and the Exeter road went to the left, through Staines.

The first coaching and posting stage out of London, and the last in, for the Exeter road, was at Brentford, which was full of inns. At Staines were the Angel and the Bridge House. The long main street of Egham was lined with inns, of which the Red Lion was the most important, a vast building with a large assembly and ballroom, magnificently imposing staircases and beautifully panelled walls. There was enormous cellarage and stabling for two hundred horses, with cottages for the postboys in the yard. And it was here that George IV often entertained his hunting friends from Windsor.

Through Virginia Water the travellers came to Bagshot, with its King's Arms and the Jolly Farmer. The Jolly Farmer was once a farmhouse owned by William Davis. But Davis was a farmer by day and a highwayman by night. He was wounded and captured on Bagshot Heath and when he was brought to the King's Arms everyone was astonished to discover who he was. He was tried and hanged and left on a gibbet in front of his own house, but the sting in the tail of the story was that the farm later became an inn in rivalry to the King's Arms.

All the way to Basingstoke were little hamlets with large inns, dependent entirely on the coach traffic: and in Basingstoke and Andover the inns were larger still. In Salisbury the inns included the White Hart and the old George, the fourteenth-century inn, much rebuilt, where, in 1668 Pepys had slept 'in a silk bed' and the food was good, but he found the bill exorbitant.

Half way to Blandford was the Woodyates Inn and in Blandford itself the Crown and the King's Arms, while at

Dorchester were the White Hart and the King's Arms, where George III always changed horses during his journey from Weymouth to London.

Bridport came next. Then Charmouth, with its little Queen's Arms, where the future Charles II hid in disguise during his flight after the Battle of Worcester in 1651, Axminster and Honiton, with its Dolphin and the Golden Lion, which was once as busy as any coaching inn in the country. At Exeter, sixteen miles on, were the Elephant, the Mermaid and the Half Moon.

On the Bath road, after Hounslow, Colnbrook was an important stage for changing coach and post horses, either at the eighteenth-century George or the Ostrich, which had once been a medieval hospice. At Slough was the Crown. Salt Hill, a few miles on, was another busy coaching village, though the inns have long since disappeared. The Old Bear at Maidenhead, the Coach and Horses and the George at Reading and the Angel at Woolhampton all had their day. Approaching Newbury there was the stately King's Arms and next to it the Pelican, of which Richard Quin, the foremost actor of the London stage in the early eighteenth century, appalled at his bill, wrote in the visitors' book:

> The famous inn at Speenhamland,
> That stands beneath the hill,
> May well be called the 'Pelican',
> From its enormous bill.

On the main road just outside Hungerford stood the Bear and on the other side of Savernake Forest was Marlborough, with its aristocratic Castle Inn. Here had once stood the medieval castle of Marlborough, but in the seventeenth century Lord Seymour had built on the site his red-brick mansion, attributed to Inigo Jones or his son-in-law Webb, where

Charles II was received during one of his western progresses. The house was rebuilt and greatly enlarged during the reign of William and Mary and in 1740 it came into the possession of the Hertford family. Lady Hertford remodelled the grounds in the formal eighteenth-century manner and created a fashionable sylvan retreat, on the lines of Marie Antoinette's arcadia at the Trianon some years later. To Marlborough Lady Hertford invited the fashionable and the literary lions of the day, to play at milkmaids and shepherds and dally in her grottoes, but when the poet Thomson was found one day with Lord Hertford, exceedingly drunk in one of her sylvan glades, Lady Hertford decided the game had gone too far and he was very quickly requested to leave.

The property passed to the Duke of Northumberland but in 1751 he leased it to Mr. Cottrell, an innkeeper, who opened it as the Castle Inn. One of his first customers was Lady Vere, who stayed there when it had been opened only a fortnight. She described it as a 'prodigious large house' but was indignant that the Duke should have allowed the beautiful house to become an inn, however exclusive.

Cottrell did not stay there long, for in August of the next year the *Salisbury Journal* carried the following advertisement:

> I beg leave to inform the public that I have fitted up the Castle of Marlborough in the most genteel and commodious manner and opened it as an inn where the nobility and gentry may depend on the best accommodation and treatment, the favour of whose company will always be gratefully acknowledged by their most obedient servant George Smith, late of the Artillery Ground. Neat postchaises.

Not for the ordinary stage-coach traveller was this grandeur. The Castle Inn was furnished with much of the furniture of the original mansion and the catering and service were soon famous. Only the rich, such as Horace Walpole and Lord Chesterfield, could afford to stay there. On his way back from

Bath, where he failed to find a cure for his chronic gout, the elder Pitt, the Earl of Chatham, was a guest for several weeks, but during his stay no other visitors were allowed and the entire staff of the inn were clothed in his own livery.

Even before the end of the coaching days, the fortunes of the Castle began to fade, for most of the guests had been visitors to Bath, and Bath was no longer fashionable after the Prince Regent had made Brighton so popular. Thomas Cooper, who was the landlord during the 1820s, could not maintain its splendour and he moved to Thatcham: and by 1842, when the railways were already bringing ruin to so many of the old coaching inns, the illustrious Castle had no tenant. At this time a group of founders were seeking a site for a new school. They bought the Castle and it became the nucleus of the Marlborough College buildings.

From Marlborough it is thirty-one miles to Bath. A great number of visitors to Bath took rooms in private houses, but there were many inns, the finest being the White Hart. It stood opposite the Pump Room and when Simond, the French traveller, arrived there in his post-chaise, in 1815, he said that 'two well-dressed footmen were ready to help us alight, presenting an arm on either side. Then a loud bell on the stairs, and lights carried before us to an elegantly furnished sitting-room where the fire was already blazing. In a few minutes a neat-looking chambermaid, with an ample white apron pinned behind, came to offer her services to the ladies and show the bedrooms. In less than half-an-hour five powdered gentlemen burst into the room with three dishes, etc., and two remained to wait. Our bill was £2 11s. sterling, dinner for three, tea, beds and breakfast. The servants have no wages—but depending on the generosity of travellers they find it to their interest to please them. They (the servants) cost us about five shillings a day.'

Some years later, Mr. Pickwick and his friends set out from the White Horse Cellar in Piccadilly to the White Hart at Bath and when they arrived Sam Weller was mystified to find that the proprietor was another Mr. Pickwick. Moses Pickwick was indeed the last proprietor of the inn, until its final days in 1864, and it was in one of his coaches that the party had travelled.

The journey was uneventful, but they did not have enough time to eat their dinner on the way. 'It would have been cheap at half-a-crown a mouth, if any moderate number of mouths could have eaten it in the time.' However, by seven o'clock that evening, Mr. Pickwick and his friends retired to their sitting-room at 'the White Hart Hotel, opposite the Great Pump Room, Bath, where the waiters, from their costume, might be mistaken for Westminster boys, only they destroy the illusion by behaving much better.'

Moses Pickwick maintained the eighteenth-century manner of his hotel till the end, dressing his waiters in knee-breeches and silk stockings and his chambermaids in muslin mob caps.

On the Dover road, after the Southwark inns, most of which were badly run down by the beginning of the nineteenth century, those at Rochester were the Bull and the George, on opposite sides of the High Street, and the Old Crown, next door to the Bull. It was at the Bull that Mr. Pickwick and his friends stayed on the first night of their adventures. It was built during the Regency, and from the roof of the wide central archway fowls and large uncooked joints of meat dangled from hooks, to keep them cool, a usual practice at inns which had to cater for a large but unspecified number of visitors.

The Pickwick party enjoyed their stay at the Bull, for as their friend the stranger told them, it was 'a good house—nice beds'. In the evening they attended the charity ball being held there that night and found the ballroom 'a long room, with crimson-covered benches, and wax candles in glass chandeliers. The musicians were securely confined in an elevated den, and quadrilles were being systematically got through by two or three sets of dancers. Two card tables were made up in the adjoining card-room, and two pairs of old ladies, and a corresponding number of stout gentlemen, were executing whist therein.'

The Old Crown next door was originally a galleried inn of the fourteenth century, where Queen Elizabeth had once stayed, but about the same time that the Bull was built the Crown came into the possession of a landlord called Wright who converted it into a characteristic flat-fronted Georgian coaching inn.

Sittingbourne was the next large town on the Dover road, with some very important coaching inns, one of the oldest being the Red Lion, where Henry V stayed on his way home from the victory at Agincourt, and, in the next century, Henry VIII stayed and held a Council. It was rebuilt and was a popular coaching inn, along with its neighbours the George, the White Hart, the Bull, the Saracen's Head, the Horn, the Rose and the Lion.

Canterbury was as full of inns as in the days of the pilgrims, those of eighteenth-century fame including the Fleur-de-Lys, the Royal Fountain, the Red Lion and the Rose: and at Dover the most frequented house for travellers to the Continent was the Ship Inn.

Along the Portsmouth road there were splendid coaching inns at Kingston, Esher, Cobham and Ripley. At Guildford the two most important were the Angel and the Red Lion, the Red Lion little changed since the days when Pepys had stayed there. On May 4, 1661, he wrote: 'and so to Gilford, where we lay at the Red Lyon, the best Inn, and lay in the room where the King lately lay in. . . . So to supper and to bed, being very merry about our discourse with the Drawers concerning the minister of the Town, with a red face and a girdle. So to bed, where we lay and slept well.' The following day being Sunday, when people did not travel, they went to the 'red-faced Parson's church, and heard a good sermon of him, better than I looked for.' Back at the inn, they had a good dinner and afterwards walked in the garden. . . . Then to supper in the banquet house. . . . Then to walk in the fields, and so to our quarters, and to bed.'

On August 7, 1688, he came again to Guildford, late at night, 'where the Red Lyon so full of people, and a wedding, that the master of the house did get us a lodging over the way, at a private house, his landlord's, mighty neat and fine; and there supped and talked with the landlord and his wife: and so to bed with great content, only Fitzgerald lay at the Inne.'

At Godalming were the Angel, the Red Lion and the King's Arms, where Peter the Great stayed on his way to London, when he lived for a time in John Evelyn's house at Deptford, studying the ship-building in the dockyard. At Liphook was the distinguished Anchor, where Queen Anne sometimes stayed and where the Duke of Clarence, in his sailor days, dropped in for bread and cheese.

Petersfield had its Dolphin and its Castle Inn, where, in 1661, Pepys and Elizabeth 'lay in the room the Queen lately lay at her going to France'.

The George, at the foot of Portsdown Hill, was the popular haunt of sailors, when they first landed at Portsmouth, but Portsmouth itself was not renowned for its inns, for most of the visitors were naval personnel who were given accommodation within the locked gates of the dockyard. Pepys was there in 1661 and lodged at the Red Lyon, 'where Haselrigge and Scott and Walton did hold their council, when they were here, against Lambert and the Committee of safety. Several officers of the Yard came to see us to-night, and merry we were, but troubled to have no better lodgings.'

On the Hastings road was the old Bell at Bromley and at Sevenoaks the Royal Crown and the Royal Oak. At one time there was also the Three Cats, the inn sign being derived from the leopards in the arms of the Sackville family, but early in the eighteenth century the Three Cats became a private house. At Tonbridge was the Tudor Chequers.

All along the Brighton road there were coaching inns and during the Regency, when the popularity of Brighton was at its height, the Old Ship was built.

Along the Norwich road there were coaching inns equally large and important at Brentwood, Chelmsford and Witham. At Colchester the Red Lion, which had once been a pilgrim inn, was a wealthy merchant's house in the fifteenth century but a public inn by the seventeenth, for it was in the inn-yard here that the Royalists laid down their arms, in 1648, at the end of the siege of Colchester. The Marquis of Granby, at Colchester, had also once been the private house of a Tudor merchant.

At Ipswich there were several coaching inns but the most important was the Great White Horse. Dickens, who knew a great deal about English inns and described them faithfully, disliked it intensely. It was, perhaps, going through a bad phase when he visited it.

'In the main street of Ipswich on the left-hand side of the way, a short distance after you have passed through the open space fronting the Town Hall stands an inn known far and wide by the appellation of The Great White Horse, rendered the more conspicuous by a stone statue of some rampacious animal with a flowing main and tail, distantly resembling an insane cart-horse, which is elevated above the principal door,' he wrote. 'The Great White Horse is famous in the neighbourhood, in the same degree as a prize ox, or county paper-chronicled turnip, or unwieldy pig—for its enormous size. Never were such labyrinths of uncarpeted passages, such clusters of mouldy, ill-lighted rooms, such huge numbers of small dens for eating or sleeping in, beneath any one roof, as are collected together between the four walls of the Great White Horse at Ipswich.

'It was at the door of this overgrown tavern that the London coach stopped, at the same time every evening. . . .'

Dickens went on to describe Mr. Pickwick's arrival, a description so vivid that it must almost certainly have been part of his own experience. A corpulent man preceded them 'down a long dark passage, ushered them into a large, badly-furnished apartment, with a dirty grate, in which a small fire was making a wretched attempt to be cheerful, but was fast sinking beneath the dispiriting influence of the place. After the lapse of an hour, a bit of fish and a steak were served up to the travellers, and when the dinner was cleared away, Mr. Pickwick and Mr. Peter Magnus drew their chairs up to the fire, and having ordered a bottle of the worst possible port wine, at the highest possible price, for the good of the house, drank brandy and water for their own.'

However, Mr. Pickwick's bedroom was a 'tolerably large, double-bedded room, with a fire; upon the whole, a more comfortable-looking apartment than Mr. Pickwick's short experience of the accommodations of the Great White Horse had led him to expect'.

In later years the Great White Horse reformed itself and survived the end of the coaching era to become a comfortable hotel for the motoring age. As with most of the surviving coaching inns, the old coachyard was roofed in to form a lounge.

Some twelve miles farther along the Norwich road from Ipswich was the White Hart, Scole, a beautiful mid-seventeenth-century inn which, with its five Dutch gables and pillared portico, surmounted by a stone balustrade, looked like a private mansion. It was built by James Peck, a Norwich merchant, in 1655, to accommodate the nobility and gentry, and with its wide well staircase and carved balustrades, was as elegant and well-appointed inside as its exterior promised. A famous feature of the inn was the enormous gallows sign stretching across the road, the largest and most elaborate that had ever graced an English inn. It cost over £1,000 and was surmounted by carved figures from Classical mythology, with a leaping White Hart swinging below. The sign stood there for a hundred and fifty years, for it was removed only in 1801. The inn's other claim to distinction was an enormous bed, which was said to be large enough for twenty couples, though whether forty people ever tested this history does not record.

On the outskirts of Norwich was the beautiful Dolphin, a Tudor mansion which, with its two wings, formed three sides of a courtyard. It was rebuilt in the seventeenth century and was the palace of Bishop Hall until his death in 1656, when it became an inn. The other important inn in Norwich was the Maid's Head, standing on the site of a thirteenth-century inn which late in the fifteenth century John Paston had recommended.

The Cambridge, Ely and King's Lynn road ran northwards from London to Edmonton and Ware, and at Ware, in the Saracen's Head, you could still see, as late as 1869, the Great Bed. It did not aspire to the claims of the Great Bed at Scole, but suggested it could sleep ten or twelve people comfortably. On the Trumpington road was the medieval Black Bull, which was given a brick frontage in Georgian times, and in Cambridge itself there were numbers of excellent inns, including the Blue Boar and the Red Lion, the Eagle, the Bath and the Hoop.

At Ely were the Lamb and the Bell, and at King's Lynn, which was a busy port during the seventeenth and eighteenth centuries, was the stately Duke's Head standing in the Tuesday market place. In Stuart times it was built as a private mansion, a magnificent brick building designed by Bell, but during the eighteenth century it became an exclusive inn.

These are some of the inns which the coach travellers of the eighteenth and early nineteenth centuries used on their journeys. Many have survived into the motoring age and, proud of their tradition, still maintain their excellent service. Others have disappeared entirely. Some have been pulled down, others have become private houses, while a number have degenerated into ordinary public houses, retaining few traces of their former importance, when English inns gave such a vital service to the country: for it was in the coaching days that the population and economy of England began to expand so quickly, and communication, which the inns made possible, was increasingly necessary to a country which was climbing rapidly to its brief years of glory as the most important in the world.

It was early in the nineteenth century that the more exclusive inns began to call themselves hotels, and although ordinary coaches still used them as posting-houses for changing horses, only private coach travellers stayed at the newly-styled hotels, the public coach travellers using the less pretentious, old-fashioned inns.

At the same time commercial inns became recognized. Commercial travellers did not usually use the mail or post-coaches but their own coaches or traps, with their own or hired horses, and they were given special terms and privileges at the inns where they stopped, the proprietors putting a room aside for their exclusive use. Thus the first commercial hotels came into existence with the distinctive 'commercial' rooms. It was in 1836 that the *Pickwick Papers* first appeared and Dickens' description of the commercial room at the fictitious Peacock at Eatandswill was a true picture of the less romantic side of life on the road.

'Most people know what sort of places commercial rooms usually are,' he wrote. 'That of the Peacock differed in no material respect from the generality of such apartments; that is to say, it was a large bare-looking room, the furniture of which had no doubt been better when it was newer, with a spacious table in the centre, and a variety of smaller dittos in the corners; an extensive assortment of variously shaped chairs, and an old Turkey carpet, bearing about the same relative proportion to the size of the room, as a lady's pocket handkerchief might to the floor of a watch-box. The walls were garnished with one or two large maps; and several weather-beaten rough great coats, with complicated capes, dangled from a long row of pegs in one corner. The mantelshelf was ornamented with a wooden inkstand, containing one stump of a pen and half a wafer: a road-book and directory: a county history minus the cover: and the mortal remains of a trout in a glass coffin. The atmosphere was redolent of tobacco-smoke, the fumes of which had communicated a rather dingy hue to the whole room, and more especially to the dusty red curtains which shaded the windows. On the sideboard a variety of miscellaneous articles were huddled together, the most conspicuous of which were some very cloudy fish-sauce cruets, a couple of driving-boxes, two or three whips, and as many travelling shawls, a tray of knives and forks, and the mustard.'

Chapter Eight

TRAVELLERS' TALES

W HEN ARTHUR YOUNG made his tour of southern England during the 1760s, he listed the inns where he had stayed and reported thirty-seven of them to be bad, dirty or too dear, but twenty years later, after his travels in France during the French Revolution, he wrote: 'Go in England to towns that contain 1,500, 2,000 or 3,000 people, in situations absolutely cut off from all dependence or almost the expectation of what are properly called travellers, yet you will meet with neat inns, well-dressed and clean people keeping them, good furniture and refreshing civility.'

It is true that, generally speaking, the prosperity of the country was rising at this time and many of the roads improved, although in the remoter parts of the country they were still very primitive. In 1770 the road from Preston to Wigan moved Arthur Young to an almost frenzied eloquence. 'I know not in the whole range of the language, terms sufficiently expressive to describe this infernal road,' he wrote. '. . . let me most seriously caution all travellers who may accidentally purpose to travel this terrible country to avoid it as they would the devil; for a thousand to one but they break their neck or their limbs by overthrows or breaking down. They will meet here with ruts, which I actually measured four feet deep. . . . I passed three carts broken down in these eighteen miles of execrable memory.'

For the most part, travellers are disappointingly reticent

about the food they were given at the inns, but at the turn of
the eighteenth century Lord William Lennox described 'the
plain and perfect English dinner down the road' which consisted generally of 'mutton broth, rich in meat and herbs, of
fresh-water fish in every form—eels stewed, fried, boiled,
baked and spitch-cocked; and water-souche; salmon, the purest
butter, green gooseberries, the earliest cucumbers, saddle of
Southdown mutton, kept to a moment and done to a turn;
mutton chops, Irish stews, rump-steaks, tender and juicy,
chicken-and-ham, plum pudding, fruit tarts and trifle, and
gooseberry-fool.' However, Lord William, no doubt, stayed
at the most expensive and exclusive inns.

When Professor Frederick Von Raumer of the University of
Berlin visited England in 1835 he described a journey to
Nottingham, the 124 miles being accomplished in one day. 'I
now proceed to the manner and inconvenience of the mode of
travelling', he wrote in a letter home.

'Outside and inside, subject and object—these great opposites
are rendered more striking, and are more felt by the English
mode of travelling with the stage, than by any other in Europe.
It seems that the outside is preferred, as is fitting in a commercial country; nay, even females do not hesitate to ascend the
ladder, and take their seats on the outside, at the risk of very
awkward exposure. A connoisseur may perhaps think this to be
the most agreeable part of the mode of travelling.'

But he found it extremely uncomfortable. 'A travelling
cushion is, in England, a most indispensable article,' he insisted.
'If in England the greatest praise is due to the beautiful horses,
the elegant harness, the smooth roads, the rapid progress; in
Prussia to the security of the seat, which is taken and numbered,
and to the coaches; what, it may be asked, is the best in France?
Without all doubt the bill of fare. A Frenchman, educated in the
art of eating, would surely have been horrified, if nothing were
set before him for his dinner but roast mutton at the top of the
table, and boiled lamb at the bottom. In France eating and

drinking has become a refined enjoyment, ennobled by art. Nay, they sometimes appear to travel solely for the pleasure of eating and sharpening their appetite.'

When Pückler-Muskau, another German traveller, had visited London nine years earlier, he seems to have been more fortunate in his choice of inns, and of those in London he was enthusiastic. He found them far better than Continental inns—the beds large, comfortable and clean, large porcelain ewers and basins, taps which supplied water, plenty of towels and a bath available when needed, but he does not mention the food.

Accommodation in London was easier for foreign visitors than it had been a hundred years earlier, when Misson, visiting London in the late seventeenth century, complained that 'there was not among all the taverns in London a single *auberge* where a man could lie and eat at set hours at so much a head, although he admitted that the cook shops were good and would send food to one's lodgings, if one were too proud to eat it on the spot. No Frenchman of distinction, said Misson, would be seen in a cookshop in his own country, but in England 'any gentleman could dine for a shilling'. There were usually four spits, each carrying five or six pieces of meat—beef, mutton, veal or lamb. 'You have what Quantity you please cut off, fat, lean, much or little done; with this a little Salt and Mustard upon the Side of a Plate, a Bottle of Beer and a Roll and there is your whole Feast.'

By the end of the eighteenth century there was the German Hotel in Suffolk Street, Pall Mall and a French inn in Leicester Square called La Sablonnière, where German and French visitors seem mostly to have stayed.

Macky described a typical day in London for a foreign visitor, for Macky, though English born, spent many years of his life abroad, as a government spy, and wrote through the eyes of a foreigner.

'I am lodged in the Street called Pall Mall, the ordinary Residence of all Strangers because of its vicinity to the King's

Palace, the Park, the Parliament House, the Theatres and the Chocolate and Coffee Houses, where the best Company frequent,' he said. 'If you would know our manner of Living 'tis thus: We rise by Nine, and those that frequent great Men's Levees find Entertainment at them 'till Eleven, or, as in Holland, go to Tea Tables. About Twelve the Beau Monde assembles, in several Coffee or Chocolate Houses; the best of which are the Cocoa-Tree and White's Chocolate Houses, St. James's, the Smyrna, Mrs. Rochford's and the British Coffee House, all these so near one another that in less than an Hour you see the Company of them all. We are carry'd to these Places in Chairs (or Sedans) which are here very cheap, a Guinea a Week or a Shilling per hour, as your Gondoliers do at Venice. .... At Two we generally go to Dinner: Ordinaries are not so common here as Abroad, yet the French have set up two or three pretty good ones, for the Conveniency of Foreigners, in Suffolk Street, where one is tolerably well serv'd; but the general way here is to make a party at the Coffee House to go and dine at the Tavern, where we sit till six that we go to the Play, except you are invited to the Table of some great Man, which Strangers are always courted to and nobly entertain'd.'

Although visitors from the provinces tended to stay at the London inns where they were deposited by their coaches, there was an increasing trend during the latter part of the eighteenth century for people to take rooms in private houses and have their meals sent in from the cook shops.

By the time of the Regency, there were one or two more fashionable hotels in London for foreign visitors, such as Brunet's Hotel in Leicester Square, but also the term 'boarding house' was coming into use, where one could lodge very cheaply. A bedroom and a small sitting-room, facing the street, 'both very clean and neat', could be had for 14s. a week. There were restaurants offering French cooking, where dinner could be had for 4s. or less, and foreigners were beginning to appreciate English fish and York ham. The eating-houses and cook-shops still gave good, hot dinners for 1s. and the standard of catering at the big coaching inns was generally excellent.

After 1815 there were many French visitors to England. One of them, General Pillet, hated nearly everything about the English, with a most venomous loathing, but he had been a prisoner of war for six years, and after he had broken his parole, he had suffered a good deal, which explains his extreme bias. His book *L'Angleterre vue à Londres et dans ses Provinces*, published in 1815, was so scurrilous that it was banned by the French police, but even after alleging that all the English were criminally minded, that the excess of women over men was made necessary by the natural tendency of Englishmen to murder their wives, and that English women were awkward and dowdy, adept in shop-lifting, usually tipsy and utterly shameless, he had to admit that our roads were excellent and our carriages and inns convenient and comfortable.

At the seventeenth- and eighteenth-century spas, such as Tunbridge Wells, Epsom and Bath, although towards the end of their popularity there were hotels such as the magnificent White Hart at Bath, many people stayed in rooms. And when, in the days of the Regency, fashion deserted Bath and fled 'with a sort of feverish rage to the unmeaning, treeless and prosaic Brighton', again most people took rooms or rented houses. This held true for the other watering-places which developed in the late eighteenth and early nineteenth centuries—Lyme Regis, Hastings and Margate—for it was not for another century or more that the habit of taking an annual holiday became general amongst all classes except the very poor, and the crop of seaside hotels and boarding houses arose to accommodate them.

The Reverend William MacRichie, who made a tour of Great Britain in 1795, seemed at every stage well pleased with what he found. He came down from Perthshire as far as Sharrow in Yorkshire by horse and then took the coach to

London. At Gretna Green, as we have seen, he dined sumptuously. He arrived at Kendal about eleven o'clock and stayed at the White Hart. At Preston he dined at the Black Bull where, he said, there were two superb rooms, one for dining great company, the other for private assemblies, and also a good assortment of bedrooms.

At Sheffield he dined at the Tontine. This was one of the many 'Tontine' inns, so called because the money for their erection was subscribed on the 'tontine'[1] system: and the Tontine at Sheffield, which was completed in 1785, appears to have been one of the best of the day.

At Sharrow he left his horse with a friend, and at half-past three in the morning set out for the turnpike on the Yorkshire and Derbyshire border to meet the London coach, on which he had already booked his seat.

All the way to Mansfield he enjoyed the company of a blind man called Stevens, 'who sang like a nightingale and played the fife and fiddle'. They dined at Nottingham and had tea at Leicester. From Leicester they drove on through the evening to Harborough and then all through the night to Northampton, where they arrived at three in the morning, and with only a brief stop, drove on to Newport Pagnell for breakfast. The journey took them through Woburn with its dignified Bedford Arms, standing almost at the gates of the Duke of Bedford's park, and then to Dunstable, 'where enter Hartfordshire. From Dunstable set out for St. Albans, and pass on three miles beyond to a good inn, where dine. After dinner set out for Barnet. Haymakers on every hand busy; a fine crop appearing everywhere.'

Here, despite a dreadful thunderstorm, he took the outside of the coach for his first view of the Thames, the City and St. Paul's. At half past five in the afternoon the coach arrived at the Bull-and-Mouth Inn near Aldersgate, and here he stayed for

[1] A tontine is a loan or fund, the surviving subscribers of which receive annuities increasing as they become fewer.

the night and enjoyed 'comfortable repose, having had none for the two preceding nights, and having in the course of thirty-six hours travelled one hundred and sixty-five miles.'

He spent three weeks in London, seeing all the sights, and one day took a trip to Eton and Windsor, boarding a coach from Piccadilly at half past six in the morning and arriving, by way of Kensington, Turnham Green, Hammersmith, Brentford, Hounslow and Maidenhead, about eleven o'clock, where he breakfasted at the White Hart, Windsor. At 4 p.m. he mounts the stage-coach again and enjoys a 'delightful evening ride to London. Arrive at Hyde Park Corner in the evening. St. James's Park and Hyde Park crowded with company walking: elegant show of fashion and beauty.'

He left London for home on August 10. 'Rise at six o'clock a.m. and pack up for my departure. Leave Mr. Brodie's at seven, and arrive at eight at the Green Dragon, Bishopsgate, where set my foot on board of the Cambridge stage-coach. Breakfast at Hoddesdon. . . . Dine at the Angel, Barkway. . . . Arrive at Cambridge at five p.m. No coach sets out for the North till to-morrow.

'12 August. At five a.m. set forward aboard the coach to Hunting-don to breakfast. . . . Then Stilton and Stamford, where dine in a great company of travellers from different parts of England.

'Thursday, 13th August. Get up early in expectation of a place in the Mail coach at seven o'clock. Two Mails arrive, but the places all occupied. Obliged to wait here till ten a.m. Heavy coach arrives at ten; have a berth on board. Arrive at Grantham to dinner. One lady and eleven gentlemen, dine all together; hearty entertainment. Two English clergymen; a Swiss gentle-man. Set out all in company; six on board, and six in the hold. Night comes on as we approach to the boundary of York-shire . . . converse about robbers: no guard attends us: all of us unarmed. Arrive at Doncaster at eleven p.m., thank God, without any untoward accident having befallen us. Sup, ten gentlemen together.[1] At three quarters past eleven, the coach sets forward with my fellow-travellers, whom I recommend to the protection of Heaven, and rest here all night in a good comfortable inn.

'Friday, 14th August. Doncaster. Slept soundly for eight hours at the Angel Inn, one of the best inns in England'.

His next stop was at Harrogate. High Harrowgate, he says, contains 'three capital inns, with very large rooms, and numerous accommodations for strangers. The Dragon Inn, the Granby, the Queen's Head, etc. In the Queen's Head there is a room that dines with ease one hundred and twenty persons with fifty servants attending. The houses all crowded at present with Company at the Waters. . . . Take up my quarters at Low Harrowgate, just in the vicinity of the Spaw. Here are also a great number of commodious inns for the company during the watering season, which continues from June to the end of September. At Harrowgate a very elegant Theatre, fit to contain fifty people (on the stage) with pit and pit-boxes, boxes and gallery. The Company here have frequently Plays, both public and private. When there is to be a public Play, cards are sent to the different houses to give notice to the Company.'

At Sharrow he picked up his horse again. 'Leave Hoard Inn after dinner and set out for Helmsley, fourteen miles to the north-west of Hoard Castle. Rain continues pouring without mercy; the road runs in streams. Night comes upon me in thick darkness as I approach Helmsley. Put up at Wilson's. A good comfortable fire in the kitchen; take this as the best room in the house. Get tolerably dry before supper. Talked to a fellow at inn till eleven o'clock. Then go to bed.'

When he reached Chillingham, in Northumberland, there being no inn in the village, the Rev. Dr. Thomas, the Vicar of the place, 'receives myself and my horse, and entertains both with the most hospitable attentions. We may boast of our

[1] The lady and her clergyman husband had left the coach just after Newark.

Scottish hospitality as we please', says William MacRichie, 'but I have repeatedly found hospitality in England too.'

It was in 1826 that William Cobbett set forth from Kensington on his *Rural Rides*. At Eversley in Wiltshire he stayed at the inn he had visited eighteen years previously. 'This inn is one of the nicest, and, in summer, one of the pleasantest, in England', he said. '. . . the house is large, the yard and the stables good, the landlord a *farmer* also, and, therefore, no cribbing your horses in hay or straw and yourself in eggs and cream. . . . I am now sitting at one of the southern windows of this inn, looking across the garden towards the rookery. It is nearly sun-setting; the rooks are skimming and curving over the tops of the trees; while under the branches I see a flock of several hundred sheep come nibbling their way in from the down and going to their fold.'

The Deptford Inn, near Salisbury, was 'a famous place of meeting for the *yeomanry cavalry* in glorious anti-jacobin times, when wheat was twenty shillings a bushel, and when a man could be crammed into gaol for years for only *looking* awry'.

At Andover he went to dine at the ordinary at the George Inn, 'which is kept by one Sutton, a rich old fellow, who wore a round-skirted sleeved fustian waistcoat, with a dirty white apron tied round his middle, and with no coat on; having a look the *eagerest* and the *sharpest* that I ever saw in any set of features in my whole life-time; having an air of authority and of mastership which, to a stranger as I was, seemed quite incompatible with the meanness of his dress and the vulgarity of his manners: and there being visible to every beholder, constantly going on in him a pretty even contest between the servility of avarice and the insolence of wealth.'

At Lyndhurst, he and George had to sleep in an inner room, 'the access to which was only through another sleeping room, which was also occupied.' They had been riding all day, since very early in the morning, so went early to bed. But, says Cobbett, 'I was, of course, awake by three or four; I had eaten little over night; so that here lay I, not liking (even after day-light began to glimmer) to go through a chamber, where, by possibility, there might be a "lady" actually *in bed*; here lay I, my bones aching with lying in bed, my stomach growling for victuals, imprisoned by my *modesty*. But at last I grew im-patient; for, modesty here or modesty there, I was not to be penned up and starved: so after having shaved and dressed and got ready to go down, I thrusted George out a little before me into the other room; and through we pushed, previously resolving, of course, not to look towards *the bed* that was there. But as the devil would have it, just as I was about the middle of the room, I, like Lot's wife, turned my head! All that I shall say is, first, that the consequences that befell her did not befall me, and, second, that I advise those who are likely to be hungry in the morning not to sleep in *inner rooms*; or, if they do, to take some bread and cheese in their pockets.'

Breakfast was not ready but Cobbett could wait no longer. He went to the nearby butcher and bought a loin of mutton. He and George cooked and ate about two pounds of it and gave the rest to a poor woman in the village.

At Tring, 'which is a very pretty and respectable place', Cobbett had urged the use of home-grown straw instead of straw imported from Tuscany, for the straw-plaiting cottage industry. 'I am the more desirous of introducing this manu-facture at Tring on account of the very marked civility which I met with at that Place', he says. On the occasion of his visit there in September, 1829, to inspect Mr. Elliman's plantation of the locust-tree, 'which Mr. Cobbett claims the merit of having introduced into this country', his Tring friends gave him a dinner at the Rose and Crown inn. 'It was the best that ever I saw called a *public dinner*, and certainly unreasonably cheap', recorded Cobbett. 'There were excellent joints of meat of the finest description, fowls and geese in abundance; and finally, a very fine haunch of venison, with a bottle of wine for each person; and all for *seven shillings and sixpence per head*. Good

waiting upon; civil landlord and landlady; and, in short, everything at this very pretty town pleased me exceedingly.'

When the officers of the Bucks Yeomanry gave a dinner to
Lord Blaney at the White Hart, Aylesbury, in September, 1815,
though the menu was more elaborate, the value was as good,
for including wine it was only £1 10s. 0d. a head. It began at
five o'clock and must have lasted for the rest of the day, for
this is what they ate and drank.

First Course

	Turtle Soup	
	Potatoes	
Lobster Sauce	Melted Butter	Lobster Sauce
	Turbot	
	Butter	
	Potatoes	
	Turtle Soup	

Second Course

	Boiled Fowls	
Haricot Mutton	Oyster Sauce	Beef Olives
	Tongue	Turnips and Carrots
	Mint Sauce	
Greens	Saddle of Lamb	Stewed Pigeons
	Salad	
Veal Olives	Boiled Leg of Pork	French Beans
Potatoes	Pease Pudding	Cauliflower
Tremlong of Beef	Road Fowls	

Third Course

Sweet Sauce	Brace of Birds	Bread Sauce
Potatoes	Hare	Potatoes
	(Flowers)	
Bread Sauce	Hare	Bread Sauce
	Brace of Birds	

Fourth Course

Jelly	Gooseberry Pie	Blancmange
Custards	Baked Apple Pudding	Apricot Tart
Apricot Tart	Plum Pie	Custards
Blancmange	Boiled Plum Pudding	Fruit in Jelly
Port	Sherry	
Claret	Champagne	
	Turtle Punch	

About twenty guests took this gargantuan meal and each course was placed on the table complete—sauces, vegetables, entrées and joints. Everything was carved and served from the table, nothing being handed round by the waiters, and the curious setting out of the Bill of Fare was to guide the waiters in placing the dishes on the table.

There was little wheeled traffic in Scotland during the early part of the eighteenth century, for although General Wade had ordered some improvement to the roads in the Highlands, after the 1715 rebellion, roads generally were very bad throughout the country for many years to come.

In 1754 Hosea Eastgate inaugurated a new fortnightly stage-coach service to run from the Coach and Horses in Dean Street, Soho, London, to John Somervell's inn in the Canongate, Edinburgh, which took ten days in summer and twelve in winter. It was a 'new genteel Two-end Glass Machine, hung on Steel Springs, exceeding light and easy' but the inns in Edinburgh were appalling. 'Mean, dirty and dismal', declared one traveller, and a stranger might well be shocked 'by the novelty of being shown in by a dirty sunburned wench, without shoes or stockings'. When Johnson stayed at the White Horse, said to be the best inn in Canongate, he was disgusted and Boswell had to apologize for the 'evening effluvia' from the uncovered drains.

By about 1760 communication had been established between

Edinburgh and Glasgow by way of Falkirk, but there had been no sizeable inn in Glasgow until Mr. Tennent had established the Saracen's Head, in 1755.

Sylas Neville, who was studying medicine at Edinburgh in the 1770s, travelled a good deal between London, Norwich, Newcastle and Edinburgh, and at some of the inns he was annoyed because he felt the landlords failed to show proper respect to the coach passengers, even to those who were 'really gentlemen and ladies in dress and behaviour'. The White Horse in Edinburgh was a dismal place and very dirty, he declared, and the George at Dunbar 'the nastiest house on the road—it stank horribly; meat, fowls etc. were hung up in the passage.'

He found English inns very much more attractive and his favourite, he said, was the Crown at Epping.

In 1784 Faujas de Saint Fond, the naturalist and geologist, set out with three companions to visit Fingal's Cave on the island of Staffa. They reached Edinburgh in the early autumn and a few days later set off for the Highlands. Late at night they came to a small inn at Luss, on the banks of Loch Lomond, which looked more like a fisherman's hut. They knocked loudly but the hostess hurried out to tell them that the inn was full and they must keep quiet as the Lord Judge, who was on circuit, was sleeping there. 'May you be happy; be off', she said quickly and thereupon shut the door on them and locked it. At the next village, fifteen miles on, the inn was full of jurymen on their way to Inverary, but by this time it was pouring with rain and the travellers had had enough. Two spent the night in the carriage and two on mattresses on the inn floor, but the horses were given stabling.

The next day was fine and sunny and they were enchanted with the beauty of Loch Lomond. 'The superb Loch Lomond,' wrote Faujas, 'the fine sunlight that gilded the waters, the silvery rocks that skirted its shores, the flowering and verdant mosses, the shepherds beneath the pines . . . will never be effaced from my memory, and make me cherish the desire not to die before seeing Tarbet again. I shall often dream of Tarbet, even in the midst of lovely Italy with its oranges, its myrtles, its laurels and its jessamines.'

But as they pressed on to Loch Fine they found the country grim and forbidding and at Inverary the inn was again full of jurymen. However, Faujas had a letter of introduction to the Duke of Argyll at Inverary Castle and here for the next three days they enjoyed the best of Scottish hospitality.

The journey to Oban was beset with troubles and the carriages were overturned in an abyss, but they came upon a very good inn and a friendly host who found them a guide, the local school-master, who spoke both English and Gaelic. Faujas' companions went on to Mull but Faujas stayed at the inn for a few days, working and exploring, and was comfortable enough except for the piper who marched up and down outside the inn every evening until midnight, playing his pipes and never changing the tune, till Faujas was nearly demented. In desperation, Faujas took him by the hand and led him firmly away, but the piper, indicating by signs that he was not tired, came back and started playing all over again. Faujas could do no more than endure.

His friends were storm-bound in Staffa for two days and had to take refuge in a cottage which was so dirty that when they returned to the mainland they had to rid themselves of the vermin, but when Faujas made the crossing—the first geologist to visit the island—he was more fortunate and made his observations in fine weather. From Mull they went on to St. Andrew's, where to their dismay they found the city in a state of ruin and desolation. St. Leonard's chapel was used as a dwelling by a gardener, the Cathedral was in ruins and the university in poor shape. Over everything hung, as Dr. Johnson had observed, 'the silence and solitude of inactive indigence and gloomy depopulation'.

In 1792 a young Breton *émigré*, the Chevalier de la Tocnaye, arrived in England and decided to explore Scotland on foot. At an inn in Glasgow, being young and cheerful, he burst into song, but an outraged landlady stormed into his room, shut the window and ordered him to be silent. "Fie for shame, you sing . . . God forbid to sing on the Sabbath", she said sternly.

For the greater part of the remainder of his six weeks' tour Tocnaye was given hospitality in private houses, for strangers were rare in the Highlands and he was an engaging young man with good credentials.

He found that whisky was so cheap that many men were drinking two bottles a day. It shortened their lives so drastically that few lived to be old men and at Bonholm, north of Montrose, a minister told him that 'through premature deaths, most properties had changed masters three times within ten or twelve years.'

At Aberdeen he was entertained by Sir William Forbes and at Banff a farmer he met on the road mistook him for a Turkish doctor and asked his advice about his wife's jaundice. Tocnaye did his best and the farmer was so impressed that at the next inn he found a crowd of prospective patients waiting for him, hoping for treatment, one farmer offering his daughter in marriage by way of payment.

Whisky, he learnt, was the Scottish panacea for all childish complaints and the best drink for new-born infants. Moreover, if it were given at the right time, it would prevent a baby from crying while being baptized.

The city of Edinburgh to the north of the Royal Mile, known as the 'new town', was being built by the time these French travellers were visiting Scotland and it was fast becoming a very beautiful city: and during the 1820s there were many more visitors, both from England and the Continent, most of them intent on seeing the Lothians or even the great Sir Walter Scott himself.

The Lake poets made the Lake District also popular and the lakeside inns flourished. Southey, describing Espriella's tour of the lakes, said that the roads were good for walking and for coaches and liked the inns, despite the crowds of visitors. He and his companion enjoyed spotted char for supper at one stop and slept well, and when they came to Keswick and found that the inn was full, they secured a good lodging with the local barber, who shaved their chins 'in the English fashion', while his wife cooked their meal and prepared the beds.

Espriella is, of course, reflecting Southey's own views, and his first impression of an English inn was at Falmouth, where he complained of the constant noise and bustle—'doors opening and shutting, bells ringing and calls for the waiter, the boots running in one direction, the barber with his powder bag in another, and his boy with hot water and razors in a third'—but after he had settled down to his tour he had little but praise for the inns he visited.

In Wales it was a very different story, to judge from the trials of Rowlandson and his friend Wigstead when they set out, in 1797, for a tour of Wales. As they approached Tan-y-Bwlch, tired and hungry, they began to plan their supper. Should it be chicken or chops? It was to be neither, for at the only inn the surly landlord told them he had no room and, in pouring rain, they had to journey another three miles to Festiniog. It was almost dark when they reached the inn, which they nearly passed, taking it at first for a barn or outhouse. The landlady, looking like one of the witches from Macbeth, was none too pleased to see them, but by this time they 'were not a little satisfied at being under any kind of roof'. For supper they were offered 'a small leg of starved mutton and a duck, which by their smell had been cooked a fortnight'.

'Our bedrooms were most miserable indeed', recorded Wigstead. 'The rain poured in at every tile in the ceiling.' And the sheets were so wet that they discarded them and slept between blankets, in their clothes.

Some days later, when they came to the inn at Llannon 'the cook on our arrival was in the suds, and, with unwiped hands, reached down a fragment of mutton for our repast: a piece of ham was lost, but after a long search was found amongst the worsted stockings and sheets on the board. . . . A little child was sprawling in the dripping pan which seemed recently taken from the fire: the fat in this was destined to fry our eggs in. Hunger itself even was blunted.'

'I devoted my attention to a brown loaf,' continued Wigstead, 'but on cutting into it was surprised to find a ball of carroty-coloured wool; and to what animal it had belonged I was at a loss to determine. Our table cloth had served the family for at least a month, and our sitting-room was everywhere decorated with the elegant relics of a last night's smoking society, as yet unremoved.' Only at Neath did Wigstead find himself able to declare 'with strict propriety' that he found an inn that was comfortable.

However, they found much of interest during that trip and at the village of Newcastle Emlyn in Carmarthenshire they came upon a 'decent inn' where, in the kitchen, a dog was being used as a turnspit. Rowlandson's drawing of 'The Kitchen of a Country Inn' shows the unfortunate dog, set in a cage high up in the wall by the kitchen fire, working the treadmill which turned the spit and the roasting joint, a practice not uncommon in large inns until mechanical spits were devised.

Here, on a happier note, is the detailed description of life at the White Hart at Harwich, when a Dutch traveller arrived there, after a stormy passage, in 1815, a few months after Waterloo.

'I have just landed and have been shown into The White Hart inn. The boatswain has returned to the packet for my luggage, which is to get to the Customs House. First, I will breakfast, and then view the town. I ring the bell and a person dressed like a gentleman comes in. He is of enormous bulk—a typical John Bull. I make this man a bow, taking him for the host, and dismiss him to send a waiter to me. "I am the waiter, sir," he replied. He then disappeared, and within five minutes

served up a most elegant breakfast. There was a teapot of a kind
of black earthenware, which I have since learned to be of
Wedgwood make, with a low relief of classic figures; the cream
pot was of silver, the cup and saucer of Staffordshire ware, but,
oh, how large the cup! The tea-caddy was of neat lacquer work,
and, in the divisions, I found excellent green and black tea with
a scalloped silver spoon for ladling out the exact measure. There
was a china plate with toast, top and bottom, upon a china
bason, and another with slices of thin bread and butter, also a
bason of very fine loaf sugar. All this was brought to me on the
neatest tray. I made the tea myself to my taste. Another waiter
then brought in a copper scuttle shaped like a Roman helmet.
I felt very comfortable, such was the elegance of the fireplace,
the polished steel grate, the fender of polished steel and the
poker, shovel and tongs, with vase tops, with which it was such
a delight to stir the fire.

'I had leisure to inspect the private room. It was spread with a
pretty carpet worked to a uniform pattern, with a large White
Hart at the centre. Breakfast over, I asked to be shown to my
bed-chamber. There I found comfort and elegance. A carpet
covered the centre of the floor, on which stood a mahogany bed
with a painted cornice and dimity curtains, and a most whole-
some counterpane as white as snow, with a beautiful design of
flowers. On the right was a bow-fronted mahogany chest of
drawers with a stand glass of the finest workmanship upon it;
on the left, a closed-up wash-stand with blue Staffordshire jug
and bason; at the side was a towel-horse with two towels neatly
folded. The sash windows were hung with dimity, and besides,
had white blinds to let up or down at will. There were two
light chairs with cane bottoms, a night-stool and a small table
for writing. The fireplace had a hob grate with two figures, one
on either side, cast with the metal. What a contrast to the hotels
of my own country, where everything is so antique! Oh, I
thought, if the rooms of the public inns are like this, what must
the apartments of the nobility be like!

'Well satisfied, I gave notice of my intention of spending the rest of the day in seeing the town. Dinner was on the table when I came back, but soup and table napkins I did not see. The waiter, the fat one, did stare when I asked for these, but it appears that the White Hart did not understand my wants, so I was forced to use my handkerchief. But the table was crowded with things. It had a cotton cloth, quite clean, and many utensils which looked like silver, including an epergne with glass dishes in which were grapes, apples and sweetmeats. There was an immense joint of roast beef at the head of the table, and a leg of mutton of equal bulk at the bottom, both awaiting and defying the guests. The table was set for ten persons, and each set of knives and forks was flanked with two different sorts of fruit pies. There were two large dishes of potatoes, and French beans, and wedged among these was a mahogany waggon in which rode an enormous Cheshire cheese. With the potatoes was butter sauce, and in glass jars I did notice some pickled onions and some walnuts, which give a particular relish to the beef. The company being seated, we fell to. For drink, there was London porter, and for wine, some port, which I found to be mixed with brandy. The meal over, three waiters appeared and whipped the cloth from over our heads. It was done so dexterously that no one seemed to mind. Then they brought on the dessert—grapes, walnuts, apples—and crackers with a special service of highly decorative plates, as well as napkins of checked pattern, evidently of wool, which were of no use, and so with eating, drinking and talking, the time did pass till tea was ready, and there was no great difference between this meal and my breakfast. Then at nine o'clock, being tired, I retired to my bed-chamber with a plated candlestick I had seen outside on a table in the corridor, awaking next morning to find my boots jet black with some polish, and so again I took my breakfast in the private room and prepared for my journey to London. The bill was most reasonable, amounting to some twenty-six shillings per day, including the service, but I was perturbed at the number of persons who came with me to the door—the cook, the chambermaid, the under-waiter, the head-waiter, the boots—all claiming a fee. I got rid of this legion for ten shillings. The coachman, he asked the guard if all was right, and then we started on the great road. On the right and left as we passed along I noticed country houses of brick, with neat gardens. There were orchards and wheat and turnip fields. People all appeared plump and well-fed, the children being very attractive. There was a vast number of private carriages and post-chaises, as well as elegant gigs on the road. One thing struck me in particular; it was the neatness of the fences and the gates, as well as the design of the toll-houses and the turnpike gates, all of which were painted in white. We stopped at Colchester, at Chelmsford and at Brentwood, and so came into London by Romford, Stratford-le-Bow and Whitechapel, the houses in this part appearing exceptionally old.'[1]

[1] Quoted in *The English Inn*, A. E. Richardson and H. D. Eberlein (Batsford, 1925).

Chapter Nine

HIGH NOON OF THE COACHING INNS

THE HEYDAY OF coaching was from about 1824 to 1840. By the 1820s Telford and McAdam had vastly improved the roads for the Turnpike Trusts, and in some places had shortened the routes. The mail and stage coaches were infinitely more comfortable and the horse-breeders had produced an especially strong and efficient coach horse, from a breed reared in the Cleveland hills.

Over the entire country a network of prompt and regular mail and stage-coach routes had been organized, which was the envy of every other country in Europe. With each year of the increasing momentum of the industrial revolution and the industrialization of the North and the Midlands, transport and communication became more vital, and while heavy goods still used the canals, the coach services provided the passenger transport: but it was only possible because of the competent service of the posting-inns.

By the late 1820s the speed of coach journeys reached the highest it was ever to attain. During the eighteenth century the average speed of a mail coach was seven miles an hour. In 1812 the 404 miles from London to Glasgow took three nights and two days of continuous driving—a total of fifty-seven hours—and it cost an inside passenger £10 8s. od. for the fare alone, apart from tips and food and drink on the way. By 1838 the time had been reduced to forty-one hours, but even so few people were stalwart enough to stay the course without dropping off on the way for at least one night's sleep at an inn. In 1825 fast day coaches began to run, in competition with the mail, and from the outset they were a success. Changing horses was sometimes accomplished in under a minute and there were no delays on post-office business. Their daytime speed soon equalled and sometimes outstripped the mails, and for those who did not like travelling at night anyway, they were preferred. The mail coach passenger business began to suffer and the post office allowed more outside passengers, to make up revenue. At first one had been allowed, beside the driver. Then two more were given places at the back. A fourth was soon allowed and eventually the mails were carrying eight or twelve outside passengers, like the stage-coaches.

All this additional traffic meant more business for the posting inns, and in the country towns not only were they places of importance, but their proprietors wielded a great deal of influence, for most of them had a large amount of capital invested in the town. They were men of education and substance, employing a great deal of labour and owning an average of twenty-five to thirty pairs of post-horses. The innkeeper had to be a good judge of a horse as well as of food and wine. He was the friend of the neighbouring gentry and often rode to hounds, while always retaining the personal touch in greeting his guests and ordering their comfort, however large his establishment.

As well as a resting place for travellers, the inn was still the social centre of the town, for there were seldom any other public rooms available to serve as meeting places. Here was the booking-office for intending coach travellers. It was the headquarters of local clubs and political parties. In Birmingham, for example, the Leicester Arms in Bell Street was the meeting place for the Jacobins and the Minerva Tavern in Peck Lane the centre for the anti-Jacobins and Tories, while the Priestley riots of 1791 began at the Royal Hotel.

At election times candidates established themselves in the inn of their choice and throughout the campaign kept the staff busy providing the prodigious quantities of food and drink which were always offered to the voters. A parish council often used its village inn as a council chamber and in a town as large as Birmingham, the business of the Town Council was all transacted at the Woolpack Inn during the early part of the nineteenth century, while at Darlaston the White Lion served almost as a Town Hall.

The inn was also a place where men could transact their business and a place of entertainment where public dinners and balls were held.

Many new inns, some now calling themselves hotels, were built at this time and others altered, enlarged and modernized. Architecturally most of the important inns of the early part of the nineteenth century are distinctive, for although still retaining the arch into the courtyard, they had many features of the contemporary Classical taste, very often with an assembly room on the first floor which had windows opening on to the roof of a pillared portico.

The Stamford Hotel at Stamford was built with a dignified pillared frontage. It had a vaulted vestibule and impressive staircase, lit from above by a dome. To left and right were the coffee room and a sitting-room, with the assembly room on the first floor. The Grosvenor at Shaftesbury, the London Inn at Exeter, the Royal at Plymouth, Webb's at Liskeard, the White Lion at Upton-on-Severn, the Cups at Lyme Regis and the Royal at Falmouth all bore a classical air, to match the important civic functions which they fulfilled.

Despite all this dignity, there was great rivalry between the inns to catch the private coach trade. On the Great North Road, for example, all along the line from London to York there were rival posting establishments, though usually not more than two at any important stopping place, each of which had an interest in its own line of posting-houses along the route. Post boys, who were usually elderly men, were paid to bring a carriage with two or four horses to the first change at the right inn of the line. They wore distinctive uniforms—a blue jacket with a white top hat or a buff jacket with a black hat. A 'blue' boy at one of the inns at Barnet, the first stop out of London, would be given ten shillings to take a coach to the next stop on his line. When the carriage arrived at the second change, the post-boy, returning to Barnet with the horses, brought 7s. 6d. Five shillings was sent from the third posting-house and 2s. 6d. from the fourth, by which time it was considered that the coach was well on the way of the right line, and it seldom strayed from it. The post-boy also had to present his tickets to the toll-keepers, for up until 1839 innkeepers had to pay a post-horse duty of $1\frac{1}{2}$d. a mile for every horse.

Elections were bitterly contested and the bribery was outrageous. At the borough elections at Aylesbury in 1802 the candidates were the old sitting members, Mr. Bernard, who made his headquarters at the George, Mr. Du Pré, who established himself at the White Hart, and a Liverpool merchant, Bent, a stranger to the town, who put up at the Bull's Head. The eating and drinking was almost continuous and on certain nights of the week each of the agents would appear at his inn with a bowl of punch and a bowl of guineas. The punch was ladled out to all comers, the guineas distributed rather more circumspectly. The probables received one guinea, those who needed a little more persuasion anything up to five guineas, but as these ceremonies were held at different inns on different nights there was nothing to prevent the enterprising voter from receiving his punch and guinea from all three candidates. Excitement rose as election day drew near and on the day itself everyone was primed for the orgy of eating and drinking, at the candidates' expense, and the free fights which always took place.

It was in 1808 that Louis XVIII caused a stir in Aylesbury by arriving to spend his exile at Hartwell House, two or three miles away. With the Queen and the Prince de Condé, he occupied the mansion and the other members of the royal family and their entourage lived in cottages or lodges on the estate or in neighbouring houses, the Duchesse d'Angoulême in a small cottage in the woods, the Duc de Berri in one of the lodges, the Duc de Blacas in another. While at Hartwell, Louis XVIII continued the strange custom, which in England had ended with William III, of dining in public, people being allowed to file past while the Royal family were at the dinner table.

Although it was here that the Queen died, the French were happy during their stay at Aylesbury. 'Toujours Heureux' carved one of the party on a Hartwell beech tree and on another tree was found the simple thought 'Quel Plaisir'.

Yet the only one in Aylesbury who could speak to them in their own language was young John Fowler of the White Hart, who had learned French at Berkhamsted school, and the King often sent for him to discuss business matters.

When the Allied armies entered Paris in 1814, Aylesbury rejoiced for King Louis. As his carriage procession from Hartwell House passed through the narrow street, later called Bourbon Street, to the market square, on its way to London, John Fowler and five of his friends were ready mounted and waiting outside the White Hart to escort him.

The first change of horses was at the King's Arms, Berkhamsted. It was kept by Mr. Page, and King Louis was greatly attached to one of his three very pretty daughters, Polly. On his journeys to and from London he always stopped with her for a time and this occasion was no exception. John Fowler and his escort rode discreetly on but the King's carriage and four overtook them before long and they made their way through Watford to where the Prince Regent and his Officers of State were waiting to greet the King at the Abercorn Arms at Stanmore. Crowds had gathered round the portico of the inn to watch the historic meeting and then they all continued to London, the Aylesbury escort accompanying King Louis to Grillion's Hotel in Albermarle Street, where the royal party stayed during the preparations for their return to Paris.

King Louis never forgot little Polly Page of the King's Head and after his restoration he invited her to Paris, where she stayed for a time, but on this day of 1814, after leaving the King in the grandeur of Grillion's, John Fowler and his friends took themselves to their favourite London inn, the old Bell in Holborn, which was the resort of nearly all the travellers to London from Buckinghamshire and the adjacent counties, as was the King's Arms, Snow Hill, for the people of Northampton and Warwickshire, and the Spread Eagle, Gracechurch Street, and the Swan with Two Necks for the Essex folk.

During the Parliamentary elections of 1818 the candidates for the borough and hundreds of Aylesbury were Lord Nugent, William Rickford and the Hon. Charles Cavendish, and Charles Cavendish and his committee made the White Hart their headquarters. Elections lasted several days, for all the polling took place in the county town. This meant that for a large county such as Buckinghamshire many people had to make journeys of thirty or thirty-five miles to reach Aylesbury, and some had to stay the night.

The Cavendish committee first met in March and their bill at the White Hart for the next three months was £287 2s. 2d. There was an additional 'executive committee' which ran up a bill for £108 4s. 6d. and the cost of entertaining the voters during the four days of the election came to £545 17s. 0d.

On the first day, June 23, 1818, the bill was:

	£	s	d
25 breakfasts, solicitors, clerks, etc.	1	17	6
40 freeholders, solicitors, clerks, etc.	3	0	0
384 freeholders, dinners, clerks, etc.	58	12	0
52 freeholders, solicitors, clerks, etc.	13	0	0
Beer	15	0	0
Wine, port and sherry	130	0	0
Rum, brandy, etc.	6	0	0
50 stavesmen, breakfasts, dinners and beer	16	5	0
	243	14	6

Second Day's Poll

As before but only 230 voters dined	176	5	0

Third Day's Poll

Only 120 voters dined	95	5	6

Fourth Day's Poll

Only 25 voters dined	30	12	0
	545	17	0

On the day of the declaration of the poll and the chairing of the winning candidate the food and drink cost £56 13s. od. and the posting and baiting of the horses £105 8s. 8d., so Charles Cavendish's expenses for the election, which he lost, were well over £1,000. Some 750 voters were entertained but only 420 voted, so the campaign worked out at 26s. a vote, but at the time this was considered reasonable and the food was magnificent. For one day's dinner alone the White Hart provided twenty dishes of fish, ten dishes of boiled fowls, ten dishes of roast fowls, one boiled leg of pork and peas-pudding, two boiled hams, two haunches of mutton, six geese, ten pigeon pies, three dishes of boiled beef, three dishes of roast beef, two fillets of veal, one loin of veal, two roast legs of pork, two fore-quarters of lamb, two dishes of roast turkey, one dish of boiled turkey, two dishes of roast pigs, sixteen plum puddings, sixty custard puddings, twenty fruit pies, ten dishes of custards, fruit, blancmange and jellies.

John Kersley Fowler, son of John Fowler of the White Hart, who records all this in his books *Records of Old Times*, published in 1898, and *Echoes of Old County Life*, published in 1892, also records that Charles Cavendish paid his bill promptly.

In 1835 the Royal Hunt Club was formed at the White Hart, meeting for a week in November and again in February. The hotel had stabling and forage for 160 hunters but on these occasions they were always full and the inn had to take houses in Aylesbury to accommodate the influx of visitors.

Amongst the members of the club was Count d'Orsay, gay,

charming and generous and always so immaculately dressed that he was known as the 'King of the Dandies', and at the White Hart during the 1830s he cut a fine figure, in his 'scarlet coat, white waistcoat and richly-embroidered satin scarf, irreproachable leathers and boots.'

'It was a fine sight to see the horses led round the market square in the morning, after breakfast, and brought up one by one to the portico of the hotel and there mounted by their owners,' wrote John Kersley Fowler.

On one occasion, when d'Orsay had come down to the White Hart for two days' hunting, he was persuaded to stay on for the meet at Aston Abbotts on the third day. But he had a problem. He sent for John Fowler and explained his predicament. He had no clothes with him except those he had worn on the previous two days. John Fowler said he was sure they would do but the Count could not face the indignity of being seen wearing the same clothes again and asked him to send an express to London for his valet to bring down a change. At six o'clock in the evening, therefore, Humphrey, the old post-boy of the White Hart, was sent off to London on a saddle-horse. He changed horses at Berkhamsted and Watford and reached London, forty miles away, by ten o'clock. The valet, he discovered, was having an evening off at Drury Lane theatre, but Humphrey managed to reach him, and by nine o'clock the next morning he had arrived at the White Hart in a yellow post-chaise and pair, with a change of dress for the Count, a vanity which cost him at least £10.

The Royal Hunt Club dinners held in the Rochester Room at the White Hart during the 1830s cost the forty-odd members from twenty-five to thirty shillings a head and were elegant banquets prepared by the old cook who had come from Merton College, Oxford, when John Fowler had first come to the White Hart twenty years earlier. Count d'Orsay used to stroll into the kitchen with his friends to introduce them to 'the finest specimen of the English cook he had ever seen in his life.'

9. Two well-known landmarks on the Great North Road. (*Left*) The George at Stamford, described by Daniel Defoe as 'one of the greatest inns in England', and (*below*) the Angel and Royal at Grantham, the stone façade of which still exists.

AND POSTING HOU
GUILDFORD.

J. AND M. BONNER

Wine and Spirits of the first Quality

NEAT TOWN CHARIOTS & POST CH

10. Three famous coaching inns on Guildford High Street. (*Above left*) The Re
Lion (*above right*) the White Hart and (*below left*) the Angel (extant). (*Bottom right*
The trade card of the proprietor of the former Red Lion, with coaching timetabl
on the reverse.

E. GINGER Guildford SURR

Post Chaises to Lo

RED LION

LINE OF POSTING

To and from London, Portsmouth, Southampton, Brighton, B

He lived at the White Hart for forty-seven years and his cooking was famous throughout the county.

The old London coaching inns were as busy and prosperous as the county inns during the 1830s. John Kersley Fowler was born in 1818 and he has left a vivid description of the Old Bell at Holborn, where his father sometimes took him. The coffee room 'was fitted with mahogany divisions, partitioning off the place into "boxes", as they were called, some holding two persons, some four, and one held six or eight, who could find room to dine; they had stuffed horsehair seats fitted to the walls and partitions, and a fixed dining-table in the centre, whilst the waiter was obliged to hand the viands and the wines over the shoulders of the occupants; these were always ample and of the best quality. The proprietor, Mr. Bunyet, was proud to bring in the bottle of old port himself, and was often asked to sit down and partake of it. A typical dinner I can well remember, when my father and three of his fellow townsmen, who always made a point of coming to London together when business called them [sic]. These little parties were for social companionship, and arrangements were made some time beforehand, that they might book their places by the stage coach, and have no disappointment. Leaving home by the four-horse coach at 7 a.m. arriving in town about 1.30 p.m., in time for luncheon of a clever mutton chop, then making a hurried visit to the wholesale business houses, where they were in the habit of doing business, during the afternoon; making their appointments for the next day; returning to the "Old Bell" about five o'clock, having ordered dinner to be ready at six o'clock sharp. Mock turtle, cod and oysters, or salmon and lobster sauce, a good rump steak and pancakes to follow, with Cheshire or Stilton cheese to finish. Old brown sherry, with soup and fish; fine old port with the cheese, and another bottle afterwards. Then to the "Play" at 7.30, Drury Lane preferred. The real old hackney coach with pair of horses.' 'These coaches, with the driver and coat of four or six capes, the horses and appurtenances, would scarcely be credited in the present day', he concludes, writing in 1898. 'They had originally been the big family carriages of old-fashioned noblemen or country gentlemen.'

There were few new hotels built in London during the first forty years of the nineteenth century and the capital was regarded as remarkably deficient in accommodation for people who came for pleasure, but round about St. James's Street and Piccadilly there were a number of exclusive, private hotels. Before about 1820 it was considered rather pretentious to talk of an hotel, and the distinction between an inn and an hotel is not definable, but by the time of the Regency these establishments were in existence in fair numbers, as an alternative to houses which let rooms to visitors. They were different from the coaching inns in that they had no common dining-room. A resident took a suite and kept to himself, either going out for meals or having them sent to his sitting-room. He did not meet other residents except by chance in the hallway, on entering or leaving the hotel. Luxurious inns such as the White Hart at Aylesbury also offered suites to their guests, and Mr. Pickwick and his friends nearly always had a private sitting-room at the inns where they stayed, but the posting-inns were inevitably busier, noisier places than the quiet hotels which unobtrusively came into existence in the West End of London, many of them just as quietly closing down after a few years.

Byron used the address of a hotel in St. James's Street in his correspondence. When Nelson returned from Naples, 'the first interview between Lady Nelson, the Admiral and his father took place in the hall of Nerot's hotel,' announced the *Morning Post*. This was in King Street, St. James's. A few days later they moved to a furnished house, Number 17 Dover Street, for the custom of letting London houses furnished, while the owner retired to the country, was becoming general.

A few weeks later, when the breach between Lord and Lady Nelson had widened, Nelson wrote to his friend and agent, Alexander Davison: 'there are nonsensical reports . . . that you are going to buy a fine house for me. . . . I should not think of a House at this time, the best thing for Lady N, when she is in Town, is good Lodgings, next to that to hire a very small ready furnished house.'

Emma and Sir William Hamilton were living at Number 23, Piccadilly, of which Sir William had bought the lease, and Nelson moved to Lothian's Hotel close by.

Later, during the preparations for his departure from England for the last time, to meet his death at Trafalgar, he was dividing his time between the *ménage à trois* at Merton and Gordon's Hotel in London: and when Emma's fortunes were fast sinking, with Sir William, her mother and Nelson all dead within a few months, she went from one lodging to another—in Bond Street, Albemarle Street, Clarges Street and Dover Street.

Osborne's Hotel in John Street, Adelphi, later to become the Adelphi Hotel, was built early in the nineteenth century, a large, solid, four-storey block, its frontage decorated with Classical pilasters in the contemporary fashion: and it was here that Emily Wardle fled from her angry father and where her affair with Mr. Snodgrass ended happily.

An exclusive private hotel which was to endure until the present day, unchanged in atmosphere, despite all its extensions and modernizations, was Brown's, which James Brown opened at 23 Dover Street in 1837. James Brown had been a gentle-man's servant, his wife a lady's maid to Lady Byron, and it is possible that Lady Byron helped the young couple to launch their new venture.

The hotel was a success from the beginning. By the following year Brown acquired the lease of the house next door and by 1845 had control of Numbers 24 and 21. Brown's Hotel now consisted therefore of four similar terraced houses, each with four floors, attics and basements. He and his wife, who seems to have been the dominating influence and organizer of the pair, divided them into sixteen suites, each with its room for the visitor's personal servant travelling with him: and if the visitor were a distinguished foreigner accompanied by a courier, a room for the courier was also provided.

In 1859 Brown, with deteriorating health, sold out to J. J. Ford, who had been running Ford's Hotel in Manchester Square, and Ford and his family continued to maintain the reputation for comfort, seclusion and excellent service which the Browns had established.

Women of the middle classes did not travel a great deal, generally speaking, in the early part of the nineteenth century. They had no part in business and holidays were rare. Moreover, coach travel was expensive. A woman living more than twenty or thirty miles from London would make a visit perhaps once in three or four years. This meant that the inns and hotels catered almost exclusively for men, though at some of the coaching inns rooms were put aside for the entertainment of women travellers.

'The first house which, as far as I remember, laid itself out for the reception of ladies and their families was Bacon's Hotel in Great Queen Street', writes John Kersley Fowler. 'It was next door to the Freemason's Tavern, of which Mr. Thomas Bacon was then the proprietor. He was a very gentlemanlike man of excellent address and manners, and his wife was a charming lady, well fitted to attract ladies and their families to their comfortable and homely establishment. This hotel was then followed by the Golden Cross.'

He does not give a date for the establishment of Bacon's Hotel, but the new Golden Cross was built in 1832.

Chapter Ten

THE COMING OF THE RAILWAYS

D URING THE HALCYON days of the coaching inns only a handful of people realized the significance of the age of steam which had already arrived and the calamitous effect it was to have, in the early days, on the hotel business. In the year of Waterloo the first steamboat had been seen in the Mersey. In 1819 an American steamboat, the *Savannah*, crossed the Atlantic from New York, calling at Liverpool on its way to St. Petersburg. By 1825 the General Steam Navigation Company of Britain had fifteen small steamers plying between London and Europe and in the same year the first goods railway was opened, to make the short run between Stockton and Darlington. The maximum speed was sixteen miles an hour and during the first year these locomotives were condemned as being too expensive, unreliable in a high wind, a danger to grazing cattle and against all the laws of Providence.

Yet many foretold that they would soon be used for passenger traffic and then Stephenson produced his *Rocket*, which reached a speed of thirty-five miles an hour, and the railway age was fairly launched.

At this time there were twenty-two regular coaches running the thirty-five miles between Manchester and Liverpool each day, taking usually about four and a half hours, though in good weather the 'flyers', with three changes of horses, had reduced the time to three hours. The cotton goods, on which the prosperity of Manchester and Liverpool depended, went by canal, at a charge of 15s. a ton, the journey taking up to thirty-six hours.

When the building of the railway between the two cities was first suggested there was an outburst of protest from the Turnpike Trusts, from the canal companies, from the owners of the land through which it would have to pass and from many members of the general public who were mortally afraid of the new steam engine. Hunting would be ruined, cows would not graze within sight of the locomotive, women would miscarry at the alarming sight of the steam and smoke, farmhouses would be burnt from flying sparks and horses would become extinct through disuse.

There were angry debates in Parliament, and Thomas Creevey, acting in the interests of his friends Lord Sefton and Lord Derby, was one of the bitterest opponents. In May, 1825, he was writing to his stepdaughter: 'Well—this devil of a railway is strangled at last . . . today we had a clear majority in the Committee in our favour, and the promoters of the Bill withdrew it, and took their leave of us. . . .'

In that same year an anonymous writer in the *Quarterly Review* snarled, with all the rancour Cresset had expended on the advent of the coach, two hundred years earlier: 'It is certainly some consolation to those who are to be whirled at the rate of eighteen or twenty miles an hour, by means of a high pressure engine, to be told that they are in no danger of being seasick while on shore; that they are not to be scalded to death nor drowned by the bursting of the boiler; and that they need not mind being shot by the scattered fragments, or dashed in pieces by the flying off, or the breaking of a wheel.'

But the battle continued, for Liverpool and Manchester cotton merchants were realizing that the railway would transfer their goods in under three hours, at a freight charge of only 10s. a ton.

Supported by their Member, William Huskisson, Parliament at last, by the Enabling Act of 1826, allowed the railway to be built, but the question of whether or not to use a steam locomotive was still not settled, for many people thought it would be safer for the coaches to be pulled along the railway by horses and deplored the high speeds claimed for the locomotives.

In the face of violent opposition, the planning of the railways began. Stephenson and his surveyors were stoned, abused and persecuted, and eventually had to work after dark, by the light of lanterns. At one stage, Stephenson was dismissed, and the Rennie brothers took over, but eventually he was reinstated and, with his army of Irish labourers, completed the railway in time for the opening day on September 15, 1830.

Grandstands were erected in Liverpool for the 50,000 spectators, and with flags flying and bands playing, eight trains were assembled to carry the distinguished guests, including the Duke of Wellington and a host of ambassadors, peers of the realm and bishops, on their historic journey. Stephenson, on the south line, drove a train with three carriages, the other seven trains, on the north line, each hauling four or five carriages, all of them full of guests.

Between Liverpool and Parkside, the trains reached a speed of 24 miles an hour and at Parkside they halted to take on water. It was here that several passengers climbed down to the track, though they had been warned not to. One of the north line trains suddenly appeared and although they had time to jump clear or climb back into their carriages, Huskisson missed his footing and fell back on to the track, receiving injuries from which he died within a few hours. It was a bad omen and those who had declared that the unnatural speed of steam locomotion was against the will of God were satisfied.

Creevey hated the sensation. '. . . the quickest motion is to me *frightful*', he wrote: 'it is really flying, and it is impossible to divest yourself of the notion of instant death to all upon the least accident happening. It gave me a headache which has not left me yet. Sefton is convinced that some damnable thing must come of it; but he and I seem more struck with such apprehension than others. . . .'

The same week a regular passenger service was put into

operation between Liverpool and Manchester, three trains a day carrying about 130 passengers, at a charge of seven shillings, and the journey taking under two hours. Soon afterwards two trains a day of second-class carriages were also in service, with seats at four shillings. The Liverpool and Manchester coach proprietors were appalled. They reduced their fares, but by the end of 1830 a thousand passengers were travelling by rail between Liverpool and Manchester each day, the fare was down and the trains were carrying both freight and the mail. The coaches had been run off the road. The canals quickly reduced their freight charges for cotton from fifteen to ten shillings a ton, but it was too late.

When Von Raumer was in England in 1835 he paid a visit to the new railway and wrote, with his usual solemnity: '. . . it makes a peculiar impression, to see this long row of wagons, loaded with so many passengers and goods, hasten along with unparalleled velocity, merely by the agency of a little fire and water. It is commendable that Germany desires to participate in the wonderfully far increased facilities of intercourse. But let us take care not to throw away large sums, if unfavourable circumstances should prevail. . . . The construction of the iron rail-road from Liverpool to Manchester, which is thirty English miles in length, cost about five and a half millions of dollars. Such a capital cannot yield sufficient interest, except where two very large cities lie at a short distance from each other, of which the one imports and the other exports an immense quantity of goods. Such a state of things is scarcely to be met with a second time in the world. No rocks can be blasted and no valleys raised, for the sake of a few individuals, who would like to travel more rapidly for their pleasure. Nothing but an extraordinary traffic makes such an enterprise practicable and useful.'

The British thought otherwise. Many enjoyed the sensation of fast travel, as well as its convenience and comfort, yet the innkeepers and coach proprietors throughout the rest of the country were still, for the most part, unperturbed.

The real blow fell with the opening of the London and Birmingham Railway in 1838. At the end of that year a newspaper reported: 'A few months ago no fewer than twenty-two coaches left Birmingham daily for London. Since the opening of the railway that number has been reduced to four, and it is expected that these will be discontinued, although the fares by coach are only 20s. inside and 10s. outside, whilst the fares for corresponding places on the railroad are 30s. and 20s.'

Nothing could stop the spread of the network of railways over the country. By 1845, at the height of the railway mania, 357 new railway companies were advertising in the newspapers, inviting investment, and nearly everyone with any spare cash bought railway shares. In some cases the companies were operating stretches of line too short to make a profit and their investors lost every penny of their money, but the big companies flourished and by 1850 there were six thousand miles of railway in Great Britain.

As the railways quickly spread, the coaches as rapidly disappeared from the roads and scores of grand old coaching inns which had depended on them for their livelihoods were suddenly faced with disaster which, all too often, was irretrievable.

One of the last coaches to go was the Brighton 'Comet', which in the early 1840s had been making the journey from London in only six hours, but these fast coaches were already being condemned by the animal lovers, who were increasingly concerned for the welfare of the horses. 'We are frequently from ten to fourteen and even sixteen persons on the top of a stage . . .', wrote one protester. 'The weight of these, together with the vast quantity of luggage stowed in every part, and the massy vehicle capable of supporting such a weight is far too much for four horses at the rate they are forced to go.'

By 1848 most of the main line railways had been established so that, within a decade, the elaborate system of stage- and mail-coach services had collapsed and died. Where the railways were late in arriving, a few coaches still ran for a time, but they knew that their days were numbered. The last of the mail coaches ran in 1874, when the Thurso and Wick Mail came to an end, with the opening of the Highland railway. In Buckinghamshire, the Aylesbury, Amersham and Wendover coach, a form of three-horse omnibus, ran each day to the Old Bell in Holborn and returned each evening at 5 o'clock, until as late as 1892, when the Metropolitan Railway opened, but by this time all the other London coaches had been off the roads for half a century.

'Steam, James Watt, and George Stephenson have a great deal to answer for,' declared *The Times*, in 1839. 'They will ruin the breed of horses, as they have already ruined the innkeepers and the coachmen, many of whom have already been obliged to seek relief at the poor-house, or have died in penury and want.'

Chaplin of the Swan With Two Necks was also, in 1838, proprietor of the Spread Eagle, the Cross Keys and the White Horse and owner or part-owner of 68 coaches and 1,800 horses, giving employment to two thousand people. He was one of the first to see that the railways could never be beaten so came to terms with them. As the London and Birmingham Railway advanced he withdrew his coaches but helped out the railway where gaps still persisted and took shares with Pickford and Company in the goods and parcel-carrying service, selling all his coaches to buyers on the Continent. He invested the proceeds in the London and South-Western Railway and eventually became its Chairman. Benjamin Worthy Horne joined him as manager of the carrying business of Chaplin and Horne, centred on Euston and Camden Town, and when they died, late in the century, they were both rich men, but the Swan With Two Necks, where Chaplin had made his first fortune, was pulled down in 1856. Sherman's Bull and Mouth in St. Martin's-le-Grand had been rebuilt in 1830 and renamed the Queen's Hotel. When he had lost all his coach passengers, the great yard became a railway goods yard but the hotel remained until 1887, when it was demolished. Mrs. Nelson's Bull at Aldgate was pulled down in 1868. The Bell and Crown, Holborn, became Ridler's Hotel, advertised as a 'Select Family Hotel', and survived for a few more years. Mrs. Mountain's splendid Saracen's Head on Snow Hill degenerated into a public house before it was pulled down. The historic Belle Sauvage went in 1850, to make way for Cassell's publishing house. The Golden Cross began to run down. David Copperfield thought it 'a mouldy sort of establishment' and his bedroom 'smelt like a hackney carriage, and was shut up like a family vault', while William Shergold called it a 'nasty inn, remarkable for filth and apparent misery'. The archway into the Strand was demolished in 1851, but the inn continued to function into the present century.

The White Hart in the Borough was rapidly declining in Sam Weller's day. 'The yard presented none of that bustle and activity which are the usual characteristics of a large coaching inn. Three or four lumbering waggons, each with a pile of goods beneath its ample canopy about the height of the second-floor window of an ordinary house, were stowed away beneath a lofty room which extended over one end of the yard. . . . A double tier of bedroom galleries with old clumsy balustrades ran round two sides of the straggling area, and a double row of bells to correspond, sheltered from the weather by a little sloping roof, hung over the door leading to the bar and coffee-room. Two or three gigs or chaise-carts were wheeled up under different little sheds and penthouses . . . a few boys in smock-frocks were lying asleep on heavy packages, woolpacks, and other articles that were scattered about on heaps of straw. . . .' It was demolished in 1865. The White Horse Cellar, which had moved from Arlington Street to the corner of Albemarle Street on the other side of Piccadilly, remained until 1884, when it was pulled down, and the Albemarle built on the site.

On the roads it was all too often the same melancholy story. The Tontine at Sheffield was only one of scores of sudden failures. It had been opened in 1785 and was one of the most important inns in the city. 'It played a leading part in the social, political, and business life of the town', wrote Robert Leader in 1901, in his book *Sheffield in the Eighteenth Century*. 'What convivialities it witnessed. To what eloquent lectures and harmonious concerts did its walls resound. Of what stirring election scenes was it the centre. How busy was the bustle when its post-chaises were called for, or when the coaches, with steaming horses and weather-worn "outsides" rattled up to its doors. The number of those who remember its plain but highly respectable brick frontage, and its capacious courtyard, is becoming very small; but to the few who can recall these, it remains the type of the stately English inn of the best days of the coaching period. . . .'

In 1838 thirteen coaches were advertised to leave daily the Tontine and King's Head offices . . . but that was the climax of a brilliance destined to speedy eclipse. For two years afterwards the North Midland Railway advertised trains between London and Sheffield, and coaching died. As Dr. Gatty has said, 'Twelve pairs of horses were wanted one day; on the morrow the road was forsaken. Thus one of the fine old English inns, in the courtyard of which a carriage and pair could be easily driven, came to grief.'

By 1850 it had been pulled down and the New Market Hall built on the site.

A most illuminating letter written in January, 1844, by Marjorie St. Aubyn to her cousin, shows how quickly the decline came to the inns. It is addressed from Thomas's Hotel, Berkeley Square, after a journey by coach from Chippenham.

'You will see that I have arrived in town, after an adventurous journey by road. My state of mind would not permit me to travel by rail, for Mr. Brunel is no hero of mine, since he has destroyed posting, put down coaches and compelled people to sit behind his puffing monsters. Two days have passed since Belinda and I left home.

' "We shan't get to Reading before three, unless we get horses," said Belinda, as we seated ourselves in the barouche.

'We drew up at The Golden Lion, which ten years since was one of the busiest inns on the road. The inn looked deserted— no ostler, no horses ready saddled as in the times when we were children and landlords took a real pride in their stables. We looked at each other in consternation. "Any horses?" shouted Richard. The landlady, a slatternly person in curl-papers, came out in a slipshod way. "No", was plainly written on her face. She seemed surprised to see an old-fashioned travelling carriage and four. "No, milady, we are new people. We are just come into the house. The people afore us was ruined; since the railway came this way nobody wants horses."

' "Will you please to unlight, if you please, milady," said the elderly postilion, a man of about fifty-five, still called a boy; "we'd take you on another stage if so be you'd bait an hour. The horses would be fresh enough. . . ." There was no alternative, so we descended and followed the landlady into the guest room. I looked around at the desolate room while the woman went off for chairs, and noted the old bell pulls which seemed to have become melancholy since the Bristol mail stopped. How different it would have been ten years since! The hour passed, and once again we took our seats, this time not so excitedly. We were now on the worst stage, a particularly hilly one, and the surface of the road had been neglected by the turnpike trust. "Ah," thought I . . . "thirty years from now the roads will be as bad as they were in our grandfather's days. . . . And who will inherit these decayed hostelries? Who will look at the ruined villages, the moth-eaten hangings and the rusty grates?" '

At the next stage they found slightly better comfort, for the inn was on a cross-roads and was still running a two-horse coach. At Newbury fresh horses were fetched for them from a livery stable and at Reading, where they stayed the night, the landlord told them that it was a great struggle to keep things going but assured them that his rooms were clean and his beds properly aired. 'With wondering steps we followed the woman-waiter upstairs into the bedroom and waited in misery while she lit the fire. . . . We made preparations for dinner, and on this being announced we made our way to the coffee room.'

They were the only travellers at the inn 'apart from several gentlemen's servants staying in another part of the house, who had been sent by their masters up to London by road.' They sat at a large mahogany table big enough for twenty and dined from 'mutton, smoking hot and tender, followed by a pudding tasting strongly of onions.'

And the next day they reached the comfort of Berkeley Square in three stages, having travelled 'ninety miles by road in the old manner, when everything goes at thirty miles an hour by steam.'

For the next thirty years the condition of the roads deteriorated and the plight of most of the inns grew desperate. During those first, bewildering days of the railway mania, the wiser innkeepers knew that they must adapt or perish. Thus the Royal Western Hotel at Bristol, which was built in the 1840s, when the dangers were becoming all too apparent, advertised with an admirable compromise between the leisured grace of the late eighteenth century and the quickening pace of the fast-approaching mid-nineteenth century:

HAM'S ROYAL WESTERN HOTEL
New College Green, Bristol

Offers superior accommodation in Suites of Apartments handsomely fitted up and combining every comfort for Families, with Coffee and Commercial Rooms not surpassed by any House in the Kingdom, to which the travelling Community are respectfully solicited.

Baths, Warm, Cold, Vapour and Shower, in the House.
Omnibuses to and from every Train.

R. P. Ham, Proprietor,
Turtle and Wine Merchant.

The inns which managed to survive the lean years were to see a return to the roads in the later part of the century and a renewed interest in the old coaching inns, as many people, hating and fearing the rapid industrialization and urbanization of the country, began to explore and discover anew what was left of the hand-made world of their fathers and grandfathers, but before that happened many very different hotels had come into existence.

Coach travellers had always tended to stay at the inns where their coaches deposited them, so it was only logical that the railway companies should begin to provide accommodation for their passengers at the stations where they arrived, but the new station hotels were of a size and luxury of appointment which staggered the Victorians.

In 1839 the Grosvenor Hotel was built at Victoria Station. Today this is owned by British Transport Hotels but operated by Grand Metropolitan Hotels. In the same year the Euston and Victoria Hotels were built on either side of the entrance to Euston Station and in 1840 they were opened by an Hotel Company composed principally of shareholders in what was then the London and Birmingham Railway.

When the station with its vast Doric portico, the 'Gateway to the North', had been built the previous year, whole streets of houses had been bought up to provide the site. People had been dispossessed and there had been a great deal of bitter litigation in regard to compensation. When the plans for the hotels became known there was more opposition, mainly from the innkeepers, for people argued that the railway companies had been granted the right to build railways but not hotels. However, the hotels were built and at first let on a twenty-one-year lease to the hotel company, but in 1861 the railway company bought the buildings and joined the Euston on the east side to the Victoria on the west side by a large, central block, spanning the roadway into the forecourt. It became known as the Euston Hotel but still kept its separate entrances to the east and west wings, and was a vast but comfortable building, with long corridors, large bedrooms, sitting-rooms, lounges and dining-rooms, which Surtees, in amazed admiration, called 'two towns or a city'.

On June 17, 1854, the Great Western Royal Hotel was opened at Paddington. 'The above new Hotel connected with Paddington Station is NOW OPEN', ran the advertisement.

These premises have been built by the Company, and are fitted up with every modern convenience for Families as well as for Single Persons, while the Terms have been fixed for every description of Hotel Business upon a very moderate Scale of Charge. Parties are strongly recommended to order their Apartments previously, by letter, addressed to Mr. Wheeler, Manager, Great Western Royal Hotel, Paddington Station, who is authorized to enter into arrangements for the reception of Parties for a given time at a rate of charge by the Week or the Day.

Passengers by the Trains can pass between the Platforms and the Hotel at once, without trouble or expense, and proper persons will be always in attendance to receive and carry the Luggage to and from the Trains.

Tariff

Ground Floor. Sitting Room, per day 6s. Small sitting room 4s.

Large apartments on First Floor—Drawing Room and Two

	Bedrooms (with water closet enclosed) *en suite* per day 22s. 6d.
On Fourth Floor	Large Bedroom per day 2s. Small Bedroom per day 1s. 6d. 1s. extra will be charged when the Bed is occupied by Two Persons.

Coffee Room Dinners etc. Joint, Chops, Steak, 2s.

Cup of Tea 6d.

Cup of Coffee 6d.

Hot Baths 2s. 6d. Cold Baths 1s. 6d.

Visitors servants meals 4s. per day.

Hotel servants not allowed to receive any Fees or Gratuities.

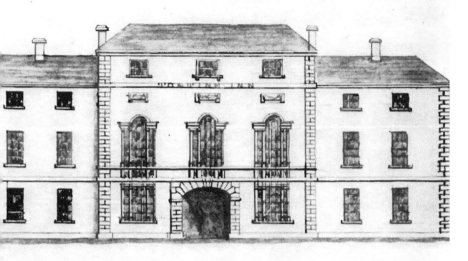

SHEFFIELD, TONTINE INN:

(*Above*) The Tontine at Sheffield, during its comparatively short life (1785–
0), was one of the finest coaching inns in the country. (*Below*) La Sablonnière,
French inn which existed in Leicester Square at the end of the eighteenth
tury, was patronized particularly by French visitors to the capital.

12. Brown's Hotel in London's West End (*above*), established in 1837. Claridge (*below*), as it appeared in the days of Mivart and Claridge.

About this time, the early railway directors, still stage-coach-minded, built a large hotel at Slough Station, once an important 'change' out of London, forgetting that it was only eighteen miles from Paddington and about half an hour's rail journey away. From the outset it was a failure and soon became an orphanage.

Existing hoteliers and innkeepers still opposed the building of railway hotels and in some cases, as at Preston, litigation went on for years, but by 1863 the Charing Cross Hotel had been opened, opposite the fading Golden Cross, and in 1865 the vast St. Pancras Hotel, with its Gothic gateway tower, which alone cost £20,000, designed by Sir Gilbert Scott. It was regarded by the Victorians with deep admiration, derided during the 1920s, when everything Victorian was anathema, and approved again during the 1970s, being considered worthy of preservation, as a splendid example of Victorian Gothic architecture.

The railway hotels set a very high standard of comfort and catering, comparable with that of the best of the coaching inns in their heyday, and for the most part people liked staying in them as much as they appreciated the comforts of rail travel, compared with the rigours and hazards of coach travel. The hotels were handsomely furnished and the service was excellent: and many of the middle-class travellers were sampling for the first time the new luxury which had been made possible by Britain's rising prosperity.

It is true that many people were already bemoaning the impersonality of the new hotels and wrote nostalgically of the old inns where the host welcomed them in person and attended to their individual needs and comforts, but coach travelling had been expensive and only the relatively wealthy had ever been able to afford it. By the time the railway hotels were opened a vast new public was on the move. The population was increasing rapidly. It rose from fourteen million in 1837 to thirty-two and a half million in 1901, and despite the millions who were too poor to travel anywhere, hundreds of thousands of people were becoming increasingly prosperous and able to enjoy the opportunities now offered them of comfortable travel and hotels.

So more railway hotels were built. At the same time, for commercial travellers and people who could not afford the larger establishments, there grew up round nearly every station in the country, a crop of privately-owned commercial hotels, many of them called 'railway' hotels, which offered amenities varying between modest comfort and near-squalor.

Soon after the Euston hotels were built, the directors of the Grand Junction Railway met in Birmingham with the London and Birmingham Railway to discuss plans for 'the erection of an Inn near Curzon Street Station'. This inn was opened in 1839 as the Victoria Hotel, but towards the end of 1840 the name was changed to the Queen's. By 1852 the railway companies decided to build a new Queen's Hotel at New Street, which was opened in 1854, the old hotel in Curzon Street being closed: and only three years later twenty additional bedrooms were added over the coffee room, 'because many passengers have been turned away from the Queen's to the Hen and Chickens Hotel and thereby diverted to Great Western lines.'

The railways were very enterprising. For many years the Furness railway had been run solely as a mineral line, carrying haematite ore. It was so profitable that, apart from a few passenger trains run for local requirements, it had no need to consider large-scale passenger traffic. Then the supplies of iron ore began to run out and it looked as though the prosperous days of the railway were over. However, the new manager realized that the line ran close to two of England's loveliest lakes—Windermere and Coniston—and along the shores of Morecambe Bay and the Irish Sea coast of Lancashire and Cumberland. Annual summer holidays were still enjoyed only by the rich and the more prosperous of the middle classes, but he saw in this railway an inducement to tourists to visit the Lake District.

In 1845 the directors of the Furness Railway Company met in London, to consider 'the subject of providing accommodation at Furness Abbey and at the terminus of Kirkby for the passengers likely to use the line of railway, by the erection of suitable inns.'

At this meeting the Chairman announced that the Earl of Burlington had proposed to build an inn at Furness Abbey at his own expense and to let it to the Company. The inn was duly built and by 1848 it was opened. It had been converted from the monastery guest house which stood within the precincts of the ruined Cistercian Abbey. Before the Dissolution Furness Abbey had been second only to Fountains Abbey in wealth and power, and apart from removing the lead from the roof, it had not been destroyed but left to the destruction of the wind and weather and casual despoilers. Alterations had been made to the guest house during the seventeenth century and it was in far better shape than the abbey, when the builders moved in during the mid-nineteenth century. It stood only fifty yards from the Abbey ruins and close to the station, by which it was approached by a covered way. It was a luxury hotel of the new order but catered for the romantics who, tired of the Neo-Classicism of the 1820s and 1830s, loved anything Gothic. It had fifty bedrooms. In the largest sitting-room, known as the Abbot's Room, stained glass and bas-reliefs from the Abbey were introduced and in another room were retained a magnificent James I fireplace and some beautiful Jacobean oak panelling.

In its day, the Furness Abbey Hotel was a delightful place. In 1864 it was leased to the Furness Railway Company by the Duke of Devonshire for seventy-five years, but in 1917, when the Furness Railway asked the London and North-Western Railway to take over its management, they declined, and the hotel did not survive: but until 1922 the Furness Railway Company and the Cavendish family between them carefully tended the remains of the Abbey, after which time it became the responsibility of the Office of Works.

In Liverpool, the Adelphi was acquired by the Midland

Railway in 1892, rebuilt in 1912 and opened in 1914. The Park Hotel, Preston, was opened in 1882, the Midland in Manchester in 1903. The Queen's at Leeds was first opened in 1865 but was closed and demolished in 1935, the new Queen's being opened in 1937.

In Glasgow, three years after New Station was built, in 1876, St. Enoch's Hotel, not unlike the St. Pancras Hotel, was opened, with five storeys above station level, two hundred bedrooms and thirty private sitting-rooms. In 1880 the Holyhead Station Hotel was built, to replace the old Chester and Holyhead Railway Hotel, which was nearly three-quarters of a mile from the landing-stage of the cross-Channel steamers.

In 1902 the North British Station Hotel was opened in Edinburgh, this great square pile, with its immense clock tower, overlooking Princes Street Gardens and the castle, claiming to be one of the largest and most palatial in Europe. In 1910 it advertised amongst its amenities 257 bedrooms, fourteen public rooms, nine private sitting-rooms, fifty-two bathrooms and many suites containing bedrooms, a sitting-room and bathroom, two drawing-rooms on the first floor, a ladies' writing-room and a library.

Few people amongst its early visitors had ever tasted such luxury. Here was a lift to take you from the station platform straight into the hotel, with an army of attendant porters to look after your luggage, so that the process was achieved with a minimum of effort. There were scores of hotel servants to attend to your slightest wish. You were encouraged to eat four gargantuan meals a day, in the tradition of the nineteenth century, and at the same time were able to enjoy the amenities of the new century, with its civilized plumbing and quick travel.

The North British at Glasgow was reconstructed from an earlier building and has a Georgian air but the later Central Hotel, adjoining the Central Station, is on the same colossal scale as the North British at Edinburgh.

Like so many of the railway hotels, the Station Hotel at Perth, adjoining the station platform, with its ballroom and banqueting-room, has become the centre of the business and social life of the city, the place of civic luncheons and receptions, conferences and celebrations, fulfilling the function that was once held by some of the larger coaching inns.

The Palace Hotel in Union Street, Aberdeen, was acquired and converted by the railway company in 1891 and in its day claimed to be the finest hotel in Great Britain, with its magnificent marble staircase sweeping up from the impressive entrance hall, complete with stained glass windows, marble walls and a ceramic tiled floor, a splendid example of a High Victorian, fashionably artistic interior, but it did not survive and its place was taken by the Station Hotel, which was conceived on simpler lines.

In 1910 a writer in the *Railway and Travel Monthly* pointed out that of the seventeen largest railways in Great Britain, only one had not created a hotel department. Railway hotels, he said, were becoming every day more popular and their numbers were steadily increasing, for they offered many more comforts to travellers than private hotels run on a purely financial and independent basis.

'What arrangement, for instance, could be more idealistic or complete for a comfortable railway journey to any of our big towns than that under which the traveller, by any of the great trunk lines, has simply, at the commencement of his journey, to hand over his luggage to the station officials, along with a note of his destination and requirements in the way of hotel accommodation at his journey's end? A telegram will be at once despatched to the hotel, free of charge, reserving the necessary accommodation, etc. while the baggage will be forwarded by the first train and delivered to the hotel also free of charge.

'But still more at his journey's end the traveller, in place of being troubled with the necessity and expense of taking a conveyance to his hotel, finds hotel porters waiting his arrival in the station, and ready to give him every assistance, and to direct him across the platform to the hotel entrance, or, as in many cases, where the hotels are placed one or two storeys above the station level, to the elevator which is in readiness to convey the weary traveller from the bustle of the busy railway station into the midst of every home comfort.

'Many of the largest and most important hotels of the country are now railway owned, with accommodation of the most elaborate and handsome description.'

The list of British Transport Hotels, as they are now known, is today very long. In London, the Charing Cross, the Great Eastern, the Great Northern and the Great Western Royal have all survived, but the Euston hotel was pulled down when Euston Station was rebuilt during the 1960s and plans for a new hotel block are still under discussion, while the mighty St. Pancras hotel, with its dauntingly long, carpeted corridors, looking as endless as those in an underground railway, was closed in 1935 for lack of customers. When it opened in 1865 it was proclaimed the finest hotel in the world, yet its life span was only seventy years and today, preserved for Sir Gilbert Scott's architecture, it houses the offices of British Transport Hotels, Limited.

All the large towns and cities of the Midlands and the north of England have their large, resplendent railway hotels, originally built for the accommodation of rail travellers, and then the railway companies established hotels for holiday-makers— the Manor House Hotel near Moretonhampstead, once a Jacobean mansion, which now offers an 18-hole golf course in its grounds, as well as tennis and squash courts and two trout streams; the even larger converted mansion, the Tregenna Castle at St. Ives in Cornwall, the Zetland at Saltburn-by-the-Sea and the Welcombe at Stratford-on-Avon.

In Scotland, the British Transport Hotels Group owns, in addition to the big station hotels, the golf hotels at Gleneagles,

Turnberry and St. Andrews and the holiday hotel on the shores of Loch Alsh, only five minutes by ferry from the Isle of Skye.

Gleneagles, the golfer's paradise, was opened in 1924. Golf had, of course, been played for centuries in Scotland, but until the beginning of the twentieth century there were hardly any clubs in England. Then it became increasingly popular and many new clubs were formed, for both men and women. The Royal and Ancient Club of St. Andrews, one of the oldest in Scotland and the premier club of the world, drew up a new code of rules and play, and the standard of performance rapidly improved: and when the railway company opened the mighty Gleneagles Hotel, golf became an important national game.

Chapter Eleven

THE FIRST LUXURY HOTELS

COMPARED WITH THE capital cities of the Continent, particularly Paris and Vienna, London still had very few hotels during the early part of the nineteenth century, apart from the coaching inns and an increasing number of private hotels for the wealthy, which came into existence in Piccadilly and the adjoining streets. There were no royal residences which could accommodate visiting royalty at this time, for George III was confined at Windsor, in the last stages of his insanity, attended by the faithful Princess Sophia, while the Queen, who was herself in declining health, spent most of her time at Kew, with Princess Elizabeth, Princess Augusta and Princess Mary. The Prince Regent was at Carlton House and Brighton, so that St. James's Palace and Buckingham House were little used during these years.

Most of the hotels of Regency London were opened by French chefs who had been in service in England or by the retired butlers of noble households, who understood the tastes and ways of the wealthy.

In Jermyn Street, for example, in 1815 there was 'a whole range of hotels. . . . All the articles of consumption are of the best, and the accommodation, much to the injury of taverns and lodging houses, combines all the retirement and comforts of home, with the freedom of access, ingress and egress, which one generally expects when abroad.'

One of the most famous of these Jermyn Street hotels was

Miller's, at Number 81, a seventeenth-century house for which Robert Miller, hotel-keeper and wine-merchant, applied for a new lease in 1811. This, with the lease of 20, Duke Street, was granted him on condition that he spent £1,500 on improvements, which included a new staircase and 'a handsome iron sky-light'. Numbers 82 and 83, Jermyn Street were leased by John Hickinbottom, who established here the British Hotel.

The name of Miller's Hotel was later changed to the Orleans Hotel, because there was a story that Louis Philippe once stayed there, though this is by no means certain. As the Orleans, it changed hands several times and in 1868, by which time it was known as the Cavendish Hotel, it was owned by Felipe Santiago Franco. And Franco's Cavendish was exclusive and expensive, for his clientele included nearly all the visiting Spanish aristocrats.

Although it is true to say that the West End clubs evolved from the eighteenth-century coffee houses, the system was not firmly established until about the middle of the nineteenth century. Neither the Naval and Military nor the Junior Athenaeum, for example, was founded until 1860. In the days of the Regency men such as Wellington, Nelson, Collingwood and Sir John Moore very seldom frequented the clubs, and men of fashion tended to meet in the numerous private hotels in and around Piccadilly, many of which had been converted from private mansions.

Palates were developing and tastes in food were changing, for despite the Napoleonic wars, people still travelled abroad, and since the days when the Grand Tour had become fashionable for the sons of the gentry, at the end of the eighteenth century, the habit of foreign travel had increased steadily.

The story goes that on one occasion some friends from White's and Brooke's clubs were dining with the Prince Regent, who asked them what the food was like at their clubs. They complained that it was dull and monotonous, 'the eternal joints and beef-steaks, boiled fowl with oyster sauce and apple tart', whereupon the Prince rang for his cook, Watier, and asked him whether he would take a house and organize a dining-club. Watier agreed. Labourie, who worked in the royal kitchens, was established as cook, and in 1807 Watier's Club duly opened in Bolton Street, off Piccadilly. The dinners at the new club were as exquisite as the Regency dandies who ate them, including Beau Brummel, and the food was said to be as good as the best that Paris could offer. Watier's was also, however, a gambling club and play was so high that the pace became 'too quick to last', and by 1819, by which time many fortunes had been lost, the club died a natural death.

More than half the houses in Albemarle Street became hotels, most of them run by men who had been butlers, amongst the more successful establishments being Gordon's, which was used by both Nelson and Byron at times.

The most famous of the Albemarle Street hotels, however, was Grillion's,[1] which Alexander Grillion, who had been chef to Lord Crewe, opened at Number 7 in 1803. This beautiful early-eighteenth-century house, with its magnificent curving staircase, is now the headquarters of the National Book League. Under Grillion's management the hotel was soon frequented by visiting royalty and aristocracy and it was here that the Grillion Club was founded, in 1813, by some members of both Houses of Parliament, who wanted to meet on neutral ground, where politics were excluded from the conversation. Every Wednesday, while Parliament was in session, the members dined together, 'the feuds of the previous day being forgotten, or made the theme of pleasantry and genial humour at a table where all sets of opinions had their representatives.' To this club belonged George Canning and many of the distinguished political figures of the Regency and the reigns of George IV and William IV, but it did not survive long into the reign of Queen Victoria.

[1] Or Grillon.

It was to Grillion's that Louis XVIII came in 1814 from Hartwell. Still accompanied by the Prince Regent, he was escorted to the crimson curtained drawing-room on the first floor, decorated with lilies of France in his honour, and was there attended by Lord Liverpool and the cabinet, the diplomatic corps and members of the French nobility. Louis stayed at the hotel for the next three days while the preparations were made for his return to Paris.

In Piccadilly, about where No. 105 now stands, there was another hotel graced by royalty, the Pulteney. It was a mansion which had once been the town residence of Pulteney, whom Robert Walpole had created the Earl of Bath in order to remove his fiery antagonism from the House of Commons. The mansion was opened as a hotel by a French chef, Jean Escudier, and at the time of Louis XVIII's restoration the Grand Duchess Catherine, sister of Alexander I of Russia, was staying there and was able to watch Louis' state entry into London from her balcony.

It was enormously expensive and cost the Grand Duchess £210 a week, but she spoke so highly of it that later the Emperor Alexander joined her there, in preference to staying at St. James's Palace.

The Pulteney did not have a long life. By 1823 it had become a private house again, known for many years as Bath House, but the hotel reopened at Number 13, Albemarle Street, subsequently becoming the Albemarle Club, where the Marquis of Queensberry left the card for Oscar Wilde which led to the famous trial.

It was to Grillion's that Princess Adelaide and her mother came in 1818, before the princess's marriage to the Duke of Clarence, the future William IV; and a few years later when, as King, he was entertaining the King of Wurtemberg, Greville noted that he 'drove all over the town in an open caleche with the Queen, Princess Augusta and the King of Wurtemberg, and coming home he set down the King (dropt him as he calls it) at Grillion's. The King of England dropping another King at a Tavern!'

The Clarendon Hotel in Old Bond Street was another famous Regency hotel, opened by Jacquier, the French cook who had served Louis XVIII during his time in England. This in its day was said to be the only hotel in England where a man could eat a genuine French dinner, but it was expensive, for even in 1815 dinner at the Clarendon cost from £3 to £4 and a bottle of champagne or claret was a guinea. It was a very large hotel—at one time the biggest in London—built on part of the gardens of old Clarendon House, with an entrance in Old Bond Street, where Cartier's now stands, and one at the back, in Albemarle Street, where the carriages drove up, because of the traffic congestion in Bond Street. It had large suites of rooms for visiting royalty and in early Victorian times official banquets were often held here.

When Peter Grillion's lease expired at No. 7, Albemarle Street he moved to the Clarendon, taking Grillion's Club with him, and the hotel lasted until 1872, when it was finally closed.

There were two other hotels in Old Bond Street in Regency times, both nearly opposite the Clarendon and both of them haunts of Byron's. Long's Hotel was a large, four-storeyed Georgian building with a classical portico. Stevens's close by was popular among army officers and Captain Gronow, in his *Reminiscences*, says that 'if a stranger wanted to dine there, he would be stared at by the servants and very solemnly assured that there was no table vacant' and it was no uncommon sight to see 'thirty or forty saddle-horses or tilburies waiting outside the doors of the hotel'. By the time Brown's Hotel was opened, however, Byron had been dead for many years, for he died in 1824.

In Old Burlington Street was the Burlington Hotel where Florence Nightingale used to stay and in Burlington Gardens the aristocratic and exclusive Bristol Hotel, which had been converted from a mansion once belonging to the Cavendish family.

In 1815 another French chef, Jacques Mivart, opened a hotel in a house on the corner of Brook Street and Davies Street, providing sumptuous accommodation. Like Grillion and the other French hoteliers, he prospered and was soon able to extend, taking over four adjacent houses. Mivart's hotel was used by visiting royalty and also by the Prince Regent, who had a suite of rooms permanently reserved for him. In the 1850s Mivart sold out to Mr. and Mrs. Claridge who maintained the high standard and prestige that Monsieur Mivart had established.

Early in the 19th century another elegant hotel was opened in Carlos Place (then Charles Street) by Wauthier and named the Coburg in honour of the Prince Consort's family. This was eventually taken over by the Grillion family and in the 1890s was rebuilt, though losing nothing of its air of quiet seclusion. During World War One the name was changed to the Connaught, and to this day it retains its atmosphere of comfort and exclusiveness.

In Regency times few of the hotels had public dining-rooms and if they did women did not appear in them. The usual custom was for meals to be served to the guests in their private sitting-rooms, and it was not until about the 1880s that women in society dined in public, in a restaurant or hotel dining-room, but a first step was taken in 1875, with the establishment of the Albemarle Club, for the 'accommodation of both ladies and gentlemen'. This was held at the Albemarle Hotel, at the junction of Albemarle Street and Piccadilly, and 'on the success of this', wrote one of the daily papers, 'depends the settlement of the question whether women as a body are *ferae natura*, or social and clubable animals'. Until 1858 the Albemarle had been Gordon's Hotel. It was rebuilt in 1889 and as the Hotel Albemarle was very fashionable for several years, visited by 'royalty, the diplomatic corps and the nobility'.

The exclusive Amphitryon Club was not founded until 1890, when it was opened by the Prince of Wales at Number 41, Albemarle Street.

The Great Western Hotel at Paddington was the first of the palatial hotels in London, and, as we have seen, within the next few years there were hotels on a similar scale at most of the London termini, for the accommodation of prosperous, middle-class travellers.

About the same time Morley's Hotel was opened in Trafalgar Square and in 1865 the Langham Hotel, where Upper Regent Street joins Langham Place. In writing of the Langham Hotel later in the nineteenth century, Edward Walford says: 'English inns have not lost their reputation for comfort and the attention paid to guests, but the almost entire alteration in the methods of travelling by the introduction of railways has left them considerably behind the requirements of the age. Except in the smaller towns and villages, they have been superseded by hotels—houses of a more pretentious kind, which contain suites of apartments for families or individuals, who choose to be alone, also a larger apartment for travellers generally.' About the year 1861 projects were set on foot for the purpose of building several hotels in London worthy of the place, and corresponding to the vastness of modern demands, and the Langham was not only one of the first erected, but has ever since remained one of the most important.

'The Langham Hotel was originally designed by a company about the year 1858, but the project proved abortive. The design, however, was subsequently taken in hand by another set of shareholders, who employed Messrs. Giles and Murray as the architects, and the foundations were laid in 1863. The hotel, which cost upwards of £300,000, is one of the largest buildings in London, and comprises no less than six hundred apartments. It measures upwards of 200 feet in the façade looking up Portland Place, and is upwards of 120 feet in height, the rooms rising to a sixth storey, and overtops by some forty or fifty feet all the mansions in Portland Place and Cavendish Square. The style of architecture would be called Italian; it is, however, plain, simple and substantial, and singularly free from meretricious ornament. It includes large drawing-rooms, a dining-room, or coffee room, 100 feet in length, smoking-rooms, billiard rooms, post-office, telegraph-office, parcels office, etc., thus uniting all the comforts of a club with those of a private home, each set of apartments forming a "flat" complete in itself. Below are spacious kitchens, laundry, etc. and water is laid over all the house, being raised by an engine in the basement. Some idea of the extensive nature of this establishment may be formed when we add that its staff of servants numbers about two hundred and fifty persons, from the head steward and matron down to the junior kitchen maid and smallest "tiger". The "Langham", on an emergency, can make up as many as 400 beds. The floors are connected with each other by means of a "lift" which goes up and down at intervals. It is as nearly fire-proof as art can render it.

'The hotel, which may be called, not a monster, but a leviathan of its kind, was opened in June, 1865, with a luncheon at which the Prince of Wales was present; and not long after its opening a dinner was given here, as an experiment towards utilizing horse-flesh by the "hippophagists" of this country and of Paris. These huge hotels are no novelties in America; indeed, the Langham is far outstripped in size by the Palace Hotel at San Francisco; but as this was the first experiment of the kind in London, though it has been extensively followed up, it may be as well to add that it has from the first paid a handsome dividend.'

The Langham remained a splendid establishment, renowned alike for its food and comfort, and it was a favourite place for fashionable wedding receptions, after marriages at All Souls, Langham Place: but with the outbreak of World War II, the hotel closed, and although the building still stands it has been turned into offices, a large number of which are used by the B.B.C.

Soon after the building of the Langham, large hotels were built at the fashionable seaside towns and other 'show' tourist towns. In 1866 the Randolph was opened at Oxford, in 1870 the Wellington at Tunbridge Wells. At Brighton, the Old Ship remained the principal hotel during the 1840s and 1850s. 'Each afternoon during the season,' writes Clifford Musgrave, 'there was a fashionable parade of handsome carriages along the sea-front, and in the evening there were balls and assemblies at the Old Ship. Most of the principal literary and theatrical figures of the day came to Brighton. Dickens gave a reading at the Pavilion, Paganini played at the Old Ship, and Jenny Lind was paid £300 for singing at the Town Hall.

'During the 60s and 70s, the nobility and aristocracy flocked to Brighton every year, especially in the autumn. One writer said "You can scarcely rest your eye on anything commoner than a Knight, and there are Commanders of the Bath enough to lift up Brill's Baths bodily and cast it into the sea!".'

In 1864 the vast Grand Hotel was built on the sea front at Brighton, a 'Cyclopean pile' of white stone, with balconies, in the Italian style, but the even larger red stone Metropole next to it did not go up until 1890. In Victorian and Edwardian days these two hotels were 'the haunts of South African gold and diamond millionaires, of wealthy speculators and race-horse owners, of the idols of the stage, and the nobility and Royalty of many lands'.

In London, which had for long borne the reputation of having few hotels, a great number were newly built or re-established in existing buildings during the second half of the nineteenth century, including the Inns of Court, the Royal, the First Avenue, the Grand, the Victoria, the Metropole, the Alexandra, Fleming's in Clarges Street, Anderton's in the Strand and Bailey's in Gloucester Road.

The 1879 Baedeker is interesting on London hotels. It says that charges for rooms vary according to the situation and the floor. A difference is also made between a *simple Bed Room* and a bedroom fitted up like a *Sitting Room*, with writing-table, sofa, easy-chairs, etc. Most of the rooms, even in the smaller hotels, are comfortably furnished. The continental custom of locking the bedroom door on leaving it is not usual, but visitors are recommended to make their doors secure at night, even in the best houses. Private sitting-rooms, it warns, are generally very expensive.

Breakfast is generally taken at the hotel, 'the continental habit of breakfasting at a café being almost unknown in England'. In most hotels smoking is prohibited, except in the Smoking Rooms provided for the purpose. Lights—candles or gas—are seldom charged for.

'The large Terminus Hotels, which have sprung up of late years at the different railway stations, and which belong to companies, are very handsomely fitted up, and have a fixed scale of charges,' says Baedeker. 'Apartments may be obtained in them at rates to suit almost every purse.'

In listing the first-class hotels of the West End, however, Baedeker warns that they receive travellers only when the rooms have been ordered beforehand or the visitors are provided with an introduction. The list begins with Claridge's Hotel, 49-35, Brook Street, which was considered the first hotel in London, patronized chiefly by royalty and the nobility and very expensive. Other 'well-conducted hotels of a similar character' were the Albemarle Hotel, 1, Albemarle Street, the York, 10 and 11, Albemarle Street, and Pulteney's, 13, Albemarle Street: and then follows a long list of establishments, mainly in the streets close to Piccadilly and Regent Street.

The price of bedrooms in these hotels varied from 3s. 6d. to 10s. a night. Breakfast was from 3s. to 4s., dinner from 5s. to 10s. and attendance from 1s. 6d. to 3s. Baedeker points out that although the charges for the best rooms in the Terminus hotels were as high, the attendance was hardly as good.

In the City of London, the guide lists hotels, most of which have now vanished without trace. De Keyser's Royal Hotel,

New Bridge Street, Blackfriars, 'was conducted in the continental fashion, was well situated, but somewhat expensive. Here, as at hardly any other London hotel, foreign newspapers were provided.'

The hotel was opened in 1874 by Sir Polydore de Keyser, a Belgian who came to London as a waiter and became Lord Mayor. The De Keyser Royal Hotel had 400 rooms and was very popular with foreign visitors. It was exclusive and at one time people had to have a personal introduction before they were given accommodation.

During World War I the hotel was taken over by the Royal Flying Corps and never reopened, for it was then occupied by Lever Brothers who later rebuilt it as Unilever House.

There was also Anderton's in Fleet Street, renowned for City dinners and smoking concerts, which survived until 1936, when it was pulled down, and several more, farther east, which have long since been demolished.

On the south side of the river was the International at London Bridge Station, but of all the inns which once lined the streets of Southwark and Lambeth, the only two which rated for a place in Baedeker, in 1879, were the Bridge House Hotel at 4, Borough High Street and Piggott's Hotel, 166, Westminster Bridge Road. With the exception of the George and the White Hart, the twenty-three galleried inns had been demolished. The White Hart went in 1889 but the south side of the George, with its balcony, has been carefully preserved, although the north and east sides of the old inn yard have been turned into railway goods sheds.

Leicester Square was still a favourite spot for French visitors, who frequented the Hôtel Sablonnière et de Provence at Numbers 17 and 18 and the Hôtel de Paris et de l'Europe at Number 9. Adjoining the Square were Bertolini's in St. Martin's Street and the Hotel Royal in Rupert Street. There was also a German hotel in Greek Street and another French hotel, the Hôtel de France et de Belgique off Bloomsbury

Square, but, says Baedeker, 'the stranger is cautioned against going to any unrecommended house near Leicester Square, as there are several houses of doubtful reputation in this locality.'

In the Covent Garden piazza were the Hummums and the Tavistock Hotel, both 'for gentlemen only', and the Bedford Hotel, recommended as 'comfortable'. The Covent Garden Hotel, at the corner of Covent Garden and Southampton Street, Ashley's Hotel in Henrietta Street and the Opera Hotel in Bow Street were all good. Evans's Hotel, above the restaurant and café, was also good but rather expensive.

Evans's was very fashionable in its day. It was founded by W. C. Evans, a comedian from the Covent Garden theatre. He retired in 1844 and was succeeded by Paddy Green who, in 1856, built a music hall in the garden at the back of the historic old Inigo Jones house, which during the previous two centuries had been the home successively of Sir Kenelm Digby, the Earl of Orford, Lord Archer and James West, President of the Royal Society, who died in 1772. When, after his death, the house was turned into a hotel, it was said to have been the first of its kind in London.

The music hall was conducted with the utmost decorum. In 1867 a visitor wrote that 'the ladies are not admitted, except on giving their names and addresses, and then only enjoy the privilege of watching the proceedings from behind a screen. The whole of the performances are sustained by the male sex, and an efficient choir of men and boys sing glees, ballads, and madrigals from selections from operas, the accompaniments being supplied on the piano and harmonium. . . . The performances commence at eight o'clock; and we recommend Evans's to the notice of steady young men who admire a high class of music, see no harm in a good supper but avoid theatres and the ordinary run of music halls. . . .'

It was here that the Savage Club was first formed, in 1857, and held its first meetings, before moving to the Adelphi.

In the Strand, the recommended hotels were Ormond's, the

Somerset, Haxell's Royal Exeter and the Golden Cross, opposite the Charing Cross Hotel: and in the streets leading from the
Strand to the Thames were a number of 'quiet family hotels',
which afforded 'comfortable accommodation at a moderate
cost'.

In Trafalgar Square Morley's Hotel on the east side, was
already popular with American visitors. The island site of
Morley's and the Golden Cross, now represented by Golden
Cross House, was acquired by the South African government
in 1922 and by 1933 the beautiful South Africa House had
arisen on the spot where Morley's once stood.

In 1879, close to Morley's, the Grand Hotel was being built,
on part of the site of old Northumberland House. This had
been the historic town mansion of the Percy family, which had
survived until 1874, when it was pulled down to make way for
Northumberland Avenue: and the Gordon Hotels Company,
who were building the Grand Hotel, promised that it was going
to be one of the most important hotels in London.

As well as many smaller and long-forgotten London hotels
Baedeker mentions an abundance of boarding-houses and also
private apartments, the best and most expensive of the apartments being still around Piccadilly, with cheaper lodgings in
the streets leading from Oxford Street and the Strand.

In regard to food, the guide says that 'English cookery which
is so inordinately praised by some epicures and *bon vivants* as
it is abused by others, has at least the merit of simplicity, so that
the quality of the food one is eating is not so apt to be disguised
as on the Continent. Meat and fish of every kind are generally
excellent in quality at all the better restaurants but the visitor
accustomed to continental fare will discern a falling off in the
soups, vegetables and sweet dishes.

'At the first-class restaurants the cuisine is generally French;
the charges are high, but everything is sure to be good of its
kind. The dinner hour at the best restaurants is 4–8 p.m., after
which some are closed. . . . Wine in England is always expen-

sive and often bad. . . . The traveller's thirst can at all times be conveniently quenched at a Public House, where a glass of bitter beer, ale, stout, or "half-and-half" . . . is to be had for 1½d. to 2d. (6d. to 8d. a quart). Wine (not recommended) may also be obtained. Many of the more important streets also contain Wine-stores or "Bodegas", where a good glass of wine may be obtained for 2d. or 6d., a pint of Hock or Claret for 8d. to 1s. 6d.'

Scores of restaurants are listed, some of which were attached to the hotels. They include Simpson's, the Hôtel de Paris, Bertolini's, Evans's, Kettner's, and the Criterion—spacious and sumptuously fitted up, with a small theatre. The Criterion was built in 1873 on the site of the White Bear Inn, one of the coaching-houses serving the west and south-west routes. The Café Monico was founded in 1879 by two young Swiss and was considered to be one of the most elegantly appointed restaurants in England, famous for both its cuisine and its wines, and it was not demolished until the 1960s. The St. James's Hall Restaurant at 69–71, Regent Street and the Burlington at 169, Regent Street both had rooms where ladies could lunch or dine. Verrey's was noted for its French cuisine but was expensive. The Grand Café Royal had first been opened by Mr. Nichol in 1865, in Glasshouse Street, but the premises were soon extended to Regent Street. After his death in 1907 it continued to be the famous haunt of Bohemian London, and even after it was rebuilt in 1925 it did not lose its character. Blanchard's in Beak Street did not permit ladies after 5 p.m. The Blue Posts in Cork Street was celebrated for its rumpsteaks and marrow bones. The Holborn Restaurant offered a table d'hôte dinner at separate tables, from 6 to 8.30 p.m., with music, for 3s. 6d.

In Fleet Street, at the corner of Chancery Lane, was the London, 'tastefully fitted up', with an à la carte restaurant and also a table d'hôte room where the London dinner of five or six courses for 3s. was served between 4 and 8 p.m. Good hock, claret and burgundy were offered for 2s. a bottle and there was also a café with newspapers and a room set aside for ladies.

Also in Fleet Street were the Cock, specializing in chops and steaks, the Rainbow, which had good wines, and the Old Cheshire Cheese, the steak and chop house which served its famous beef-steak pudding on Saturdays. The Cock, which had been on the north side of Fleet Street, where Number 201 now stands, for over three hundred years, was pulled down in 1886 and the old sign moved to the other side of the street. The Rainbow is now an espresso coffee bar but the Old Cheshire Cheese still survives, its history and traditions respectfully and affectionately preserved.

The Cathedral Hotel offered dinner for 2s. at 1 p.m. and also at 5 p.m. Dolly's off Paternoster Row was plain and quiet, specializing in chops and steaks. The Salutation in Newgate Street had good fish. The Grand Café Restaurant de Paris on Ludgate Hill gave a table d'hôte dinner with half a bottle of claret included, for 3s. 6d., from 5 to 8 p.m.

In Bishopsgate, Crosby Hall had become a restaurant, and Baedeker says it was 'very handsomely fitted up'. Crosby Hall, with its beautiful oak roof and oriel windows, was once the great hall of Crosby Place, the fifteenth-century mansion of Sir John Crosby, and later became the London home of Sir Thomas More. It survived into the nineteenth century, when it became a restaurant, but in 1910, to rescue it from demolition, it was moved, stone by stone, and re-erected in Chelsea, on the site of Sir Thomas More's mansion, which had been demolished by Sir Hans Sloane in 1740. During its years as a restaurant in Bishopsgate, Crosby Hall, like the King's Head tavern in Fenchurch Street, was equipped with smoking and chess rooms.

The Ship and Turtle in Leadenhall Street was noted for its turtle soup, Halford's in Upper St. Martin's Lane for its curries. Birch's of Cornhill were the chief caterers for civic feasts and the Three Tuns Tavern at Billingsgate fish market offered their famous 'Fish Ordinary' at 1 p.m. and 4 p.m., consisting of four or five different kinds of fish, besides meat and cheese, for 2s., with beer at 6d. a pint and claret at 1s. 6d. a bottle, but this was 'for gentlemen only'.

In 1889 the hotel situation in London, according to Baedeker, had changed very little. Minimum prices were up a little but maximum prices unchanged: and the guidebook notes that 'numerous as the London hotels are, it is often difficult to procure rooms in the Season, and it is therefore advisable to apply in advance by letter or telegram.'

The Grand Hotel had opened in 1880. It was built in the Italian style, on the lines of the most up-to-date American and French hotels of the time, and it had 300 bedrooms. The same company followed with the Hotel Metropole in 1885 and the Hotel Victoria in 1890, both in Northumberland Avenue.

At the Hotel Metropole a table d'hôte breakfast cost 3s. 6d., a table d'hôte dinner 5s., and rooms were from 3s. 6d. a night with attendance 1s. 6d. extra. The Hotel Victoria had accommodation for five hundred visitors and there were eight beautiful sitting-rooms. But all these luxury hotels were short on bathrooms, the Gordon Hotels Company not having taken enough notice of the advances in plumbing towards the end of the nineteenth century and the tendency amongst the more prosperous members of the community to bath more often.

The Hotel Victoria, acclaimed as the finest hotel in the world, had only four bathrooms for its full complement of five hundred visitors and there was no running water in the bedrooms. Under each bed was a flat, shallow bath capable of holding a few inches of water, and when the visitor required a bath the chambermaid extracted it, placed it on a blanket in the middle of the floor and produced two small cans, one of hot water, the other of cold. There was no central heating in the hotel and even though there was a coal fire in every occupied room, involving endless labour, the corridors remained permanently cold.

None of these hotels lasted for long. The Metropole and the Hotel Victoria both became government offices during World

War I and were eventually bought by the government and converted into permanent office buildings. The Grand lasted until 1928, when it was sold for conversion into offices and became Grand Buildings. At the meeting of the Gordon Hotels Company, when the decision to sell was made known, the Chairman commented that 'nowadays a great hotel resembles a battleship inasmuch as it tended to become obsolete after twenty years of existence and visitors now preferred the newer hotels in the West End.'

The Savoy receives a bare mention in Baedeker's 1889 list, for it was only just completed. The Hotel Windsor in Victoria Street is another new name and also the First Avenue Hotel in Holborn, which was one of the first to be lighted throughout with electric light and charged 15s. to 25s. a day *en pension*.

The old Claridges, not yet rebuilt, was still the most exclusive and expensive hotel in London, offering sumptuous accommodation for the wealthiest visitors and foreign royalty, but when the hotel was pulled down and reopened in its present building, in 1897 (*see* p. 214, Chapter Twelve) any historical records which may have been kept of its early days disappeared.

There were one or two other hotels in London of a similar character during the late 1880s, such as Buckland's in Brook Street, Berles' Private Hotel, the Albemarle Hotel, the York and Pulteney's, all in Albemarle Street: and the Bristol, which was being supplanted in exclusiveness and elegance by Claridges and was eventually to be turned into shops and offices, was still flourishing.

The name of the Berkeley now appears in Baedeker, which was built on the site of the old Gloucester Coffee House, the West End office of some of the west of England coach services. All the hotels in Jermyn Street are still recommended but Fenton's has disappeared and the Queen's Gate Hotel and the South Kensington Hotel are now listed, as well as Bailey's by Gloucester Road Station, which had opened in 1876 and which, like the South Kensington Hotel, now belongs to Empire Hotels, Limited.

In 1882 J. J. Ford's son Henry returned from Canada to take over the management of Brown's and by 1885 he had introduced baths, electric light and telephones. As in other hotels, these innovations were regarded with a good deal of suspicion by some of the guests, who had used candles and lamps and hip baths all their lives. They could see nothing wrong with them and disliked change.

Henry Ford also introduced a public dining-room at Brown's, which became very popular, although the private butler was retained for many years, calling at each suite every morning to take orders for the day's meals and find out at what time the guests wished to be served.

At the back of Brown's, at 32, 33 and 34, Albemarle Street, separated by only a small courtyard, was the St. George's Hotel, which had been founded in the 1850s, and in 1889 the proprietor sold out to Ford and the St. George's Hotel became incorporated in Brown's. The courtyard was roofed with glass and a fifth floor was added to both buildings. For a time it was known as Brown's and St. George's Hotel, but soon it became just Brown's again.

In 1906 three more houses in Albemarle Street were added and the dining-room, lounges and writing-room reconstructed. Henry Ford ran the hotel until he retired in 1928, by which time it had become a private limited company. The Bon family of Swiss hoteliers then bought it and in 1948 Trust Houses Ltd. acquired the company, but the unique atmosphere of the hotel has remained unchanged from the day in 1894 when Henry Ford wrote in the foreword to his booklet about Brown's: 'Notwithstanding the many innovations of late years introduced into English hotel-life, the proprietors of Brown's Hotel have always had in mind that no inconsiderable number of visitors to London would probably desire the quiet and privacy of what is known as a "Private Hotel" in place of the bustle and publicity generally associated with larger hotels, with which, however, such establishments we do not enter into competition. Messieurs Ford have appealed almost exclusively to the support of the class of visitors referred to: having spared neither pains nor expense in their endeavour to meet its every reasonable requirement and to justify the present repute of their hotel as the leading one in London.'

The list of distinguished visitors to Brown's is a long one, including, during the 1870s, John Pierpont Morgan, who introduced the young Alexander Graham Bell. Bell was still experimenting to perfect his telephone and it was from Brown's Hotel to the Fords' home at Ravenscourt Park that the first successful telephone call in this country was made.

Don Carlos, Pretender to the Spanish throne, was a resident during the 1880s and the Fords were such excellent hoteliers that he never knew that a staunch supporter of Alfonso XII was living there at the same time.

From 1886 to 1894 the Comte de Paris lived there, holding a regular Court in his suite. Arriving in the same year was Theodore Roosevelt and it was from Brown's that he was married at St. George's, Hanover Square, to Edith Carew, who was at the time staying at Buckland's Hotel in Brook Street.

In 1905 Franklin and Eleanor Roosevelt stayed there during their honeymoon, and were disconcerted when they found they had been given the royal suite, with its huge sitting-room, for they were afraid they would not be able to afford to pay for it.

Queen Emma, Regent of the Netherlands, and the fourteen-year-old Queen Wilhelmina stayed at Brown's on a private visit in the 1890s. Twenty-five years later Queen Wilhelmina brought the eight-year-old Princess Juliana to stay there. And during World War II it was in a room at Brown's that the Dutch Government in exile declared war on Japan.

During World War I Queen Elizabeth of the Belgians and her family lived at Brown's and King Albert came over to join them during his brief leaves from the western front. In 1924

King George II of the Hellenes, forced into exile when Venizelos came to power, lived nearly all the time at Brown's, until the restoration of the Greek monarchy in 1935, and the hotel was the official court of the Greek Royal family. Emperor Haile Selassie fled there in 1936, King Zog of Albania in 1940.

Who nowadays stays at Brown's Hotel? The guests are as distinguished as they ever were and come from many walks of life, but, to quote the concluding words of David Tennant's account of Brown's: 'It has been and will continue to be a cherished tradition of Brown's never to disclose the names of these guests. When they enter the hotel they can be assured of privacy as complete as if it were their own home, a factor not always easily attained in these days of mass communication.'

Chapter Twelve

CÉSAR RITZ AND THE SAVOY

IN 1850 THERE was born in the little Swiss village of Niederwald César Ritz, the thirteenth child of a small-holder. By 1867, the year of the second Paris Exhibition, Ritz was a waiter in a small, unimportant hotel in Paris and here, from a long way off, he saw for the first time the world of glittering wealth and fashion with which he was one day to become so familiar. The charming old eighteenth-century Paris had disappeared by now for the new Boulevarde Haussman had been built, the Magasins du Louvre had opened and Paris was lit by gas. Worth had been largely responsible for creating the magnificent Paris dress-making industry and was already waging war on the crinoline, which had been fashionable for fifteen years. The Empress Eugénie, the Princess Metternich and most of the Queens and Princesses of Europe, as well as the wives of the American business magnates and South African diamond millionaires wore his clothes and were adopting the new, severer fashions emerging from the Rue de la Paix, which seemed to herald the approaching tragedy of 1870 and the war with Prussia.

Ritz was a deft waiter, good-looking and spruce, and he took his work seriously, moving steadily upwards in the world of Paris restaurants until he became assistant waiter at Voisin's, perhaps the most distinguished of all the restaurants at this time. Here, under the tuition of the proprietor Bellenger, he learnt the subtle techniques of a first-class French restaurant, the finer points of carving and decanting, the appeal to the eye which stimulates the palate, and the way to attend on the needs of princes and aristocrats, including the Prince of Wales, the future Edward VII.

As in London, it was very rare for a woman of social standing to appear in a public restaurant but on occasions an actress might be seen at Voisin's, or a member of the *avant-garde* set, such as George Sand, but generally speaking the women who dined at Voisin's with the distinguished males were considered not quite respectable.

Another restaurant almost as renowned for its cuisine as Voisin's was the Petit Moulin Rouge, where a young and as yet unknown chef, Escoffier, was slowly winning recognition.

It was to Voisin's, in 1870, that the news was brought that Napoleon III and his army of 30,000 men had surrendered at Sedan, and as the Empress Eugénie fled from the back door of the Tuileries, the Prussians pressed on to besiege Paris.

Within a few weeks food was running short in Paris. In September, when the siege began, Voisin's had a great store, but by the end of November catering had become a problem and throughout the city the food queues grew ever longer.

Experiments in tinning food had already been made but during the Franco-Prussian war Escoffier, who had become chef de cuisine at General Headquarters at Metz, began to consider more seriously the possibilities of preserving meat, vegetables and sauces and made his first, highly successful experiments.

In Paris the food situation grew desperate and during that terrible winter of cold and starvation, as people died of hunger, rats were sold openly in the markets, cats, dogs, donkeys and horses were eaten and all the animals in the Jardin des Plantes were slaughtered for food, but Voisin's, despite lack of food and fuel, managed to keep going.

With the end of the war, Paris slowly returned to its old ways and by 1872 Ritz had become a floor waiter at the Hôtel Splendide in the Place de l'Opéra, which was considered to be one of the most luxurious hotels in Europe, and here, where he soon became *maître d'hôtel*, he met many of the American millionaires who were now flocking to Europe—J. P. Pierpont Morgan, John Wanamaker, Jay Gould and Cornelius Vanderbilt. He became friends with them all, and he also studied their tastes in food, wine and music, for he found them discriminating.

In 1873 he went to Vienna, at the time of the International Exhibition, and waited on half the crowned heads and princes of Europe, including the German Emperor William I, Franz Joseph, the Kings of Belgium and Italy and the future King of England. From there he went as restaurant manager to the Grand Hotel at Nice, and then to Rigi-Kulm in Switzerland, following the trail of the rich tourists, some of whom were now being conducted on luxury tours of Europe by Thomas Cook's organization.

He managed the Hotel Victoria at San Remo for a time, another luxury hotel, although, like most others in Europe, it had only two bathrooms. A number of tubercular patients came to the Victoria at San Remo, for the sea and mountain air. Little was known about the nature and treatment of tuberculosis at this time, but Ritz became convinced that it was infectious and took many precautions which were innovations, such as removing the heavy, velvet, befringed curtains and replacing them by easily washable fabrics such as silks and muslins, and personally supervising the scrupulous cleaning of all the rooms.

In 1870 Colonel Pfyffer d'Altishofen had built the Grand Hotel National at Lucerne, on the shore of the lake, a superb situation and a beautiful and luxuriously appointed building, but it was not making money. D'Altishofen approached Ritz and persuaded him to move to Lucerne and manage the hotel for him. Ritz agreed and quickly inspired the staff and the chef with his own enthusiasm and principles of good service, so that the National was soon the most exclusive of all Europe's hotels, the resort of princes and princesses, dukes and duchesses. Ritz organized weekly balls which became social events, and soon such social celebrities as the Duchesse de Rochefoucauld, the Duchesse de Maille, Lady Greville, the Duchess of Leeds and the Duchess of Devonshire were appearing in the public ball-room and dining-room, something which they could never have done at any hotel in London or even Paris.

Ritz organized the most fabulously luxurious and extravagant entertainments for his guests—rare flowers from Naples for the ballroom, an artificial moon for a boating party on the lake, ten thousand candles for one special illumination, fireworks and fountains, Neapolitan singers and exotic orchestras.

For eleven years Ritz was at the National for each summer season and during the winters he managed hotels almost as splendid in other fashionable European resorts, including Mentone and Monte Carlo. Then he moved to the Grand Hotel at Monte Carlo for the winter seasons which, though not as sumptuously decorated as the rival Hôtel de Paris, became during his eight years there the resort of the Princes and Grand Dukes of Europe and the financiers of America. When the Hôtel de Paris wooed away his chef, Ritz was undismayed, for he at once sent for Escoffier, and the Grand became even more renowned for its superb cuisine and service, for Ritz was the first man to appreciate to the full Escoffier's talents and gave him the scope he deserved.

Together they established the conventions of the modern luxury hotel, the white tie and apron of the waiter, the black tie of the *maître d'hôtel*, the morning coat of the upper staff and manager. In the kitchen Escoffier, though insisting on a basic simplicity in the presentation of dishes, reorganized the kitchen routine into departments under separate chefs.

During the 1880s women were beginning to take a far greater part in public life, and in place of the gargantuan meals which hotels had prepared for the predominantly male visitors, Ritz and Escoffier now offered food which would appeal to the palate of discriminating women. 'When Ritz decorated and furnished his hotels he always considered *first* the requirements and taste of ladies,' wrote his wife, 'and Escoffier was the first great *chef* to esteem their taste in food or to cater for it.'

Moreover, Ritz created hotels and restaurants of such elegance and restraint that women of fashion enjoyed visiting them. Dining out, in itself a great social change, became a pleasant habit.

On his marriage, in 1888, Ritz left the Grand at Monte Carlo and the National at Lucerne and bought the Restaurant de la Conversation at Baden-Baden and the Hôtel de Provence in Cannes, to which the Prince and Princess of Wales and the Marlborough House set were soon arriving. They were brilliantly successful. No hotels in Europe could compete with Ritz for décor and service, cuisine and an atmosphere of sumptuous luxury, and in England there was as yet nothing like the standards he had created.

A new venture was afoot, however. In 1875 the first of the Gilbert and Sullivan operas, *Trial By Jury*, had been presented at the Royalty Theatre by the impresario Richard D'Oyly Carte. The next operas were presented at the Opéra Comique, but by 1880 they had become so popular that the little theatre was too small for the audiences. D'Oyly Carte acquired a plot of land within the precincts of the ruins of the Savoy Palace and here built the Savoy Theatre, which was not only the first theatre to be lit by electricity, but the first public building to have the new form of lighting.

Until the quarrel in 1891, over the price of a theatre carpet, Gilbert, Sullivan and D'Oyly Carte had worked together in perfect harmony, and Gilbert and Sullivan had written and composed a new opera every year. Then the partnership broke and although the quarrel was patched up the collaboration was never again so successful. However, D'Oyly Carte and Sullivan now combined in a new venture. They planned to build a luxury hotel in London on similar lines to those which Ritz had created on the Continent.

A site was bought between the Savoy Theatre and the Embankment, a company was formed and the seven-storey hotel was built, with its main entrance in Savoy Hill. Its frontage was to the river and all the suites had flower-filled balconies. From Savoy Hill the cabs and carriages drove into a large courtyard of more than 6,000 square feet, in the midst of which a della Robbia fountain played against a background of exotic palms. To the astonishment of the builders, this new hotel was provided with no less than seventy bathrooms. The restaurant was panelled in mahogany, there were several private dining-rooms, a billiards-room, smoking room and ballroom, and there were six hydraulic lifts, said by the American Elevation Company who installed them to be the 'largest and most efficient in Europe . . . ready for use at all hours of the day and night . . . perfectly safe, their movement rapid and pleasant'. And like the theatre, electric light was installed, visitors being assured that 'the supply will be continuous during all the hours of the day and night, not only in Sitting Rooms, but in Bedrooms, the button or switch in the Bedrooms being so placed that the light can be turned on or off without getting out of bed'.

The hotel was beautifully appointed in every detail and 'with the aid of communication by speaking tubes from every floor and the installation of service lifts' there was continuous service throughout the day and night for every guest. Accommodation was arranged in suites and every suite of two or more rooms had its own bathroom. From the outset, D'Oyly Carte determined that the restaurant of the Savoy would be welcome to non-residents where, as in Europe, women could dine with impunity. There also a table d'hôte dining-room for residents and a grill room exclusively for men.

For the first few months after the opening of the Savoy in 1889 the hotel was not the success for which the directors had hoped. A few months earlier D'Oyly Carte had gone to Baden-Baden for the cure, staying at Ritz's hotel. Prince Radziwill had asked Ritz to prepare a special party for him and Ritz had composed an exquisite menu and hired a special orchestra. Then he turned the entire Restaurant de la Conversation into a woodland glade. The centre-piece was a giant fern, which he had borrowed from the horticultural gardens at Baden, round which a circular table was built. The floor was covered with turf and the walls with roses, and at one end of the room a fountain played into a pool glinting with goldfish.

"This", said D'Oyly Carte, "is the sort of thing I'd like to do at my new hotel in London."

He had asked Ritz at that time to come to London and manage the Savoy for him, but Ritz had turned down the offer, although he had attended the opening ceremonies. Now D'Oyly Carte wired him again, asking him to come at his own price, and Ritz accepted, provided he were allowed to keep control of his hotels in Cannes and Baden-Baden.

Ritz had been excited by his first visit to London and the vast possibilities it offered for his skill. "The wealth and brilliance of London are simply indescribable", he told his wife.

It was a particularly brilliant season, for there were elaborate preparations afoot for the marriage of the Princess Louise to the Duke of Fife. 'The Shah of Persia was being entertained on a lavish scale everywhere; there was a succession of magnificent entertainments, balls, dinners, processions, gala opera nights...' writes Marie Ritz in her life of her husband. 'César had gone to the opera one night to hear Emma Eames as Juliette. Never had he seen a more brilliant audience, never had he seen so many diamonds or so many beautiful women. . . . Wealth on every side. Wealth from Persia, India, Africa. It was all pouring into the lap of London.'

Of the hotel, Ritz had said to his wife: "The equipment is excellent. The staff is fairly good and could easily be whipped into shape. Needs a little weeding out, that's all. The *cuisine*—is uninteresting. It should be much better. The directors are eager to make a success of it and seem very generous in their ideas.

But, in my opinion, the management and organization will have to be improved, or the thing will not be successful."

When Ritz arrived in London to manage the Savoy he brought with him his own wine connoisseur, Echenard, as *maître d'hôtel*, Autour as his assistant, Agostini as his cashier and the incomparable Auguste Escoffier as *chef de cuisine*. In foggy, lamplit London, where Society was still unashamedly ostentatious, the Savoy quickly became an unqualified success. London at last acquired the restaurant habit and the stars of the stage and the opera, the American and South African millionaires, exiled Royalty and the beauties from the Marlborough House set, including Lily Langtry and Mrs. Keppel, were all to be seen at the Savoy.

Other hotels followed quickly. 'It is of no little advantage to ladies coming to London for the evening, from the suburbs or outlying districts, to know of a place where they may dine in evening dress without seeming conspicuous, or intermingling with those whom they might be indisposed to meet', wrote a newspaper correspondent in 1890. 'Either at the Grand Hotel or the Hotel Metropole they may be sure of the proprieties being very carefully observed. The tables, for the most part, are reserved to family parties, and visitors staying in the hotel; and the service of the dinner is so arranged as to allow of a very fair margin of time for partaking of it without hurry or discomfort.

'The Bristol Hotel, in Burlington Gardens, has a reputation among fashionable diners-about; but is somewhat expensive; and we may add that the chef of Brown's and St. George's Hotels in Dover and Albemarle Streets is equal to providing anything in the way of dinner the most accomplished practiser of the art of Dining might devise.'

Yet none of these establishments, including even the exclusive Hotel Bristol, could compete with the splendour of the entertainments which Ritz was asked to provide for the guests of the Savoy during the glittering 'nineties. Dinners sometimes cost £20 a head, flowers alone for these occasions cost hundreds of pounds and the price of galas sometimes ran into thousands.

Alfred Beit, the South African millionaire, conceived the idea of flooding the Savoy Court, which is now the lower dining-room, and creating a Venetian scene with the guests seated at tables on gondolas and entertained by the songs of genuine gondoliers, a party which cost him £1,500.

Ritz also brought to the Savoy many of his guests from Europe, who were prepared to stay at any hotel which he managed, and one of the first royal residents was the Comte de Paris.

In 1895 the Comte gave a dinner and reception for sixty-four guests at the Savoy, to celebrate the marriage of his sister, Princess Helen, to the Duke of Aosta. He gave Ritz only a few days' notice and the best reception rooms had already been booked for a regimental dinner at which the Prince of Wales was to preside. The Comte and the Prince disliked each other and it required all Ritz's tact and ingenuity to solve the situation and prevent the Comte from turning to the Hotel Bristol for his party.

Ritz consulted Echenard. They discovered two unused basement rooms in the Savoy, shabby, unattractive and almost unfurnished. Within two days, Ritz had arranged for the windows to be enlarged, a door cut and the rooms to be redecorated. It was high summer and very hot, so banks of ferns, palms and flowers, concealing huge blocks of ice, were ranged round the walls, between large mirrors, and the tables were laid with fleur-de-lis and La France roses arranged in vases of sculptured ice. After hours of hard work and brilliant organization, the party, at which the Princess of Wales was present, turned out to be one of Ritz's outstanding successes.

Escoffier devised many famous dishes for the Savoy, including his famous *pêche Melba*, but perhaps the most exotic was his *cuisses de nymphes à l'Aurore*, prepared especially for Edward VII when he was Prince of Wales. The Prince and his guests ate the 'nymphs at dawn' with wondering delight and then asked what they were, having not the slightest idea. They turned out to be frogs' legs served cold in a jelly of cream and Moselle, coloured with paprika—and soon all fashionable London was eating frogs' legs.

There is little doubt that Ritz changed the style of hotels in London and at the same time the social habits of society. He went further and changed the law, so that a hotel of the Savoy's class was allowed to keep its restaurant open until half an hour after midnight, thereby making possible the establishment of the famous Savoy theatre suppers. The Savoy was also allowed to open its restaurant for dinner on Sunday nights, and after Lady Grey and the Duchess of Devonshire had been seen there, Sunday dinner at the Savoy became high fashion. And the story goes that the Duchesse de Clermont Tonnerre was the first woman in London to be seen smoking a cigarette in public, when she lit one at her dinner table, one Sunday evening in 1896, at the Savoy.

In the days of the old coaching inns, foreigners had complained of the silence which usually prevailed when the British were eating. Ritz noticed this too and to the dismay of some but the delight of many, he introduced music to the restaurant. For Ritz nothing but the best was worthy of consideration and he engaged Johann Strauss, who was in London from Vienna for a series of public concerts and private entertainments. So now the elegant company of guests at the Savoy, eating superb food and drinking choice wines, lingered longer than ever at their tables, as Ritz had predicted, to listen to one of the best orchestras in Europe.

In 1891, Lily Langtry, who often stayed at the Savoy, sent Ritz a cutting from the San Francisco *Chronicle*, reporting a discussion at a hotel in California, during which General John Cutting declared that 'although I only visited London and Paris, I maintain that for service there is no hotel in the United States to compare with that Hotel Savoy in London. There is no rush or excitement when you arrive. You are courteously escorted by an attendant to your apartment, not by an officious bell-boy who wants to wear his whisk-broom out on your clothes for the expectation of a tip. You open your trunk and lay out your crumpled clothes and go to your breakfast. Every wish seems to be almost anticipated, and you don't feel like being obliged to lay down a fee for attendance. You return in the early evening to dress for dinner, and your dress suit is there freshly pressed and ironed for use. In the morning your day suit is similarly fit for wear. You couldn't have your wants better attended to if you were at home. In fact, the hotel supplies special attendants for every want, and I never had to call for any special service—you don't have to ring for ice water; it's there. That's the way to keep an hotel.'

There were, of course, almost inevitably, the grumblers who resented some of the new ways, amongst them, surprisingly, Oscar Wilde, who complained to Madame Ritz about the "modern Improvements" at the Savoy, which he said "were invariably ugly".

"Who wants an immovable washing-basin in one's room?" he grumbled. "I don't. Hide the thing. I prefer to ring for water when I need it."

He had little use for electric light either, which he thought 'a harsh and ugly light: enough to ruin the eyes'. And he bemoaned the fact that there was no candle or bedside lamp for reading in bed. 'Even the lifts,' he said, 'moved too fast for him.'

When the Savoy Company decided to develop the Grand Hotel in Rome and appointed Ritz its managing director, he sold his hotels in Cannes and Baden-Baden and established the new Grand Hotel as the social centre of Rome, while also finding time to advise Herr Adlon on the new hotels he was building in Berlin.

When Claridge of Claridge's Hotel died in 1895, the Savoy Company bought the property. The old hotel was pulled down and the present building, planned as the most luxurious hotel yet in existence, was opened in 1897, with a staff organized by Ritz.

It was in this year that Ritz resigned from the Savoy, on the climax of a long period of tension with the housekeeper, who had been at the Savoy from its first days, before Ritz had arrived there, and Escoffier left with him. For the next few months Ritz was busy in Paris with the building, decorating, furnishing and organization of the sumptuous Hotel Ritz in the Place Vendôme, while Escoffier helped with the plans for the new Carlton Hotel, at the corner of Pall Mall and the Haymarket, which Ritz's newly-formed Hotel Development Company was building.

The Paris Ritz opened in 1898 with Olivier as *maître d'hôtel* and Gimon as chef. Olivier had learnt his business at the Hotel Bristol and then at the Amphitryon Club, where he worked under Emile: and amongst the stories he had to tell of those days was the one about the dinner which King Milan of Serbia once gave for eight or ten people at a private room at the Amphitryon, when the walls were entirely covered with orchids. "He had absolutely no sense of the value of money", remarked Olivier. At the Bristol he had served scores of famous people, including Melba and the Duc d'Orléans, who liked to have an after-theatre supper in a private room, usually choosing *homard à l'Américaine* and champagne.

The Carlton Hotel, with Escoffier as *chef de cuisine*, was opened in July, 1899, on part of the site of the Prince Regent's Carlton House. It was the first hotel in London to have baths to every apartment, and they were, moreover, large and very luxurious bathrooms. The hotel was furnished mainly in the style of the English eighteenth century and every detail of linen, silver and glass was exquisite. The entrance hall was a palm court with green and cream walls and a red carpet, and at the top of the steps leading to the dining-room was a narrow, secluded balcony where, said Ritz, the Prince of Wales and his friends could take their coffee and listen to the orchestra undisturbed.

When one of his directors asked him how often he thought the Prince would be coming to the new hotel, Ritz replied, with sublime confidence, "very frequently". And he was right.

The clientele at the Carlton was brilliant throughout the next few years and included the Prince of Wales, who in 1901 was to become Edward VII, the Duke of Cambridge, the King of Spain, the Emperor of Ethiopia and a string of princes, dukes and marquises, as well as all the important theatre and opera stars, Caruso, the De Reszkes, Beerbohm Tree and Coquelin, Sarah Bernhardt, Melba and all the society beauties, Lady Curzon, Lady Randolph Churchill and Lily Langtry.

Hotels were at last completely respectable, as the night porter, Frank, who had been butler to the steward of the Queen's household, the Marquis of Breadalbane, confided one day to Madame Ritz. "When I first came here to take employment in a public hotel, I thought I was taking a bit of a step down, begging your pardon, Madame", he said. "You see there seemed to me a deal of difference between being a footman to a gentleman in his private house and being an employee in a hotel to which anybody might come! I hesitated quite a bit, ma'am, before I could bring myself to decide. But I've never regretted coming here, not for a moment."

Frank had dreaded the ignominy of "having to take orders from anybody", but he found that at the Carlton things worked out differently and declared that he had met there "some of the finest people that ever lived. Princes all of them."

The Carlton was so successful, both socially and financially, that the directors were soon looking for a site for yet another hotel. The Old Walsingham and Bath Hotels, where Walsingham House had once stood, just west of Arlington Street and overlooking the Green Park, were about to be pulled down. The directors bought the site and after Ritz had finished his survey for the remodelling of the Hyde Park Hotel, which had been occupying his attention at this time, he set about the plans for his new Ritz Hotel. It was the first steel-framed building in England, with a colonnaded frontage like the Paris Ritz and the Rue de Rivoli, but before it was completed César Ritz suffered a nervous breakdown from which, although he lived for another fifteen years, he was never to recover.

The Ritz Hotel was opened in 1905. César Ritz was well enough to put in an appearance at the opening celebrations, but he was never to enjoy the triumphant success that the London Ritz, like all his other hotels, including the Ritz-Carlton in New York, was to enjoy. As his mental condition gradually deteriorated, he retired from all his business ventures, and he died in Switzerland in 1918, only a week or two before the Armistice.

The Carlton remained an elegant and exclusive hotel all through the first four decades of the twentieth century but in 1940 the Palm Court was destroyed during an air raid. The hotel was then closed and requisitioned by the Government for the rest of the war and in 1948 it was bought by the New Zealand Government. In 1959 it was demolished and the fifteen-storey tower block of New Zealand House built on the site.

The Ritz survived the war years and throughout all the changes and tribulations of the century has maintained its impeccable standards.

After Ritz had left the Savoy, the directors brought Joseph of the Marivaux Restaurant from Paris, together with his chef, Thoraud. Menge became General Manager and he also managed the new Claridges for the Company.

There was room in London for all these luxury hotels and the Savoy went from strength to strength, maintaining its position as an important part of London's social life.

In 1892 the Hotel Cecil had been built on the Embankment, next door to the Savoy. It was a vast hotel with over a thousand bedrooms, two hundred private sitting-rooms, a large ballroom and restaurant and a terrace overlooking the river, but it began under a cloud, for it had been promoted by Jabez Balfour's Liberator Permanent Building and Investment Society which failed for £8,000,000 and in 1895 Jabez Balfour was sentenced to fourteen years' penal servitude. However, the hotel opened in 1896 and was very popular for a number of years, but it closed in 1930 and was demolished, Shell-Mex House being built on the site.

In 1901, a few months before his death, Richard D'Oyly Carte invited George Reeves-Smith, who had been manager of the Hotel Victoria and then managing director of the Berkeley, to join the board of the Savoy. Shortly afterwards the Savoy Company bought the Berkeley and Reeves-Smith became managing director of the Savoy, though continuing to live at the Berkeley. Thus the three distinguished hotels, the Savoy, Claridges and the Berkeley came under one control, but through the years they have each maintained their distinctive personalities.

Several books have been written about the excellence of George Reeves-Smith's direction of the Savoy, where he remained until his death in 1941. Arnold Bennett's *Imperial Palace* was dedicated to him and Compton Mackenzie pays a glowing tribute to him in his book *The Savoy of London*. He had perfect taste in food and wine and through all the years of bewildering change he maintained the Savoy's high standards, at the same time imbuing the hotel with its atmosphere of unobtrusive friendliness, which is one of its most valuable though intangible assets.

During the Strand widening scheme which began in 1899, the Hotel Cecil extended its frontage on the Strand and in 1902 the Savoy Company acquired property in the Strand which included old Beaufort House, the Fountain Tavern and Simpson's Chop House. Simpson's was rebuilt and opened again but the other two buildings were pulled down and on their site was built Savoy Court, which was originally designed as a block of self-contained residential chambers, but in time became incorporated into the hotel. The old grill room became the Café Parisien and was opened to women, and then was once more known as the Savoy Grill. A new entrance to the hotel was made from the Strand, between the Court and the theatre, by a private roadway.

All through the Edwardian years, the hotel expanded, until its original accommodation was doubled. The restaurant was enlarged until it swallowed up most of the old winter garden. Its mahogany panelling was changed to a lighter scheme of decoration, with mirrors, and the Embankment frontage was brought forward to allow more bathrooms to be added, an eighth storey being built on to the hotel at the same time. On the site of the old courtyard a new ballroom and banqueting room was built, large enough for five hundred couples to dance or four hundred and fifty guests to be seated at a banquet.

Some of the Savoy parties during the Edwardian years have become part of social history. At Krupp's party in 1906 the fountain in the old courtyard spouted forth champagne. To celebrate Commander Peary's discovery of the North Pole, the Pilgrims' Club gave a dinner for which the winter garden was transformed into a polar scene of snow and ice, and the waiters were dressed like Eskimos: and at another of the Club's dinners, to honour the American Naval Squadron's visit, twenty tables were modelled into replicas of famous British and American battleships.

Henry Irving, Whistler and Sarah Bernhardt were among many famous residents at the Savoy and Lily Langtry, Melba, Tetrazzini, Caruso, Gigli and Chaliapin all stayed there when they were in London. Actors and actresses, singers and dancers were all to be seen there and then came the film people, both American and English.

During World War I the Savoy became a centre for visiting Americans and the meeting place of the American

Luncheon Club and the American Society, and after America's entry into the war, in 1917, it was a haven for many a young subaltern during his short leaves from France.

At first dancing took place in the Lancaster ballroom, on a beautifully sprung floor, after dinner, but during the nineteen twenties the habit developed of dancing during the meal, in the restaurant, and when the British Broadcasting Company began operating from Savoy Hill people were able to listen each night to the Savoy Orpheans, first under the direction of Debroy Somers, and two years later, in 1924, under Carroll Gibbons.

By 1927 the Savoy had copied the Metropole and introduced a cabaret, which performed on a section of the restaurant floor ingeniously built to rise two feet above the dance floor, so that everyone could have a clear view.

Between the wars the theatre was rebuilt and canopies added on two sides of the pavements surrounding the courtyard. A new entrance to the hotel was made, surmounted by the statue of Peter of Savoy, and the foyer built.

During World War II the Savoy was again a friendly haven, despite a good deal of bombing. Many American war correspondents made it their home. Sir Winston Churchill was often to be found there and one of the most famous residents, all through the bombing, was Lady Oxford.

'Today', writes Compton Mackenzie, 'the Savoy has the unmistakable stamp of a well-bred host by whom every guest is made to feel particularly welcome.'

There is a strong feeling of continuity among the directors and staff who have been responsible for this imaginative direction. When Richard D'Oyly Carte died in 1901 his son Rupert succeeded him, and on Rupert's death in 1948 his daughter Bridget joined the Board, while many members of the staff belong to families who have been connected with the hotel during the three generations of its existence.

The organization behind the scenes at the Savoy is enormous.

It has its own laundry, building and decorating departments, and makes its own beds and bedding as well as some of its other furniture. It has over 2,000 rooms and endless corridors to be equipped, and the furnishing department deals with carpets, curtains, covers, lampshades and bedspreads. The flowers come mostly from Covent Garden, though some are especially grown for the Savoy by private growers. The head of the restaurant kitchens controls nearly a hundred cooks and the output of the bakery alone includes 4,500 rolls a day, baked freshly for every meal. The cellars are vast, for there are few hotels in the world that can offer such a wide variety of wines and the Savoy is probably the largest wine buyer of any European hotel.

As Compton Mackenzie says, in the conclusion of his book, 'Today the hotel is as much as it ever was a centre of international life.' At the same time, it is a survival of that comfortable London world in which it was opened more than eighty years ago.

Several other large hotels were opened in London before the outbreak of World War I. On the north side of the Strand the Exeter Hall had stood since 1831, between the two parts of Haxell's Hotel, which was connected by a corridor running across the upper floor of the Hall. In 1907 the Exeter Hall was pulled down and the Strand Palace Hotel built on the site, by J. Lyons and company. Later the two parts of Haxell's Hotel were demolished and by 1930 the Strand Palace had extended over the sites, a huge hotel of nine storeys with nine hundred rooms, at moderate prices.

After the construction of Kingsway and Aldwych and the widening of the Strand from the Law Courts to Wellington Street, which took place between 1900 and 1905, the large and comfortable Waldorf Hotel was built, in 1906, between the Strand and the Aldwych theatres. In 1911 Baedeker described the Waldorf as 'a palatial edifice with 400 bedrooms, 176 bathrooms, a palm-court, restaurant and grill-room'. Luncheon cost 3s. 6d., dinner 5s. and afternoon tea in the palm court was 1s.

Between 1905 and 1908 the Piccadilly Hotel was built, on the site of the St. James's Hall and Restaurant, which had opened in 1858.

The building of the Regent Palace Hotel, also by Lyons, with its nine storeys and nearly a thousand rooms, just off Piccadilly Circus, was begun in 1913 but not completed until 1915, after the outbreak of World War I.

'The standard of comfort, or at least of magnificence, in London hotels has risen in recent years, and the large first-class houses are fully equipped with modern luxuries and comforts, such as electric light, lifts, central heating, ample bath accommodation, telephones in the bedrooms, and, in several cases, private orchestras,' reported Baedeker in 1911. 'Even in the older and smaller hotels most of the rooms are fairly well-furnished, while the beds are clean and comfortable'.

It goes on to say that private hotels, by which is meant those without a licence, are often as comfortable as the first-class licensed houses, but there is a tendency for establishments which are really ordinary boarding houses to describe them-selves as private hotels. Temperance hotels are less pretentious and generally cheaper than the genuine 'Private hotel'. They are usually only second class in regard to cuisine and appoint-ments, but many, especially those in Bloomsbury, may be safely recommended. The so-called Residential Hotels are often 'large blocks of separate suites or flats, let furnished with attendance, and frequently have restaurants for the convenience of tenants'.

Claridges, the resort of visiting royalty and the very rich, was still regarded as the leading, exclusive hotel, with a room and bath costing 10s. 6d. a night, luncheon 5s. and dinner 8s. 6d., and the prices at the Ritz and the Carlton were the same. Rooms at the Berkeley cost from 8s. 6d. a night and at the Savoy from 9s. 6d. but dinner at the Berkeley was 10s. and only 7s. 6d. at the Savoy. Charges at the Piccadilly were much the same as those of the Berkeley but at the Hotel Cecil rooms cost from only 6s. a night, luncheon was 3s. 6d. and dinner 6s., and at the Waldorf Hotel rooms were from 4s. 6d. The Hotel Metropole, the Hotel Victoria and the Grand Hotel all charged from 5s. to 6s. a night for a room, the Charing Cross Hotel and Morley's 4s. 6d., the Golden Cross 5s. and the Strand Palace 6s. for a room, bath and breakfast, with the added attraction and innovation of no gratuities.

In the streets between the Strand and the river there were still a number of quiet, comfortable and reasonable hotels, three newcomers being the Arundel in Arundel Street, the Norfolk in Surrey Street and the Howard in Norfolk Street, all charging about 6s. a night, with dinner from 3s. to 3s. 6d.

At the corner of Victoria Street and Tothill Street was the Westminster Palace Hotel, built in 1860 on the site of Caxton's house, to provide accommodation for members of Parliament and people attending the law courts, which at that time were centred in Westminster. It had 400 rooms and at the time was considered the last word in modernity, but with the outbreak of World War I it was taken over by the National Liberal Club and then became the shops and offices of Abbey House. In Buckingham Gate was the large Buckingham Palace Hotel, with prices much the same as those of the Westminster Palace. In Caxton Street was the St. Ermin's Hotel, which is now converted into flats, and at the corner of Victoria Street and Palmer Street was the Windsor Hotel, which has now been turned into offices. The Hotel Belgravia in Grosvenor Gardens closed in 1936, but the Goring Hotel in Ebury Street and the Wilton Hotel survived.

In Kensington, the Hyde Park Hotel at Albert Gate, the Hans Crescent Hotel, the Cadogan, the Alexandra, the South Kensington Hotel, the Royal Palace, the De Vere and Bailey's were all flourishing, as well as the Park View at Hyde Park Corner Station and the Royal Court in Sloane Square.

Between Oxford Street and Regent's Park there were a number of recommended hotels but the Langham was still the most important, apart from the large railway hotel, the Hotel Great Central, at Marylebone Station, with 700 bedrooms.

In Bloomsbury the large Hotel Russell was built in 1898, an eight-storey building with 500 rooms, a restaurant, winter-garden and orchestra, charging only 4s. 6d. a night: and in 1907 Harold Walduck built the 350-roomed Imperial Hotel next door to it, on the site of the old Bedford Hotel which at the turn of the nineteenth century had been the Bedford Coffee house. The Russell survives but the Imperial was recently demolished.

Of the three railway hotels in this area, the Euston, the Great Northern, and the Midland, the Midland was considered at this time to be the best.

There were a number of good temperance hotels in Bloomsbury during the early years of the century, including the West Central in Southampton Row, the Kingsley in Hart Street and the Thackeray in Great Russell Street, both of which belonged to the same proprietor; the Ivanhoe, the Kenilworth and the Waverley, all three belonging to another proprietor, the Endsleigh Palace and the Coburn, both in Endsleigh Gardens, and the Bonnington in Southampton Row.

Some have not survived. The Thackeray, for example, opposite the British Museum and invaluable for people who had come to London to research in the Reading Room, closed on the outbreak of World War II, but many are today as busy as they have ever been, a number being used as the London stopping place for overseas visitors arriving for a motor tour of Britain. Amongst the largest, with more than two hundred bedrooms each, are the Ivanhoe and the Kenilworth. Others are the County, the Ambassadors and the Cora in Upper Woburn Place, the Bonnington and the Bedford in Southampton Row, the starkly plain Royal Hotel in Woburn Place, which opened in 1927, and the Tavistock

Two hotels built in the grand manner. The Langham in London (*above*) opened 1865 and the Grand Hotel at Brighton (*below*) in 1864. Napoleon III of France 1 the Empress Eugénie are shown arriving at the Grand.

14. Two of the railway hotels. (*Right*) The North British Station Hotel at Edinburgh and (*below*) the Great Western Hotel at Paddington.

Hotel, which was built by the Imperial London Hotels Company, a modern hotel with a private bathroom to each bedroom, and opened in 1951, the first London hotel to be built after the end of World War II.

In 1911 the Thackeray was charging 8s. 6d. a day *en pension* (without luncheon) compared with De Keyser's, which varied between 12s. 6d. and 25s. a day. Anderton's, the favourite resort of many dining clubs and masonic lodges, charged 10s. 6d. a day, the First Avenue Hotel in Holborn and the Inns of Court Hotel in High Holborn, for many years the favourite lunch-time meeting place of barristers, from 15s. to 25s. a day. The Inns of Court Hotel did not survive World War I. Anderton's went in 1936 and the First Avenue Hotel was sold by the Gordon Hotels Company in 1940, the new proprietors turning it into offices.

No account of the hotels of Edwardian London would be complete without a mention of the Cavendish and that extraordinary and much loved character, Rosa Lewis.

Rosa was born in 1867 at Leyton in East London, the fifth child of lower middle class parents, who seem to have descended in the social scale during the previous few generations, though Rosa spoke with a cockney accent which she never lost. At the age of twelve, after four years at a Board School, she went as a general servant to a small villa in Leyton, where she lived in and received a shilling a week wages: and apart from a half-day off a week and a whole day every month, she worked from half past five in the morning until nine o'clock at night, after which time she was free to go up to her small attic and read by the light of a single candle.

Her reading was mostly her employer's discarded copies of the *Morning Post*. The Court circulars fascinated her and set her dreaming about the remote world of high society. By the time she was sixteen, with the help of an uncle who knew the chef, she had moved from Leyton to become under kitchen-maid at Sheen House, Mortlake, where the exiled Comte de Paris and his family were living. Her wages were 12s. 6d. a week and her main job was to scrub the kitchen floor, but her romantic soul was exultant. Her dreams were beginning to come true, for she was working for the heir to the throne of France.

She was very successful at Sheen, quick to learn French and the techniques of the kitchen, and very soon she was taking the responsibility for some of the cooking. The Prince of Wales was a visitor at Sheen House and on one occasion, when the chef was absent, Rosa, still only seventeen, was called upon to cook the dinner. The Prince enjoyed it so much that he asked to meet the chef, whereupon the butler brought the surprised but imperturbable Rosa from the kitchen to be presented to him. The Prince shook her by the hand and gave her "a present Sovereign from your future Sovereign". "And that", said Rosa, reminiscing in later life, "was how I first met the King".

After four years at Sheen, during which she was lent to the Comte's uncle, the Duc d'Aumale, for a spell, to work in the kitchen of his château at Chantilly, Rosa felt she was ready to move on. She had learnt a great deal about French cooking and was supremely confident in her own skill. Against the wishes of her family, she went to London and, through an agency, took a temporary post as cook to Lady Randolph Churchill, while her chef was taking time off. The first meal she cooked was for an important dinner party, and it was so successful that other hostesses were soon eager to acquire the services of the brilliant cook, who by this time had become a beautiful and immaculately dressed young woman. She was soon charging high sums for her temporary services to society hostesses but for a time she went into the permanent employ of Lady Randolph Churchill, at 50, Grosvenor Square. The Prince of Wales was a frequent guest and Rosa soon began to learn his tastes in food, as well as that of many other members of the nobility on the Churchills' long visiting list: and she was the first cook to experiment with putting a dash of sherry into the *consommé*, to stimulate their jaded appetites, although most people still considered it vulgar to use wine in cooking.

When she was twenty-five, Rosa married Excelsior Lewis, a friend of her family, four years older than Rosa and butler to Sir Andrew Clarke. Lewis had a certain amount of money saved and an ambition to run a lodging-house. Together they took the lease of 55, Eaton Terrace, which they opened as an expensive and exclusive lodging-house for clients whom they took great care to select. Although the guests were provided only with breakfast, the Lewises employed five servants, including a woman to help in the kitchen, and there was little for Rosa and Excelsior to do. Rosa, already bored with her husband, who seems to have been a grievous disappointment to her, returned to her career, and Excelsior took to drink, while to deepen the rift his sister Laura, whom Rosa heartily disliked, came to live with them.

Rosa's catering service expanded. There were as yet no hotels where hostesses could entertain their guests and Rosa's service was unique. She had soon acquired a staff of young assistants. As much as possible of the meal was prepared in the kitchen at Eaton Terrace and then, on the afternoon of the party, she and her team would move into the house where the party was to be held and take over the kitchen, often to the fury of the resident cook and kitchen staff.

From the old Negro cook of William Low, an American friend of the Prince of Wales, at whose house in Warwickshire Rosa did some catering, she learnt how to prepare Virginia peach-cured ham and waffles with maple syrup, American dishes which were becoming increasingly popular in London. And the more successful she was, the gloomier and more indolent grew Excelsior.

In 1902 Rosa heard that Franco of the Cavendish Hotel in Jermyn Street wanted to retire and that the nine remaining years of the lease of the hotel was for sale and could be renewed. At this time its reputation was very high and it differed from the new luxury hotels, such as the Savoy, Claridges and the Carlton, because it was a 'private hotel', arranged in suites and with no public rooms or even a dining room. Rosa decided to persuade Excelsior to leave the house in Eaton Terrace. She would buy the lease of the Cavendish in his name, and he and Laura could run it while she continued her lucrative profession. Excelsior agreed, but as an hotelier he was a failure and began drinking more heavily than ever. He ran into heavy debt and Rosa, in sudden desperation, turned him and Laura out of the place and settled down to rebuild its declining fortunes, spending nearly all her savings and continuing with her catering service, in order to pay off Excelsior's £5,000 debts.

In less than two years she was solvent again and able to concentrate on her hotel. It was to be quiet, intimate and exclusive, for she had been able to preserve some of Franco's distinguished clientele, despite the havoc of Excelsior's brief reign. 'Franco had a marvellous Spanish clientele—all the Grandees of Spain and the most wonderful American clientele that has ever been,' she told Michael Harrison many years later, 'Bishop Potter, Stuyvesant Fish, Pierpont Morgan, Joseph Choate, and heaps of others. . . . King Edward came here too— before my time—when he was Prince of Wales.

'Everybody had a Town house; and there were only a few hotels and the clientele was of the very best . . . the kind . . . that has *chicken*—they don't have a *piece* of chicken—they had to buy the whole of it. If you had roast beef, you had to have the whole joint.'

When Rosa set about modernizing the Cavendish 'there were no bathrooms, so we made one; then two, and then three. No telephones either.

'There were no dining-rooms; all the meals were served in the sitting-rooms, being taken from room to room on large, round tables, like the old Bristol Hotel in Paris, where the Prince of Wales used to stop.

'No public sitting-room, but wonderful china, old teapots

and old Sheffield-plate, and everything beautiful and comfortable—and everyone had baths in their rooms. Tubs.

'People used to go about in their dressing-gowns in those days, it was all so simple. Then we had only three bathrooms; now (1923) we have forty-six—and we are no happier with the forty-six than we were with the three!

'I put in beautiful chintzes, and made it look like an English country house. It had all the charm of a Georgian mansion, combined with modern conveniences.

'All the furnishings were beautiful, stately and dignified; and everything was very comfortable.

'On the walls were choice engravings, and very valuable works of art; Chinese pottery, bronzes, tapestry etc.'

One of Rosa's first permanent guests was the elegant Lord Ribblesdale who wrote an interesting comment on the effect of hotels on social behaviour. He had been writing about the half-cross, half-tired expression which Queen Victoria often wore, when she was over-driven and over-tired and added a footnote: 'In this respect—crossness—I notice a great improvement in these latter days. In my youth, people were frequently —almost generally—cross to one another. I attribute the change to the urbane sway of the Ritz and corresponding establishments, restaurant life and music-halls, to the Riviera Express and winter sports—the world is more amused and so better pleased.'

Rosa came to know Escoffier. 'I consider Escoffier one of the greatest chefs of France, and one of the greatest gentlemen among the bourgeoisie, and one of the few Frenchmen I ever had any respect for', she once said. In return, Escoffier had a great admiration for Rosa's skill and referred to her as the Queen of Cooks.

In 1901 the Ligue des Gourmands, an association of the great French chefs in London, was founded, and under the presidency of Escoffier they gathered each year to dine, after which a reception was held. Around the table gathered the chefs of the Russell Hotel, the Union Club, the Midland Hotel, the Grand, the Carlton, the Hyde Park Hotel and restaurants such as Prince's and Romano's. Women were not invited to the dinner, but in 1903 Escoffier invited Rosa to the reception of the Ligue, as his personal guest.

By 1909 Rosa was rich. She still had her catering service. At the suggestion of King Edward, she had cooked for the German Emperor when he was staying in England at Highcliffe Castle. She had cooked for the King and she had prepared dinners for the Foreign Office and Admiralty banquets. She had cooked for W. W. Astor at Hever Castle. On occasion she would take a large empty house and furnish the reception rooms for the one night of a party or ball, providing not only the food and wine, but the china, glass, silver, tables and chairs.

In 1904 George Evans of the British Hotel next door, Numbers 82 and 83 Jermyn Street, sold out to Felix Sartori, who proceeded to modernize the old Regency building and re-named it the Hotel André. The next year Elio Gelati at Number 84 took a partner and together they transformed the hotel. At numbers 85 and 86, the old Waterloo Hotel came into the hands of Jules Ribstein, who opened the smart new Restaurant Jules on the ground floor and converted the upper floors into the Waterloo Residential Chambers. By May, 1910, Rosa had bought the Hotel André and shortly afterwards acquired Gelati's house at Number 84. The Cavendish now consisted of three eighteenth-century houses and she was able to build a fourth wing at the back, to surround a central courtyard garden. With this greatly enlarged hotel she made a public dining-room with windows overlooking the courtyard, a pale grey, mirrored room which soon became very fashionable.

Rosa's personality, her cockney wit, her superb cuisine and service made the Cavendish like no other hotel in London. The stage adopted it—Ellen Terry, Mrs. Pat Campbell and Pauline Chase—as well as the writers, artists and playwrights, wealthy Americans and visiting foreign Royalty.

Colonel Newnham Davies described a luncheon party at the Cavendish, to which Rosa had invited him. 'Our first dish was of grilled oysters and celery root on thin silver skewers, and then came one of those delicious quail puddings which are one of Mrs. Lewis's inventions and for which King Edward had a special liking. . . . This was followed by a dish of chicken wings in bread crumbs and kidneys, before the pears and pancakes, an admirable combination, with which our lunch ended.'

Rosa's quail pudding was one of her most famous original dishes and in 1909 the recipe was published in the *Daily Mail*.

> Take your quails or snipe, and truss for braising, and leave in a marinade for a few hours. Make an ordinary suet paste, line a basin with it, then place your quails or snipe, one for each person, in slices of beef as thin as paper, which when cooked dissolve into the sauce; put some fine, chopped mushrooms, parsley, shallots and good stock, and put a paste top and boil for one hour. Serve rice or barley with it.

By 1914 Rosa was thinking of retiring but with the outbreak of the war she decided to carry on. She was kind to young subalterns on leave and often, when she knew they could not afford her prices, charged them little or nothing at all, though she stiffened her charges to the rich by way of compensation. When America came into the war, many young Americans were as fond of the Cavendish as the Savoy. Nevertheless, Rosa lost money during these years and had to keep on working.

After the war, the Cavendish was never the same, although the young Prince of Wales, later Edward VIII, was sometimes to be seen there and she kept the custom of some of the old county families. During the 1920s it became the resort of the Bright Young Things, and although many of them were of impeccable lineage they brought with them a retinue of raffish hangers-on, who used the hotel for secret rendezvous and amorous adventures.

Several books have been written about Rosa and the Cavendish, including Michael Harrison's *Rosa* and Daphne Fielding's *The Duchess of Jermyn Street*, both of which brilliantly evoke the Edwardian atmosphere of the place; and Evelyn Waugh's Lottie Crump in *Vile Bodies* was based on Rosa Lewis.

In 1932 Aldous Huxley stayed there and later he wrote:

> It was like staying in a run-down country house—large comfortable rooms, but everything shabby and a bit dirty. We were not bibulous, so must have been a disappointment to Rosa Lewis. However, she put up with us. Once, I remember, a young man in what the lady novelists call 'faultless evening dress', top hat and all, came swaying into our bedroom at almost 2.30 a.m. and had to be pushed out. How sad, but how inevitable, that the hotel should now be doomed to destruction.

Yet Rosa and her hotel survived World War II, despite some considerable bomb damage. She died in 1952 and it was not until early in 1963 that the old hotel was demolished.

'Poor Cavendish—I passed the spectral darkened hostelry where Christmas used to be celebrated with all religious and pagan rites', wrote Sir Shane Leslie.

'The name-plates had been wrenched away like the shoulder décor of a degraded officer. The windows are like blinded eye sockets curtained by dust. The hospitable doors have clashed for me the last time. Every room has been engaged for Christmas by a ghost. Old crumpled waiters move through the corridors carrying out commissions forgotten in the past. The stairways are thronged but never a creak do they give. The never silent telephone is as dead as Rosa's old heart. With the New Year the last of the Edwardian palaces will tumble into chaos and broken brick and wizened wood and the Cavendish will all be gathered to such as the Mermaid Inn.'

In its place has been built a new Cavendish Hotel of fifteen storeys, with 250 bedrooms, modern in every detail, which was opened in 1966, but as a salute to Rosa's memory one of the bars has been named the Sub Rosa, the telegraphic address is Rosatel and the two tall lamps which used to stand on either side of the pillared portico have been preserved to stand outside the entrance of the new building.

Chapter Thirteen

BACK TO THE ROADS

D URING THE LATE Victorian and Edwardian days of
Society opulence, when the luxury hotels were being
built in London and the large cities of Britain, many
things were happening which were to bring new life to the
long-neglected coaching inns on the deserted roads.

Although the rich went to Europe or Scotland every summer,
ordinary middle-class families had not yet adopted the habit
of taking a summer holiday each year as a matter of course.
The custom developed gradually and when they did decide
to go away they usually took apartments at one of the seaside
towns, more often than not buying their own food which the
landlady cooked for them and served in a private sitting-room.

There were not many boarding houses at the seaside and
holiday resorts in late Victorian times and the hotels were far
too expensive for most people. As for the huge mass of the
working population, they seldom caught a glimpse of the
countryside or the sea, and thousands never saw either in all
their lives.

It was with increasing wages, holidays with pay and the
cheap excursions offered by the railways that people began to
form the habit of holidays away from home, and at first they
favoured the seaside rather than the country, which meant that
at the coastal resorts boarding houses were soon established and
many more small hotels opened, catering mainly for the
summer holiday trade.

The old coaching inns, buried deep in the countryside, were for the most part too remote and inaccessible still, and those that had not already died were lapsing into a mortifying neglect.

Then came the sudden popularity of the bicycle. Throughout the nineteenth century various types had been invented but they were cumbersome affairs of iron and wood, in which few people took much interest. But early in the 1890s a steel model was designed in Coventry, at first with solid tyres and later with pneumatic tyres. These new bicycles were far easier to ride than the old bone-shakers and penny-farthings and a good deal safer, and they soon became popular.

At first only the rich indulged in them, including those *avant-garde* young women who had begun to flaunt convention by appearing in public in hotel restaurants, but prices fell and bicycles were soon being bought by the middle and working classes. Under pressure from the trade unions, wages were rising and more people could afford to buy the new free-wheel model which soon appeared on the market. The cycling craze spread. It gave people a freedom of movement they had never thought possible. They found themselves able to visit places they had never seen before and some of which they had never even heard. It awakened new interests and now, with the slowly acquired increase of leisure time and longer weekends, thousands were able, for the first time in their lives, to explore with delight the countryside surrounding the towns and cities where they lived, which even the railways and bus routes did not reach.

The Cyclists' Touring Club was formed and the cyclists began to travel ever farther afield, into the farmlands and woods, the lonely hamlets and villages, and the market towns with their coaching inns, which their grandfathers had known and used sixty years earlier. In the country towns a good many of the inns had survived, especially those standing at the cross-routes not yet served by the railways, but in the smaller places nearly all of them had given up all thought of catering or providing accommodation, and they existed solely on their liquor trade. The bedrooms were unused, the stables empty and dilapidated, the courtyards overgrown with weeds.

But now the Cyclists' Touring Club needed accommodation for its members, because travellers, whatever their mode of transport, need somewhere to sleep at their journey's end. The officers of the Club began to tour the inns and examine their possibilities. It gave new life and new hope to many of them and as, with varying degrees of success, they gradually came back into business, the Club compiled a list of those which would be suitable for the cyclists, and it maintained this register for many years.

While the cyclists were roaming the countryside, the rich had found a new diversion, little realizing that, within half a century, it was to change almost every aspect of social life. The motor car had arrived.

By 1901 cars had assumed their modern shape, with the engine in front of the driver, but they were high and had no roofs, so motoring on country roads which had not been macadamized was a dusty and uncomfortable business, but soon the roads were improved, cars became more comfortable and by 1904 there were eight thousand on the roads of Great Britain, their maximum speed limit twenty miles an hour.

In 1897 the Royal Automobile Club was formed, soon to be followed by the Automobile Association. Like the Cyclists' Touring Club, the motoring clubs published a register of likely inns for their members, and as cars became cheaper and more reliable and their popularity spread, the innkeepers and hoteliers saw the new opportunities that were dawning for them. The registers and classifications were a challenge. They influenced charges and amenities, and among the long-neglected inns of Britain the art of inn-keeping was born again, though in the early years of the century it was a slow and painful process, for the countryside that the motorists and cyclists were discovering anew was very different from that of the last days of the coaches, in the 1830s, which foreign visitors had so much admired for its neatness and prosperity.

With the free-trade policy of the last quarter of the nineteenth century and the import of cheap food from the Empire, the farming industry had been nearly ruined and a blight of despair and bitterness had crept over the farming community. Although it had kept going, mainly by turning to dairy farming, half a million men had left the land and thousands of small farmers had sold out. This depression had helped to hasten the decay of the old roadside inns and for many their only hope of survival had been to sell more and more drink, for it was their main source of livelihood. Barmen were encouraged to give credit to men whose wages were barely above subsistence level. They offered overfull measures—the long pull—and made up their losses by watering the beer and adulterating the spirits; and drunkenness was as common in English villages and country towns as in the gin palaces of the industrial slums.

It was the fourth Earl Grey who, realizing the extent to which drunkenness was sapping the vitality of the country, and also lamenting the continued decline of the roadside inns, many of which were so rich in history and architectural beauty, decided to take practical steps to try and cure the double problem, and at the same time provide accommodation for the increasing numbers of people who were seeking it. His aim was to improve the public house, using that term in its widest sense, to include hotels, inns, taverns and alehouses.

He maintained that inns could now do equally good business serving tea, coffee, soft drinks and food as well as alcohol. He wrote to the Lords Lieutenant of the counties, suggesting that every county should found a Public House Trust Company, the money to be used to buy inns and put in paid managers, who should receive a salary and a commission on food and lodgings but not on liquor. Where landowners had let houses to the brewers, these should be sold to the County Public

House Trust when the leases expired, and the magistrates be asked to transfer the licences.

In 1904 the scheme was put into operation in Hertfordshire, by the renting of a small inn at Ridge Hill, sixteen miles from London, on what had once been the busy mail road to Holyhead. The Waggon and Horses at Ridge Hill was a square white Georgian house, with a slate roof and bow windows on the ground floor, on either side of a small porch, and it had once been a rest house for the waggon freight-carriers.

The Hertfordshire Public House Trust re-decorated and re-furnished the Waggon and Horses, added the county sign of the hart couchant and put in an ex-policeman and his wife to manage it.

Very soon it was transformed from an ordinary public house to a place where travellers could have a drink in the bar, tea in the tea-garden, a more substantial meal in the dining-room, or could stay for the night in one of the three available bedrooms. It had become an English inn again.

There were not many cars on the roads yet, but the Waggon and Horses became so popular with cyclists, particularly at weekend tea-times, that the little well in the garden, which was its only water supply, was sometimes in danger of running dry.

Several more Trust House Companies were formed, the directors being gentlemen of the counties, their shareholders people who believed in Lord Grey's ideas and were content to risk their capital and accept only a small profit.

The Hertfordshire company acquired a second house—the Battle Axes at Elstree. Then Lord Rothschild rebuilt the Rose and Crown at Tring and presented it to the Trust.

Before long the county units amalgamated and formed themselves into a company, which by 1913 owned forty-three houses. They were not making much money but their influence on the running of other hotels was out of all proportion to the relatively small number they owned, for their reputation for good food, rooms and accommodation was gaining ground quickly.

It was not until after World War I that, despite the years of the depression, motoring became really popular and the pastime of the people. The first British-made cars had been expensive to buy and maintain, but after 1918 Ford's exported cheap cars from America and then established an assembly plant at Manchester. William Morris began the manufacture of his Morris Cowleys and Morris Oxfords in competition with Ford's and as the slump of the early 1920s began he reduced his prices, to promote sales, so that by 1925 he was selling 50,000 a year.

It was cheap motor cars which brought about the new style of hotel industry, for people now embarked on touring holidays throughout the relatively empty roads of Great Britain for their summer holidays, as an alternative to staying in one place, and they needed accommodation at reasonable prices. They seldom booked in advance, for there were still more hotel rooms available than visitors to fill them. Nevertheless many people now saw the possibilities of the hotel business. They moved into old-established, run-down inns, spent more than they could usually afford on renovating them and establishing a synthetic 'old-world' atmosphere, with sometimes, though by no means always, the amenities of modern plumbing, and waited for business.

Catering for this casual trade in the early days of motoring must have been a nightmare, for it depended on unpredictable factors such as the weather and economic crises. There were black days when no one arrived, the staff was idle and good food had to be wasted. Prices were low and the margin of profit very small, so that many a brave venture foundered before it had a fair chance to become established and well-known, despite the good intentions and genuine enthusiasm of a proprietor to offer good food and service. The vagaries of the motor-car trade compared with the regularity of the old coaching trade made his task well-nigh impossible.

Even the Trust Houses, which by 1919 were a limited company with over a hundred hotels and a capital of £1,000,000, ran into troubled waters. They had been charging 2s. 6d. to 3s. 6d. a night for a single room and the maximum charge at any of their hotels was £2. 18s. 6d. a week with suppers or £3. 3s. 0d. with dinners.

By 1921 they found that they were losing money and for the next two years, which were the beginning of the post-war slump, they had to retrench and reorganize. These years also saw the end of the great ducal mansions in the West End of London, for death duties and high taxation made it impossible for their owners to maintain them.

By the late 1920s, however, there was a new boom in the hotel business, for in London and the south-east economic conditions were beginning slowly to improve again. In 1927 Grosvenor House, once the London home of the Dukes of Westminster, was sold and demolished and on its site the Grosvenor House Hotel was built. In the same year the Mayfair Hotel went up, at the lower end of the Devonshire House garden. Two years later Dorchester House was pulled down and Gordon Hotels built the Dorchester Hotel, with its 400 bedrooms.

On the north side of Piccadilly the Green Park Hotel, where the old Pulteney had once stood, was remodelled and opened in 1927 as the Hotel Splendide, but it did not survive World War II and has since been turned into offices. The building of the huge Park Lane Hotel had begun before World War I but work stopped with the outbreak of war and was not resumed for several years, so the Hotel did not open until 1927. In 1935 the Junior Athenaeum was pulled down and Athenaeum Court built in its place, a ten storey block of flats, part of which is now a hotel.

In 1933 J. Lyons and Company (Strand Hotels, Ltd.) opened the vast Cumberland Hotel at Marble Arch, with 1,000 bedrooms, all with private bathrooms, and a few months later

Two outstanding hoteliers. César Ritz (*above left*) and Rosa Lewis, 'the Queen
Cooks' (*above right*), of the Cavendish Hotel in Jermyn Street. Ritz created
reputation of the Savoy (*below*), the Carlton and the Ritz in London.

16. London's Hyde Park area
abounds with huge modern hotel
cluding the multi-storey Hilton (le
Park Lane. The twentieth-century 'r
to the roads' has produced a crop of
houses, like this one near Norwich (be

Mount Royal close by was opened, with its eight upper storeys containing 750 small service flats, run on the lines of a hotel, and offering accommodation for 1,200 people.

By 1923 the Trust House Company was making a profit again, for more people than ever were buying cheap motor cars. The motor car age had arrived and exploring the country-side was probably the most popular week-end pastime.

In 1924 the Trust Houses adopted their familiar sign, which, until a modern version was introduced during the 1960s, hung outside every Trust House Hotel—a stag rampant against a background of the sun and a star, symbolic of day and night service, and a sprig of traveller's joy; and by 1926 they were paying a five per cent dividend again.

For the hundreds of hotels throughout the countryside during the 1920s and 1930s, most of which were adapted from old-established inns, fortune was variable.

John Fothergill who in 1922 tried his hand at inn-keeping for the first time, when he bought the dilapidated Spreadeagle at Thame, Oxfordshire, suffered some heart-breaking years. He was a perfectionist. He planned to run an inn with furnishings and appointments as irreproachable as the service, the im-peccably cooked food and the wine. And he hoped that his guests, in the benign atmosphere he created, would all behave with elegance. In fact, he wanted only those who were capable of appreciating his aims. The vulgar and the querulous were discouraged and the couples engaged in illicit love affairs were turned away, notwithstanding those who tried to insist that an innkeeper had a legal obligation to receive them.

In a small, comparatively remote town like Thame, an inn on these lines was made possible only by the motor car, and when the Spreadeagle became famous, people motored many miles to visit it, but in the early days Forthergill had to wait for custom, depending on the weekly 'farmers' ordinary' on market days, when some sixty farmers, dealers and corn merchants would arrive and fill his beautifully furnished dining room for a 2s. 6d. meal, for which they expected three different joints to be prepared, which they carved themselves in huge portions. Other regular customers were the local free-masons and the commercial travellers, and the Grammar School held its biennial dinner there. There was also the bar, on which there was very little profit.

The farmers took offence when Fothergill moved their weekly meeting place to another room and never came back, but gradually his old friends from London and Oxford sought him out, enjoyed his food and wine and good conversation, and his plans began to take shape. Nevertheless, it was a hazardous business. He was often accused of being an insufferable snob, but he argued that he wanted the kind of people he would have received in his own home and he was doing no more than many of the pre-war hotels such as De Keyser's, who had insisted on personal introductions before accepting visitors.

In post-war England, however, where country hotels like the Spreadeagle depended so much on passing motorists, he could not be entirely selective. Prices were competitive. Tea was only 1s. 6d., luncheon 3s. 6d., dinner 5s. and bed and breakfast 6s., yet many of the casual visitors, unappreciative of the quality they were offered, grumbled at the high prices and one young man complained bitterly at being charged 6d. extra when he asked for an egg with his tea.

The requirements for keeping a good inn, said Fothergill, were the ability to work fourteen to sixteen hours a day, with rarely even a half day off, capital with which to have good food ready, which might have to be wasted (On one Sunday, for example, he wrote in his diary '. . . a lovely day . . . and instead of sixty people, six came to lunch'), a mind for the tiniest details, an ability to form a policy and the courage to carry it out, and a natural love of the job.

Although, through skill and hard work and the success of his first book *An Innkeeper's Diary*, Fothergill achieved renown, it did not bring him financial success and after nine years he found that he was losing money and had to sell, but there is no doubt that many enterprising hotel keepers were influenced by the high standards he set. During the 1930s, as more and more people owned cars, an increasing number of hotels began to concentrate on providing good and well-cooked food, interesting wine, well-appointed bedrooms and more bath-rooms. For them, inn-keeping became an art as well as a means of livelihood, and the widespread use of refrigeration helped to combat the losses of fluctuating custom during periods of unseasonable weather.

The Trust Houses gained a high reputation during these years for reliability and good value for moderate charges. By 1938 they had acquired 222 hotels, but during World War II 176 of them were requisitioned and some of them never re-opened.

From 1939 to 1945 the hotels of Great Britain made as good a show as possible with reduced staff and rationed food, and when peace came they made gallant efforts to recover their pre-war standards, but only a few succeeded. As food was freed from rationing, prices rose. Staff shortages remained an acute problem, particularly in the smaller country towns, yet by the 1950s there were thousands more cars on the road and a steadily increasing demand for hotel accommodation. Success came to the hotel keepers who were able to acquire staff for good, quick service and well-cooked meals, and in the final analysis it is the personality of the proprietor and his wife with an ability to select and control the right kind of staff and keep them contented and courteous, which makes for a good hotel.

Many new Trust Houses were established during the 1950s and 1960s. They have been built or acquired in the Cathedral cities—Winchester, Canterbury, Hereford, Norwich, Salisbury and York—the University cities, with the Randolph at Oxford and the Blue Boar at Cambridge, at the spa cities of Bath, Cheltenham, Harrogate and Leamington, at the beauty spots in the south-east and the south-west, the ancient towns of East

Anglia, including the Swan at Lavenham, the Brudenell at Aldeburgh and the Duke's Head at King's Lynn, in the Lake District, the Derbyshire Peak district and in Ireland, Wales and Scotland.

By 1971 Trust Houses Limited controlled 181 hotels with 10,299 rooms. Some of these are modern buildings but many are ancient inns which we have already met in this account of British hotels, and which have been rescued from obscurity and decay and restored to modern standards, including the old pilgrim hostel, the Star at Alfriston, the Angel and Royal at Grantham, the Lion at Buckden and the magnificent sixteenth-century Luttrell Arms at Dunster.

In London the company owns Brown's Hotel, the new Cavendish, where Rosa Lewis once reigned, Grosvenor House, the Hertford Hotel in the Bayswater Road, the Hotel Russell, the Hyde Park Hotel, which had been built in 1890 by Jabez Balfour about the time that he built the Hotel Cecil, as a block of flats, but was re-opened as a hotel in 1902, Kensington Close Hotel, Quaglino's and the Hotel Meurice in Bury Street, the Waldorf and the new St. George's Hotel in Langham Place, built on the site of the old St. George's Hall, which had been destroyed by bombing during World War II. The St. George's was opened in 1963, the first seven storeys being occupied by the B.B.C. and the six storeys above comprising the hotel.

These ten hotels provide 2,408 bedrooms and at Grosvenor House there are also 140 luxury service flats.

The problem of every hotelier today is that of staff, for most British men and women do not take kindly to domestic service, but for middle-class pockets Trust Houses are useful and still fairly reliable, and one must always be grateful to the company for saving a great many beautiful buildings which might well have been lost for ever.

Forte Holdings was founded by Sir Charles Forte in 1935 as a catering service and since 1945 the business has expanded to include catering services at twenty airports and airway terminals in the United Kingdom and Europe. The company entered the hotel industry in 1958 and by 1970 had 43 hotels with accommodation for 12,500 guests, as well as an interest in a number of hotels at home and abroad which were operated in partnership with BEA and BOAC. In 1970 Trust Houses and Forte's merged to become Trust Houses Forte, Limited, the largest hotel group in the United Kingdom and one of the biggest in the world.

Since 1945 catering for British holiday makers has become big business, one feature of the industry being the holiday camp companies, the best known of which is Butlin's.

There are nine Butlin holiday camps in the British Isles, five in England, one in Scotland, two in Wales and one in Ireland. These are for people who like their amusements arranged for them, for the camps are vast and contain all the diversions one could want for relaxation and entertainment. Accommodation is arranged in separate chalets and guests can have full board, taking their meals in the dining hall, or rent a chalet with a kitchen and cater for themselves.

The camps have swimming pools, boating lakes, skating rinks, ballrooms, discothèques, cinemas, music halls, repertory theatres, bingo halls, putting greens, rooms for snooker, billiards and table tennis and amusement parks. There are coffee bars and cocktail bars, pubs and shops, launderettes and hairdressers, restaurants, cafeterias and grill rooms for those not on full board, and church services are held for all denominations.

No aspect of the lighter side of western civilization seems to have been overlooked and although for the individualists it all sounds like a nightmare, the camps are immensely popular among the gregarious.

A special feature of the camps is that there are imaginative facilities for children—cinemas, a free fun fair and all manner of organized games and competitions. There are special nurseries for the babies and a supervised playroom for the older ones, with nurses to look after them, a service which is greatly appreciated by hundreds of young mothers.

Butlin's also have hotels at Cliftonville and Saltdean, each with accommodation for about 800 guests and the Metropole at Blackpool, with rooms for 500 guests.

In providing even cheaper holiday accommodation for young people the Youth Hostels Associations are doing valuable work.

One of the first hostels was Idwal Cottage at the head of the Nant Ffrancon Pass in Caernarvonshire, which opened in 1931. Two years later Black Sail, a shepherd's hut at the head of Ennerdale Pass in Cumberland became a hostel and in 1934 the beautiful Tudor mansion, Hartington Hall in Derbyshire, as well as the 17th century Houghton Mill in Huntingdonshire.

During World War II a great many of the hostels were requisitioned but the Association kept going and by 1943 membership had risen to 100,000. With the end of the war, the Association began to set its houses in order and many were redecorated by members themselves, working in voluntary weekend working parties.

Since 1953 school parties have increasingly used the Youth Hostels and a number of 'adventure' holidays have been organized, the adventures including sailing, canoeing, pony-trekking and under-water swimming.

Today there are over 250 Youth Hostels in England and Wales, providing simple accommodation for walkers and cyclists. They range from cottage to castle, from converted mill to purpose-built hostel, and include rectories and historic mansions. The smallest accommodate only ten people, the largest two hundred. All provide dormitories, washing facilities, a common room and a kitchen, where members can cook their own meals, and some hostels also supply meals cooked by the warden. They are closed during the day and there is usually a limit of three nights stay at any one hostel.

They are not commercial undertakings and members themselves run them, mostly doing their own cooking and cleaning, so that a minimum of staff is required and charges can be kept very low.

Chapter Fourteen

THE NINETEEN-SEVENTIES

THE PROGRAMME OF hotel building in Great Britain since the end of World War II has increased rapidly with the phenomenal rise in the number of cars on the roads, the habit of taking more and longer holidays, higher earnings and, most important of all, the steadily developing tourist trade, made possible by cheap air travel and 'package' tours and given an added impetus, in 1966, by devaluation, which suddenly made Britain one of the relatively cheaper countries of Europe for overseas visitors.

The hotels throughout Britain's countryside, which between the wars often had a hard struggle to survive, are today seldom short of customers during the holiday months, despite the thousands of people who now take their holidays abroad: and it is unwise to embark on a motor tour without booking accommodation in advance.

Hotels still suffer from staff shortages but labour-saving devices help the situation, for as well as deep refrigeration there are now micro-wave ovens where food which has been cooked and refrigerated can be reheated and ready for the table in a matter of seconds. This means that meals can be provided at all hours of the day by any member of the staff available to turn on a switch, while the qualified and highly-paid kitchen staff are off duty. Whether or not the customer enjoys food treated in this way is another matter. Some find it tasteless but a growing number of people seem unable to tell the difference between fresh and refrigerated, reheated food and are well satisfied.

The motoring clubs keep their rating of hotels under supervision and inspect them periodically for service, quality of food, amenities and cleanliness. During 1971, 135 hotels lost ground in the rating stakes and more than a hundred disappeared from the lists altogether, being considered unworthy of any rating at all.

It is difficult to define a good hotel, for customers themselves have differing standards and requirements, but today, as it has always been, the proprietor with a love for his work, a concern for his customers and the good name of his house, whether he is catering for the rich, the poor, or those in between, will usually find success.

A new feature of the motoring age is the motor hotel, which provides a bedroom and bathroom and garaging, with usually a tea-making machine in the bedroom. There is a restaurant and often a buttery as well, for lighter meals, but no other service. They are not cheap and they are utterly impersonal, but they are efficient and convenient for motorists looking for a one-night stop.

The coaches created the old posting inns and the railways ruined them. The motor-car revived them and has supplemented them with the new and inevitably soulless motels and motor post houses. At the same time the flood of foreign visitors arriving by air has created the need for airport hotels, which like nearly all new hotels catering for short-term visitors, are comfortable, clinically efficient and characterless, the inevitable result of too many people wanting to do the same thing at the same time.

In 1970 the tourist boom was Great Britain's fourth largest earner of foreign currency, representing a total of £433 million, and the hotelier's business has become a serious profession, for which degrees and diplomas are now granted. The University of Strathclyde offers a degree course in Hotel Catering and Management, the University of Surrey in Hotel Catering and Administration, and three-year courses are available at many technical colleges for the higher national diploma in hotel catering and two-year courses for the ordinary national diploma.

The number of foreign visitors in 1970 was over six million.

In 1971 it was over seven million and in 1972 it is expected to reach nearly eight million. As ninety per cent of foreign visitors spend all their time in London, the pressure on London hotels is tremendous, particularly during the three summer months, and it has resulted in the biggest hotel development in London since the building of the railway hotels more than a century ago, a development brought about by the aeroplane.

Many luxury hotels have gone up in London since the war, hotels with bedrooms all equipped with radio, coloured television, telephones and bathrooms. The mighty Hilton with 509 bedrooms was opened in Park Lane in 1963, one of a chain of more than sixty International Hilton Hotels built in the important tourist centres and capital cities throughout the world, and in 1973 the even larger Kensington Hilton, with 611 rooms, is planned.

The Royal Garden Hotel, the largest British hotel to be built since the war, cost £5,000,000, and from its basement, which is four floors below ground level, to the roof there are fourteen floors, with 500 bedrooms and four restaurants. It stands in the Kensington High Street, on the corner of Kensington Palace Gardens, overshadowing in its aggressive modernity the demure old red brick palace. This was originally the site of the King's Arms tavern, about which Thackeray wrote in *Henry Esmond*. The tavern was burnt down in 1857 and in 1890 the eight-storey Royal Palace was built, with the adjoining Empress Rooms, but these in their turn were demolished to make way for the post-war gargantuan newcomer.

The Europa in Grosvenor Square opened in 1964, the Westbury, at the corner of Bond Street and Conduit Street, in 1951. The Churchill Hotel in Portman Square with 500 bedrooms, claiming 'elegance combined with 20th-century luxury' was built by the American Loew's Corporation; the Sonasta Tower in Cadogan Place is the first London hotel of the American Sonasta Hotel Group, and the Royal Lancaster in the Bayswater Road, a skyscraper block with 432 bedrooms, is one of the new Rank chain.

These hotels are all gorgeously luxurious and comfortable, with an excellent international cuisine and splendid service, but they are expensive and by very reason of their size, they are impersonal. Only the rich tourists and British businessmen on expense accounts can afford them and they are far beyond the pocket of most overseas visitors, a third of whom are under twenty-five, either older school children or university students.

The Hilton charges nearly £20 a night for a double room, without breakfast, the Sonasta Tower about the same, compared with, for example, the Grosvenor at Victoria, now rated as a second-class hotel, which charges less than £10 for a double room with a private bathroom and a Continental breakfast.

London's old-established luxury hotels, particularly the Savoy, Claridge's, the Ritz, the Connaught and the new Berkeley, recently reopened at the corner of Wilton Place and Knightsbridge, remain in a class apart, for in the midst of all the new and noisy development they have imperturbably retained the atmosphere of quiet friendliness and superb service which has characterized them from the beginning: and unlike the new leviathans, peopled mainly by birds of passage, they have their regular visitors and remember their tastes and needs and frailties.

There are about 900 hotels in central London today, offering about 80,000 beds. In 1970 there were enough hotels under construction to provide 7,750 more beds, and on the assumption that the tourist traffic will have nearly doubled by 1975, hotels providing a total of 12,500 more beds have been planned. This is still not enough and it has been estimated that 30,000 more beds will be needed, but they must be medium-priced.

By 1971, 51 hotels in Westminster, 24 in Chelsea and Kensington, eleven in Camden, three in Tower Hamlets, two in Lambeth, one in Southwark and seven in Outer London were under construction or at various stages of planning permission, with about £40 million already invested.

In central London, however, land values are rising so steeply that the problem of building less expensive hotels defies solution. It has been estimated that the land value of a bedroom at Earls Court, apart from the £5,000 building cost, is more than £1,500. At Knightsbridge it rises to between £2,500 and £3,000, while in Mayfair it may be as much as £5,000, making the total cost of the bedroom £10,000.

The estimate for the nightly rate at a hotel is reached by dividing the cost of the room by 1,000, which means that these hotels must charge at least £6 a night in Earls Court, £8 a night in Knightsbridge and £10 a night in Mayfair.

The borough of Kensington and Chelsea, which is nearest to the London Air Terminal, already provides nearly a third of central London's hotels and there is very little space left for building any more. Between 1965 and 1968 31 hotels with 2,500 beds were opened, most of them conversions or extensions of existing properties, and by 1969 there were 24 new hotels being built, providing 1,673 beds. Planning applications for more hotels reach the borough offices at the rate of four a month, though only about a third of them are passed.

Westminster hotels, nearly all in the luxury class, provide 40,000 beds and another 6,000 will soon be available.

The airlines have come into the hotel business, in order to ensure that their passengers who take advantage of cheap group rates will have somewhere to sleep when they arrive. About ten airlines are involved with development companies who are building or plan to build hotels in central London, but they want them to be moderately priced, for the new type of 'blue collar' traveller.

The Labour Government's Hotel Development Incentive Scheme, designed to provide accommodation for the flood of foreign tourists, gives grants of up to 20 per cent of the capital cost of a hotel or £1,000 a bedroom, whichever is the smaller sum, and to be eligible for the grant building must have begun before March 31, 1971, and be completed by April, 1973. This has brought in some 2,500 applications, nearly half in the London area, and if the hotels are completed this will mean that 40,000 more beds will be available in London for the 1973 season. But one result of the incentive scheme has been to push up the price of sites, so that new hotels will inevitably be more expensive than was first planned.

There is also the problem of staff, for 15,000 additional hotel workers will be needed. Manual workers are hard to come by in central London and the wages of hotel manual workers are still below the average of manual workers in other industries, so they will obviously have to be paid more.

Foreign visitors are already complaining about the high cost of London hotels and as it is they who spend half the hotel nights in London, mainly concentrated into the three summer months, the position is beset with difficulties. The demand for West End accommodation by the native British, on business or holiday from the provinces, is rising far more slowly than the pressure of the tourists at the moment, so if the tourist traffic should decline, because of high charges, a 45 per cent to 50 per cent increase in the supply of hotel accommodation would be met by a considerably lower demand and spell disaster for many of the new ventures.

In ten or fifteen years' time the charges, based on current building costs, may not seem so high and the position might become more stabilized. In the meantime, the Greater London Council is encouraging hotel planners to build on the outskirts of London and in the east, around the St. Katherine's Dock area, where land values are considerably cheaper: and the British Tourist Association is trying to persuade tourists to stay out of London, but as it is London which they mainly want to see and very few visitors to Britain leave without seeing it, this is no easy task, for travelling into London each day may well seem a waste of holiday time.

In central London the only hope for cheaper hotels seems to be to reduce staff and use ever more automatic equipment. In a luxury hotel, the traditional ratio is two staff to one guest, but hoteliers now contemplate a reverse ratio of one staff to two guests, with even less for the cheaper hotels. The chairman of the London Tourist Board said recently that in these days of the supermarket and self-service, he believed that the hotels of the future would have the bare essentials of a bedroom and a shower, and the rest of the services would be automated, with self-service breakfasts.

This is a pretty dismal prospect and sounds as though the British hotel is heading full circle back to medieval times, when the traveller of moderate means was provided only with his straw pallet on an earthen floor and either brought his food with him or found it where he could.

But if such a state of affairs should ever come to pass, it would never remain for long. Someone would be inspired by the long tradition of the good British hostelry and the whole cycle would begin again.

And despite the pressure on London, there are thousands of men and women throughout Britain today who, against countless difficulties of rising prices and staff shortages, are valiantly maintaining the good name of the British innkeeper and offering to all comers, independent travellers, foreign and British holiday-makers on coach tours and visitors attending conferences and exhibitions, friendly hospitality and good value.

Index

You may also be interested in:

Zenon Vantini
From Grand Tour to Package Holiday

In this remarkable study, Pamela Sambrook rescues from obscurity the contribution of a former member of Napoleon's Imperial Guard to the development of specialist hotels and catering in the formative years of the railway network in England and France. In doing so, she interrogates what lies behind some of Zenon Vantini's very real achievements, legacies and disasters. She asks how far he was driven by his familial background in Elba and his involvement in the political turmoil of early-nineteenth-century France, and to what extent his whole life was known to those around him.

Vantini's extraordinary life encapsulates the change between two very different worlds – the old imperial past and the new age of entrepreneurial risk-taking. Never shaking off his old political loyalties, he believed resolutely that the mobility afforded by railway travel would change Europe fundamentally. In the long view he was a component part in the very early years of an industry which revolutionised England and arguably Europe more than did even his hero, Napoleon. Scholars and general readers of British and European social history will be fascinated by his story.

Pamela Sambrook is a former museum curator and distinguished researcher into country-house domestic offices and the lives of the servants who worked in them. She has now retired from consultancy to the National Trust, English Heritage), and from teaching adult education. She is currently an Honorary Senior Research Fellow at Keele University.

Paperback ISBN: 978 0 7188 9576 1
PDF ISBN: 978 0 7188 4837 8
ePub ISBN: 978 0 7188 4838 5
Published 2021

BV - #0021 - 170921 - C0 - 216/138/15 - PB - 9780718895808 - Gloss Lamination